Living the Dream

Living the Dream

New Immigration Policies and the Lives of Undocumented Latino Youth

Maria Chávez

Jessica L. Lavariega Monforti

Melissa R. Michelson

Paradigm Publishers

Boulder • London

Published in the United States by Paradigm Publishers, 5589 Arapahoe Avenue, Boulder, CO 80303 USA.

Paradigm Publishers is the trade name of Birkenkamp & Company, LLC, Dean Birkenkamp, President and Publisher.

Library of Congress Cataloging-in-Publication Data
Chávez, Maria, 1968–
   Living the dream : New immigration policies and the lives of undocumented Latino youth / Maria Chávez, Jessica L. Lavariega Monforti, and Melissa R. Michelson.
      pages cm. — (Critical viewpoints)
   Includes bibliographical references and index.
   ISBN 978-1-61205-711-8 (pbk. : alk. paper) — ISBN 978-1-61205-734-7 (consumer ebook)
   1. Illegal aliens—United States. 2. United States—Emigration and immigration—Government policy. 3. Hispanic Americans—Social conditions. I. Lavariega Monforti, Jessica. II. Michelson, Melissa R., 1969– III. Title.
   JV6038.C43 2014
   305.235089'68073—dc23

                                                                                    2014012419

Printed and bound in the United States of America on acid-free paper that meets the standards of the American National Standard for Permanence of Paper for Printed Library Materials.

Designed and typeset by Straight Creek Bookmakers.

19 18 17 16 15 1 2 3 4 5

Contents

Acknowledgments

We would like to thank our colleagues for useful comments and helpful suggestions as our thinking developed over the course of this project; in particular, we received invaluable assistance from Nicholas P. Lovrich, Bill Ong Hing, and Joe R. Feagin. Their tireless commitment toward working to make America's political, social, and legal reality come in line with its rhetoric through the humane and just treatment of immigrants, people of color, and the poor has resulted in life-changing benefits for many people. Thanks also to the members of the Politics of Race, Immigration, and Ethnicity Consortium (PRIEC) for their feedback and support, including Karthick Ramakrishnan, Jennifer Merolla, Adrian Pantoja, and Tom K. Wong.

We are especially grateful to our research assistants who helped us in so many ways ranging from completing interviews, doing transcriptions, providing research assistance, fixing critical file names, and making statistical tables: Martha Calderon Galassi, Annie Franco, Joe Tafoya, Landyn Rookard, Karter Booher, Wendy Martinez, Angie Jimenez, and Caesy Morphis. Nicholas Lovrich deserves another huge thanks for providing the funds to have our interviews transcribed; these transcriptions were critically important for the analysis of the interviews conducted for this project. We would also like to express our appreciation to our respective academic institutions for their support and assistance: Pacific Lutheran University, University of Texas–Pan American, and Menlo College. We are especially grateful to our publisher, Dean Birkenkamp, who was helpful and supportive from the very beginning of this research project when it was just an idea all the way to the completion of the final manuscript. Also, thanks to Ashley Moore, associate production editor, and all the folks at Paradigm Publishers who expertly helped turn our manuscript into book form. We would again like to thank Joe Feagin for his excellent guidance during each stage of this project, and for believing in the value of documenting the lives of the DREAMers.

We are most grateful to Reyna Grande for writing the Foreword that introduces this book, and for the moving memoir *The Distance Between Us*, a memoir anchored in the sadness and dysfunction that often come with being separated from your family and living on the margins as an undocumented youth. Her courage in sharing her story is a testament to the character, strength, and resilience of the DREAMers in the "land of opportunity," which cannot seem to find a political solution to their continuing uncertainties about their future.

Finally, thank you, DREAMers, for sharing your dreams and stories. This book is dedicated to you. It is our sincere hope that the insights derived from the DREAMers and recorded in this book help to shape our society in a way that will embrace you as valued members. May you never quit believing that you will one day truly belong in America.

FROM MARIA CHÁVEZ

Thanks to Michele, Donald, and Thomas for your patience as I worked on this book. Thomas, I'm sorry you couldn't be on the cover. David, thanks for your encouragement and support of this research project even when it meant sacrifices for our family. A special thanks to my friend and *hermano* Ross Burkhart. Thank you for introducing me to the work of Reyna Grande and for your unwavering support and faith in me and my work. I am grateful for the opportunity to have collaborated on this research with two brilliant scholars, Jessica and Melissa. This book would not be the same without you both. It has been a privilege to write it with you.

FROM JESSICA L. LAVARIEGA MONFORTI

I need to thank my family for all the support and inspiration they provide; my work would not be possible without them. Thanks to my husband, Belsay, for bearing with me during the research and writing—*te mando un fuerte abrazo*. I would like to thank Walter Díaz Rodríguez, Dean of the College of Social and Behavioral Sciences at the University of Texas–Pan American, for providing the generous support that was essential for the completion of this project. I would like to thank my research assistants, whom I shall not name—but they know who they are. Thank you for the numerous hours you put into this project and for your dedication and integrity. I must acknowledge the help of my consigliere, Adam McGlynn. Thank you for the advice on this project and on all on my projects. A special thanks to my mentor Dr. William E. Nelson. Many have read various drafts of this work, and we thank them as well, especially Amy Cummins and Maureen López. Last but certainly not least, I thank my coauthors Maria and Melissa for their collaboration, friendship, and patience.

FROM MELISSA R. MICHELSON

Thanks to Joshua and Zachary for enduring the many afternoons and evenings of "mommy working on her book" instead of playing with you, and to Christopher for stepping up his coparenting. Thanks especially to my outstanding research assistant, Joe Tafoya, whose natural interviewing skills and personal connections to the DREAMer community in Los Angeles generated interview "gold." Finally, thanks to Maria and Jessica for sharing this adventure with me. It's been an honor to work with you.

Foreword

Reyna Grande

The mythos of the American Dream tells us that, in this land of opportunity, anyone—no matter their background—can get ahead with hard work and dedication. For some, though, the American Dream comes at a huge price. For others—such as the young men and women you will read about in *Living the Dream: New Immigration Policies and the Lives of Undocumented Latino Youth*—the American Dream has been kept completely out of their reach.

My family's pursuit of the American Dream began when I was a toddler. In 1977, my father left Mexico to find work in the fields of California's Central Valley. Two years later, my mother joined him in the United States, leaving me and my siblings behind with a promise that soon we would all be together.

It took years before my family was reunited. I was nine years old when my father returned to Mexico for my siblings and me. In May of 1985, we found ourselves at the US-Mexico border running in the darkness. As we crawled on our bellies, hiding in bushes from the Border Patrol, what gave me strength to keep going was the dream that had sustained me through the years of separation from my parents—the dream of finally having a family.

As I struggled to learn English and find my place in this society, I discovered more American dreams: of one day going to college, having a good career, and being a homeowner. But I was undocumented. I lived in the shadows of America. I feared my dreams would never be realized and remain just that ... dreams.

In November of 1986, the year after I arrived in Los Angeles, President Reagan signed a bill into law that allowed almost 3 million people to step out of the shadows and seize their dreams. My family qualified for the Immigration Reform and Control Act (IRCA), which gave us amnesty and allowed us to legalize our status.

With a green card in hand, I embraced my responsibilities and opportunities as a taxpaying legal resident. I earned a BA and then an MFA. I bought a home. I became a teacher and, finally, a US citizen. Best of all, my new legal status allowed me to give back by becoming a published novelist and memoirist. My contribution to American literature has been honored with an American Book Award and, recently, a nomination for the National Book Critics Circle Award.

The opportunity to legalize my status allowed me to accomplish more than I ever hoped. It changed my life.

Twenty-seven years later, the word "amnesty" has become a dirty word to some, a word that time and time again has been used to defeat any proposals to legalize the status of the 11 million undocumented people living in the country today, 5 million of whom are young people who, like me, were brought to the United States as children. Opponents of amnesty argue that undocumented people violated the laws and should not be rewarded for it. They should not be forgiven. That's what the amnesty of 1986 did for those 3 million people, including my parents. It forgave them. Forgave them for being so poor in their native countries that they had no choice but to come north. It forgave them for trying to find a better life for themselves and their children. It forgave them for being so desperate to save their families that they were willing to risk their lives to do so.

It is a shame that though the 1986 amnesty allowed undocumented immigrants to step out of the shadows, giving them the opportunity to fulfill their dreams and become productive members of this society, today's immigrants are haunted by the specter of IRCA and its alleged failure. Their dreams are being held hostage by lawmakers who have been afraid to confront the so-called "dirty word" and move forward with a fair immigration process.

Through the years there have been proposals for immigration reform, but they have all stalled in Congress. One of these bills is the DREAM Act (the Development, Relief, and Education for Alien Minors Act), which would provide a path to legal citizenship for those who were brought to the United States as children. For the past twelve years, the DREAM Act has been introduced in every session of Congress without success.

The beneficiaries of the DREAM Act must continue to suffer the consequences of our lawmakers' inability to pass meaningful immigration reform. These DREAMers, the young men and women who were brought to this country as children and who are American in every way except on paper, are forced to live in fear: fear of being deported, fear of their families' being torn apart, fear of not being able to fulfill their full potential because they don't have those precious nine digits called a Social Security number. They are dreaming the American Dream in the shadow of fear, just like I did when I was still undocumented. The only reason why I am not a DREAMer is because I was lucky enough to be given a chance to legalize my status, saving me from the fear of deportation and unfulfilled dreams.

Currently, America has 5 million mostly Latino youth in legal limbo, forced to live as noncitizens. What does it say about our American values when 5 million young people raised in the United States are excluded from all sectors of society? What does it say about this country when 65,000 DREAMers are graduating from American high schools only to be faced with few or no options for their future?

This is not what this country stands for.

In *Living the Dream: New Immigration Policies and the Lives of Undocumented Latino Youth*, you will meet an inspiring group of DREAMers and through their stories, you will bear witness to their strength, their resilience, their humanity. You will bear witness to how our broken immigration system has affected the lives of these aspiring Americans and why the United States must step up to fulfill its promise that anyone, no matter their background, can get ahead with hard work and dedication. In this book, you will understand why we must not allow the DREAMers to continue to suffer the consequences of our lawmakers' inability to pass meaningful immigration reform.

As it is eloquently stated in this book, "The United States is a nation of immigrants, and we must treat our young immigrants—our DREAMers—in a way that reflects the values of this great nation."

Let us include the DREAMers in the fabric of our society—and let's give the DREAMers, and all immigrants for that matter—a fair shot at the American Dream.

Chapter 1

Introduction

"This Is the Most Important Day of My Life!"

Linda* has lived in California for the past twenty-five years. Her family is from Mexico. No one else in her family has ever gone to college. She sits at a coffee shop in Boyle Heights, California, ready to describe her "story" for this study: a successful Latina DREAMer who has earned not only her bachelor's degree, but also her master's degree. Despite growing up in poverty with a single mom who only went as far as the first grade, Linda was able to attend a private liberal arts college in Iowa and was awarded a full-tuition, merit-based scholarship for her undergraduate education. Linda was born in Mexico City and came to the United States at the age of two. The emphasis on education was impressed upon her from a very young age. Even though Linda's mother did not have a formal education, she had been saving money for Linda's education since Linda was a little girl. This changed the direction of Linda's life.

Linda decided to major in Spanish for her bachelor's degree and in Latin American Studies for her master's degree after she found out she could not earn a teaching certificate because of her undocumented status. For the time being, she has chosen to work for a nonprofit organization that focuses on helping undocumented youth by placing them in internships with other nonprofit organizations. Linda shares her passion for environmental issues, public education, and immigration reform as she describes her story to us. Her mother, who remained undocumented, has had to return to her original home in Oaxaca. Linda sends her mom money each month. Although Linda was raised in the United States since the age of two, she lived with an undocumented status until very recently.

She feels she will never truly "belong" in this country. This lack of true acceptance has taken its toll. Now in her late twenties, Linda is in the process of attaining permanent residency; however, having lived without documents for the majority of her life, Linda says, "I still kind of freak out by seeing the cops. I didn't learn to drive until about a year ago and I still get nervous. I'm like, 'Oh my God, the cops!' And I'm like, wait a minute, I have a license, like, I still freak out. Even now taking trips." In her heart, Linda still feels like an outsider in the United States. Though she loves both English and Spanish, and readily admits she dreams in English more easily, she plans to leave the United States eventually to go live somewhere in Latin America.

If she carries out her plan, what will our country lose? Linda has always had a strong level of involvement and commitment to Latino communities, to improving public education, and to environmental issues. She will use her education and talents to pursue her civic and professional commitments in another country, one where she won't have to be constantly reminded when she sees a police officer that for most of her life she was undocumented and an outcast.

We begin with the story of Linda because her story represents the experiences of many undocumented Latino youth. It represents the obstacles, the fears, and even the dissolution that this group of youth experiences in the political system and in the US government and society. Yet, it also represents the fact that even while waiting for a political solution to their circumstances, many of these youth find the motivation to go to college, and as in Linda's case, even graduate school. Estimates of the size of the overall undocumented immigrant population in the United States have stabilized in recent years to approximately 11 million. While many are adults who made conscious decisions to come to the United States without legal documentation, others are children who were brought to the United States by their families. They have lived in the United States as undocumented Americans for the majority of their lives. Because of their undocumented status they face major challenges as they transition to adulthood. For example, in many states they cannot obtain a driver's license when they turn sixteen. For many, this is when they first learn of their immigration status, having grown up in this country with no memory of living anywhere else, and believing themselves to be fully American. Often their parents end years of silence to tell them that they do not have the correct documentation to join their peers in this ritual of adolescence.

The lack of a driver's license means secondary limitations for these young adults as well, such as the inability to travel by airplane, a dependence on public transportation (or their friends and family) to get around town, and more generally a lack of freedom and opportunity for exploration and adventure that provide youth the necessary experiences to try new things. This may seem trivial, but exploring new adventures helps in the transition to becoming independent adults. Others decide to drive with false documentation or without a license, but such a conscious decision to defy basic societal rules may undermine their trust in government and means risking significant future consequences in terms of their ability to regularize their status or avoid deportation. Even among those who choose to forego the rite of teenage driving, the newfound knowledge of their status often has a dramatic negative effect on their future goals and dreams, personal relationships, and attitudes about the US government and society. Looking ahead to their lives beyond high school, they are ineligible to apply for financial aid and many other scholarships because of their lack of a Social Security number, making postsecondary education prohibitively expensive for most. Similarly, they are ineligible to legally work, even in entry-level jobs at fast food restaurants, or to intern in their preferred field. Even though employment opportunities may still be available, they are limited and generally poorly compensated, with little opportunity for advancement and rife with potential abuse on the part of employers who might take advantage of the fact that these youth do not have legal recourse. Many of these Latino youth excel in high school and dream of continuing on to become doctors, lawyers, scientists, and teachers; instead, they are left with the prospect of working "under the table" at manual jobs or domestic work, or possibly even leaving the only home they know in the United States for a country in which they were born but that they do not remember.

After twenty-five years of living in the United States without legal authorization, Linda's circumstances—along with the circumstances of hundreds of thousands of undocumented youth—were partially changed on June 15, 2012, when President Barack Obama announced that under his administration the Department of Homeland Security would no longer engage in the deportation of certain undocumented youth, effective immediately. In making this announcement, the president declared that if undocumented students met certain criteria[1] they could also be eligible to apply for renewable, two-year work permits. President Obama explained, "It makes no sense to expel talented young people who for all intents and purposes are Americans—they've been raised as Americans, understand themselves to be part of this country; to expel these young people who want to staff our labs or start new businesses or defend our country—simply because of the actions of their parents, or because of the inaction of politicians."[2]

The initial reaction to the news among the country's nearly 5 million undocumented youth was one of great relief. As twenty-year-old Victor Pealafox stated in a *NewsHour* interview, "With this announcement, with the news, you know, *this is the most important day of my life*" (emphasis added).[3] For the first time in his life, this young Latino, raised in the United States from the age of seven, was free to pursue his academic dreams without fear of being arrested or deported.

BACKGROUND OF UNDOCUMENTED YOUTH

The experiences of undocumented Latino youth are situated within the context of a long history of racist immigration policies that have especially oppressed, targeted, and exploited immigrants of color.[4] Indeed, the lives of the undocumented youth we interviewed for this study stand in direct contradiction to commonly held historical conceptions of the United States as a land open to immigrants; it's not even open to those immigrants who have, by and large, been raised in the United States. This is not the first time in US history that a group of people who see themselves as Americans has been denied legal status and the wide scope of rights that go along with it.[5] In this chapter we discuss how undocumented Latino youth and other Latino immigrants are caught up in a long-standing pattern of exclusionary immigration policies by examining the background of undocumented youth and how we came to have a group now known as the DREAMers; many undocumented youth are commonly referred to as "DREAMers" because they comprise most (though not all) of the individuals who meet the general requirements of the Development, Relief, and Education for Alien Minors (DREAM) Act. We contextualize the experiences of undocumented youth by examining assimilation theory and the racialization of immigration and Latinos as conceptual frameworks for understanding today's hostility toward immigrants, especially those who are "illegally" in the United States. We then discuss the most recent immigration bill being debated by Congress. This sets the framework for understanding the experiences shared by our sample of DREAMers, which will be detailed in this book. Our goal is to shed light on the life circumstances in which undocumented Latino youth find themselves, and also on the racializing effects generated by current public discourse on immigration.[6]

This book illuminates these important issues by analyzing the real life stories of undocumented youth in the aftermath of President Obama's 2012 Deferred Action for Childhood Arrivals (DACA) decision. It is our hope that their stories provide the understanding needed for the public to demand that our political leaders address the legal limbo in which DREAMers currently live. Marshall Ganz wrote in *Sojourners* about the power of stories in creating social change.[7] Ganz argues, "A story communicates fear, hope, and anxiety, and because we can feel it, we get the moral not just as a concept, but as a teaching of our hearts."[8] It is our hope that the stories we document here will motivate us to "break through the inertia and apathy of things as they always are."[9]

The United States is a nation of immigrants, but most immigrant groups have historically struggled for acceptance and inclusion, particularly immigrants who are not of white, Anglo-Saxon, Protestant backgrounds. In *Civic Ideals*, Rogers Smith argues that a fundamental aspect of the nation-building process is defining citizenship by deciding who will be allowed to become full and equal members of the political community.[10] Smith demonstrates that the history of US inclusion of racial and ethnic groups, particularly through citizenship policies, has reflected racial and gender hierarchies just as much as (if not more than) it has reflected liberal and republican traditions.[11] Smith's analysis demonstrates that the history of citizenship has been one of exclusion for people of color. Citizenship in the United States has never been easily achieved for racialized groups.[12] This reflects the racial frame of the United States wherein whites are understood to be the base category, the "most American" in terms of their civilization, culture, language, and work habits, while individuals of other ethnoracial groups are considered inferior (e.g., the stereotype of Mexicans as lazy, dirty criminals) and thus are not necessarily deserving of US citizenship. Citizenship in early America impacts the idea of who is considered a true American to this day. For many people, the word American is synonymous with white American.

Undocumented Latino youth who have been raised in the United States from childhood and have carved out a precarious place for themselves as Americans are constantly reminded that they are not "real Americans," challenging our ideals as a "nation of immigrants" and requiring a shift in the identity, dreams, and goals of undocumented youth, not only in terms of which country they call home but also in terms of where they see themselves fitting within the broader American society and culture. What does the denial of citizenship and full participation to American-raised immigrants teach us about our political values as a nation and about our long history of exclusion from citizenship by race and ethnicity?[13] In one analysis of undocumented immigrants' experiences in the United States, L. Chavez observes, "Undocumented settlers are tied to a society that continually questions their right to remain ... many of the children of undocumented immigrants have lived virtually all their lives in the United States."[14] His study of undocumented immigrants in San Diego found that Latinos are not being socially and politically incorporated in San Diego. They are often being excluded, used, and separated from many aspects of their own society. He describes with passionate insight the hostile climate experienced by many Latinos, documented and undocumented alike, in California during 1994's Proposition 187 Save our State campaign. Proposition 187 proposed excluding undocumented immigrants from receiving social services, including health care and education, and that government agents (including teachers) be required to report individuals that they suspected might be undocumented. This latter aspect of the proposition raised widespread fears of racial profiling, and the political debate over Prop. 187 made many Latinos—regardless of their citizenship status—feel that they were outsiders in their own country. Chavez refers to this as the "Latino Threat Narrative," and maintains that evidence of this vilification can be seen in many aspects of American society.[15]

Proposition 187 was approved by California voters but eventually declared unconstitutional; for undocumented youth, however, this same type of experience of exclusion continues. *All* Latinos—whether legal immigrants, undocumented, or US-born—are regarded with suspicion in the United States. A recent poll found that one out of three Americans inaccurately believes that most Latinos are undocumented.[16] Undocumented Latino youth in particular, because their sense of belonging in the United States is so precarious, have learned hard lessons about citizenship, political exclusion, and faith and trust in government based upon their experiences as outcasts.

HOW DID THIS GROUP OF DREAMERS COME TO BE?

The undocumented youth interviewed for this book represent a group that has come to be called DREAMers, after the Development, Relief, and Education for Alien Minors Act, a measure first proposed in 2001. The DREAMers label is evocative of the familiar concept of the American Dream, and the idea that the children brought to this country by their parents should have the opportunity to pursue that dream. Since the birth of the republic, the United States has included as part of its ethos a belief in the American Dream—that this country is an economic meritocracy, a land of opportunity where anyone can achieve economic success and a better life for themselves and their children.[17] President Obama has defined the "classic immigrant story" as "the story of ambition and adaptation, hard work and education, assimilation and upward mobility."[18] The continued flow of immigrants to the United States speaks to an enduring belief in the American Dream, and recent data indicate that "immigrants continue to realize significant gains in economic mobility between the first and second generation."[19]

Yet, the reality for most Latino immigrants is somewhat different, due to limitations related to inequalities of economic achievement, residential segregation, and discrimination.[20] The racial frame or hierarchy of the United States—with whites at the top and other racial and ethnic groups beneath them as inferiors[21]—is emphasized and reinforced throughout their lives, both formally by institutions and their processes, and informally by other individuals, such as neighbors, employers, and shopkeepers. While the majority of Mexican Americans are "pursuing the American Dream and clearly advancing beyond the humble status of the parental generation," many Mexican immigrants, "because of a lack of legal documents, the absence of economic and educational opportunities, or racial and ethnic discrimination," are unable to do so.[22] This is particularly true for DREAMers, whose ability to pursue the American Dream has been complicated by the decisions of politicians and the courts.

While comprehensive immigration reform requires an act of Congress, there are other powerful decisionmakers that have contributed to the inhumane conditions under which immigrants, especially undocumented immigrants, are currently living, including, among others, President Obama. For example, the National Council of La Raza's president Janet Murguía has recently called Barack Obama the "Deporter-in-Chief," as, according to Murguía, President Obama's administration has overseen the deportation of close to 2 million undocumented immigrants, more than any other administration.[23] However, this label has been criticized as inaccurate and even unfair. Political blogger Nancy LeTourneau recently pointed out that the Obama administration's decision to focus scarce resources and allow "prosecutorial discretion" in targeting those with criminal records for deportation needs to be taken into consideration.[24] Indeed, deportations have decreased significantly because of prosecutorial discretion from around 150,000 immigrants deported in 2009 to 10,336 immigrants deported in 2013. LeTourneau also points out that those who are being deported have changed as well with convicted criminals representing 59 percent of deportees in 2013, which is up from 35 percent in 2009.[25] However, an article by Thompson and Cohen of the *New York Times* demonstrates that prosecutorial discretion has not worked out as stated and deportations among those with minor or no criminal records continue. Through a Freedom of Information Act request analyzing 3.2 million deportations in the past decade,

Thompson and Cohen found that "since President Obama took office, two-thirds of the nearly two million deportation cases involve people who had committed minor infractions, including traffic violations, or had no criminal record at all."[26] Stated differently, the majority of those who are being deported are not serious criminals. David Nakamura of the *Washington Post* describes the political context regarding the issue of President Obama's deportation record.[27] While the Obama administration has deported record numbers of undocumented immigrants with the use of prosecutorial discretion, this approach is not always followed by the street-level bureaucrats who are conducting the arrests. All of this is taking place within the context of an ideologically divided Congress with many Republicans in the House who are not supportive of comprehensive immigration reform. Thus, President Obama is forced to implement difficult choices within the congressional constraints his administration is operating under. Critics are not convinced that President Obama is doing all he can; however, Nakamura's discussion of the context is important to remember when considering the large number of deportations.[28]

There are many other key agents who have contributed to increased numbers of deportations of undocumented immigrants, including congressional leaders, Immigration and Customs Enforcement (ICE) in the Department of Homeland Security, and private prison corporations that actively lobby members of Congress[29] whereby private detention centers are used to hold undocumented immigrants without due process, mass deportations are carried out, and immigrant families are broken apart and destroyed. This represents a classic interest-group iron triangle of congressional agents, private/economic interests, and bureaucratic interest, which results in public policy that is very difficult to change. In this case it is even more difficult to change because there are many people who hire undocumented workers in industries that benefit from this government oppression of the undocumented. As Feagin states in describing the United States' maintenance of slavery during the Founding period in our history, "Once these critical societal choices are made, the system of oppression has a strong inertial force keeping it in place ... until a major unbalancing force significantly challenges that oppression."[30] Rather than immigration reform, these powerful decisionmakers have created an immigration nightmare for millions of Latino families in the United States. As the editorial board of the *New York Times* states, "Because of Mr. Obama's enforcement blitz, more than 5,000 children have ended up in foster care."[31]

Despite this current reality, various court rulings have held that undocumented children are entitled to the same public benefits as other children, including public K–12 education. The Supreme Court ruled in 1982 (*Plyler v. Doe*) that undocumented children were entitled to free public education. However, the *Plyler* decision did not address the question of secondary educational rights or opportunities of those students. As undocumented residents of various states within the United States they are generally not eligible for in-state tuition rates or for most types of financial aid, making their continued education prohibitively expensive for most families. Undocumented high school graduates thus become

DREAMers—willing and ready to pursue their educational and life goals, yet unable to do so.

Legal scholar Michael A. Olivas has written a comprehensive monograph that analyzes the *Plyler v. Doe* case.[32] The Supreme Court decided that undocumented students had a right to a K–12 education in a case involving various independent school districts in Texas that had either outright denied undocumented school children the ability to enroll in their schools or were trying to impose a tax or fee on them for attending public school. The Supreme Court concluded that undocumented children throughout the country had constitutional equal protection rights with respect to access to public education, and the decision reinforced the principle that children should not be punished for the actions of their parents. Olivas argues that *Plyler* is significant because it "has become an important case for key themes, such as how we treat children fairly, how we guard our borders, how we constitute ourselves, and who gets to make these crucial decisions."[33] According to Olivas, *Plyler* is fundamentally about "how this society will treat its immigrant children"[34] and constitutes a "true high-water mark of immigrant rights in the United States."[35]

Olivas refers to the DREAM Act as the "postsecondary *Plyler* issue."[36] This major legislation was originally bipartisan, cosponsored by Senators Orrin Hatch (R-UT) and Dick Durbin (D-IL) in 2001; however, it has had a long and unsuccessful legislative track record, most recently failing to gain congressional passage in the 113th Session of Congress (2012–2013). Various versions of the DREAM Act have been passed in a piecemeal fashion in twelve US states, making it possible for undocumented college students to be considered state residents and hence allowing them to attend public universities and pay in-state tuition rates.[37] These states are California, Connecticut, Illinois, Kansas, Maryland, New York, Oklahoma, Rhode Island, Texas, Utah, Washington, and Wisconsin. While public opinion polls show that this legislation is favored by a majority of the public, opposition among Republicans and Congress has consistently blocked its passage.

There have been many studies of undocumented immigrants across academic disciplines. Many have sought to shed light on the complicated and divisive issue of immigration by putting a human face on the immigration debate—a debate that is often mired in bias, prejudice, and partiality. As Marquardt et al. describe in *Living "Illegal,"* undocumented immigrants are often constructed as harming Americans either as users of public benefits and contributing little to society in return, or as burdens on the economy, as criminals who erode the safety and security of our country, as cultural threats who allegedly do not assimilate into American society and culture. However, after seven years of field research among Brazilian, Guatemalan, and Mexican immigrants the authors found that the reality is quite different.[38] Similarly to other scholars of immigration policy, they stress that the United States has been promoting a contradictory set of immigration policies—both encouraging and discouraging migration with Mexico. Thus, they argue that there is no credibility to the argument that undocumented immigrants "should just get in line" and migrate legally. Their research demonstrates that the vast majority of immigrants would prefer to come here legally but because the immigration system is broken they cannot do so. For example, Massey, Durand, and Malone argue that immigration from Mexico developed over one hundred years of government policies that openly encouraged the migration of Mexicans to the United States by the official actions of both countries.[39] Furthermore, rather than posing a threat to our safety, undocumented immigrants are often the victims of violence, robbery, and theft. Their legal status makes them vulnerable in many ways. The work by Marquardt et al. demonstrates that undocumented immigrants not only are likely to contribute to American society, but they want to be legal residents. A survey conducted by the Pew Research Center in 2012 supports this finding, and goes further by indicating that *92 percent* of Latino undocumented immigrants stated they would like to become US citizens.[40]

In another study, Gonzales and Chavez provide an excellent description and analysis of how the failure to pass the DREAM Act affects the so-called 1.5 generation, a term used to characterize undocumented youth brought to this country before the age of fifteen who, through no choice of their own, were raised here but are not allowed to enjoy many of the benefits of inclusion in mainstream society at great personal and professional cost.[41] Through in-depth telephone interviews they discovered that many of these undocumented Latino youth did not understand the consequences of their lack of legal residency until it was time for them to apply for a driver's license or apply to college. As these youth approached adulthood they were more and more often required to produce official identification. The authors state in this regard, "This was a defining moment, a challenge to their taken-for-granted identity and sense of belonging. This often came as a surprise to many who were unaware of their unauthorized immigration status or its significance."[42] With this new awareness came fear of deportation and hopelessness about their futures, resulting in what Gonzales and Chavez refer to as the "Wasted Lives"[43] frame of mind. Gonzales and Chavez characterize this conceptual frame as follows:

> The voices heard here indicate bitter lessons learned. With the awakening reality of their abject status as socially constituted noncitizens, these young people came to realize they were not like their peers. Even though they may have come to believe the civic lessons learned so essential to citizenship and to hold dear the values driving the American Dream, the illegality that defined their abject status left them with a clear sense of their difference. As noncitizens, they were full of discardable potential. No matter how hard they worked or how they self-disciplined, applied themselves, and engineered their very beings, they were to remain on the sidelines, waiting, leading abject lives on the margins of society, desiring government documentation of their presences.[44]

Building on the rich scholarship of others such as these, we interviewed our sample of DREAMers across four major areas: (1) their socioeconomic background, (2) their immigrant background and experiences, (3) their views on the DREAM Act and deferred action, and (4) their political values and personal identity. We found that many of our respondents arrived in the United States as small children. Some no longer speak Spanish and many do not have any close relatives in their country of birth, or if they do have relations they do not know them. They were raised and socialized in the United States for the majority of their lives, attending public schools and living immersed in American culture; however, the US government and society do not accept them as legitimate members of society because they lack the proper documents. In many ways, they are politically, legally, and culturally in between two countries. Consequently, the undocumented youth we studied often watched their "American" friends and even members of their own families who were born in the United States go through high school, drive cars, and apply for scholarships and college programs because they have the privileges and benefits of what one DREAMer we interviewed called the "nine-digit number." These youth witnessed, but could not participate in, many of the conventional socializing processes of adulthood in US culture. These experiences were often accompanied by a sense of resentment. As this DREAMer stated,

> I feel I deserve more than some of the kids that are here that get grants and got all the scholarships just for having a nine-digit number. But their effort's not there, their passion for education isn't there and their dedication isn't there.... But I've always worked hard, like, I was trying to find a job, that there's a required pay—pretty much treated like a slave, you know, getting underpaid, not hours paid enough. You know, and you can't complain because you have no rights.

The themes in this telling statement of greater limits, vulnerability, and struggling were repeated by many of our study respondents, including Linda, the subject of the opening vignette. We found through our in-depth interviews that these young people are forever socialized as outsiders in the only country they have ever known.

WHY DOES THIS MATTER?

Why do the experiences of DREAMers matter? There are currently over 5 million undocumented youth and young adults in the United States who were brought here as minors.[45] Understanding the plight of undocumented youth is significant for a number of reasons. First, there are many widely shared misconceptions and stereotypes about immigrants and their lives, particularly about those who are not legally authorized to be here. In a study by Feagin and Cobas, they found that half of all Latinos in the United States are thought to be undocumented.[46] According to Feagin and Cobas this "collective ignorance" about Latinos combined with a systematic racialization of them in the United States has a very long history.[47] As they note, Latinos have been and continue to be situated within a particular racial frame, a "hierarchy of racialized groups in this country" that includes a lack of "racial capital" or the resources, social networks, and status systematically denied to people of color.[48] Their analysis traces the subordination of Latinos through the white racial frame, which has led to stereotypes of Latinos; to outright discrimination, theft, harm, and violence; and to continued race-based exclusion. They state, "For more than a century and a half, Latino groups' positioning on this society's racial ladder has been a powerful determinant of their members' racialized treatment, socioeconomic opportunities, and access to various types of social capital."[49]

The stereotypes and racialized stories are with us to this day in the way immigrants are viewed. For example, Iowa representative Steve King's statement in July of 2013 that, "For every one who's a valedictorian, there's another 100 out there that they [*sic*] weigh 130 pounds, and they've got calves the size of cantaloupes because they're hauling 75 pounds of marijuana across the desert."[50] This kind of anti-immigrant rhetoric is illustrative of the common stereotype that Latinos are drug-smuggling criminals who are bringing harm to American society. The national gridlock over immigration policy underscores serious differences of opinion about how best to control our borders and bring out of the shadows the millions of undocumented immigrants estimated to be here. Public opinion on these policies is sharply divided, and politicians in both major political parties have found themselves unable to achieve an acceptable compromise. Of the many aspects of immigration policy that have been considered in recent decades, however, the DREAM Act is often considered the most popular. Yet Congress's inability to pass even the most reasonable aspect—and some might argue the most crucial aspect—of immigration reform demonstrates how strong anti-immigrant sentiment is among many Americans today, and thus the fear of many elected officials that regularizing the status of DREAMers amounts to political suicide. Examining the lives of DREAMers through their own words is important to counter the widespread distorted misinformation in circulation about them that is often exacerbated by some of our political leaders and media outlets.[51]

Second, DREAMers' experiences are a broader indicator of the well-being of American democracy in an increasingly diverse ethnoracial society. The demographics of the United States are changing rapidly; the US Census Bureau reported in June 2012 that racial and ethnic minorities constituted more than half of Americans in the under-five age group, and in June 2013 predicted that the United States would lose its majority-white status by 2043. As these demographics shift, the traditional racial hierarchy is increasingly challenged, generating fear among many Americans who seek to maintain it. At the same time, it asks us as a society to reconsider how well we are living up to our core political beliefs. Earlier in this chapter we raised the important question: What does the denial of citizenship and full participation to American-raised immigrants say about us as a nation? The United States' political values have included what Feagin refers to as a strong liberty and justice frame. This liberty and justice frame can be found in the Declaration of Independence, in the Preamble to the Constitution, and in academic and popular discourse.[52] However, notions of liberty and justice have never been easy for people of color or for immigrants. Feagin notes, "From the American revolutionary era to the present, most whites have held to a cherished liberty-and-justice frame, albeit one that is usually rhetorical and hypothetical when it comes to challenges by Americans of color to racial oppression."[53] Therefore, one must ask how strong our democratic values remain with the legal, social, economic, and political exclusion of 5 million young people who were raised in the United States, but who cannot participate in it through traditional meaningful ways. Our political institutions, specifically Congress, appear to be incapable or unwilling to address their status, as illustrated by repeated sessions of failed immigration reform. What do liberty and justice really mean in the United States when there is a permanent underclass of noncitizen undocumented residents comprised of 5 million, mostly Latino, youth? Clearly, this situation falls short of our stated ideals as a country and tarnishes our political values and institutions. In fact, that this group is largely made up of one specific ethnoracial group only makes matters worse. When we disregard the lives of undocumented Latino youth by excluding them from participation in our political, economic, and social institutions we are perpetuating the centuries-old white racial framing, a way of thinking about our society and institutions that is based on a rigid racial hierarchy that places whites at the top and people of color at the bottom. The white racial frame is a paradigm that has guided our country from the very beginning. This racial exclusion comes at great moral and societal costs to us all.[54] As Ron Schmidt argues, the racialization of undocumented immigrants has resulted in their political exclusion; if we want a healthy democracy in the future it must be an inclusive ethnoracial democracy.[55]

Finally, Latino communities are becoming a more significant segment of American society as the largest ethnoracial group in the country. Yet, research about the political activism, attitudes, identities, and loyalties of the 1.5 generation of undocumented Latino youth—those raised in the United States, but born in Mexico or other parts of Latin America—remains largely absent in social science literature. The in-depth interviews described and analyzed in this book provide part of this missing piece of the puzzle. Knowledge concerning their experiences will add notably to the growing literature on Latinos' political and social experiences in the United States.[56] Furthermore, learning about the lives of undocumented Latino youth is important because this is the generation of future Latino leaders, as well as the "bridging" group between immigrants and citizens among the Latino population in the United States. One undocumented young woman we interviewed summed it up well when she observed the following:

> We are members of this society whether people acknowledge it or not, but we continue to be discriminated against, marginalized and "othered." We experience rejection on a daily basis, and although we continue to overcome barrier after barrier, it is not a way of life that any person should have to experience. We are talented individuals who want to be able to give back to our communities. Why does legislation continue to prevent us from doing so? Why let our

skills go to waste? Why not use them to improve this nation? This problem is much bigger than people want to acknowledge.... [W]e are human beings who deserve to be treated with dignity and respect.[57]

Throughout this book, we highlight the tremendous uncertainty DREAMers have faced and continue to face, even with the possibility of deferred action. The lasting impact that growing up undocumented has had on them comes through clearly in the words they spoke, which we report in this book. We argue that only by embracing DREAMers as full members of our society can the United States stay true to our founding ideals and move toward the goal of becoming a successful ethnoracial democracy.

THEORETICAL BACKGROUND—THE RACIALIZATION OF IMMIGRANTS: PAST AND PRESENT

Assimilation Theory and Immigration

In order to understand the experiences of the DREAMers in our study we must first understand how assimilation affects immigrant groups, including Latinos. Immigrant assimilation is a complex process in which immigrants not only integrate themselves into a new country, but may also lose aspects of their heritage.[58] As noted by Feagin and Cobas, broader discussions are needed about assimilation and the racialization of Latinos, including those who are "legal" and those who are contributing members of the middle class.[59] One of their central arguments is that there is a strong "assimilation perspective" in which Latinos and other immigrants are viewed (and often view themselves) in the United States. This conceptualization includes the notion of "a gradual and orderly integration of a racial or ethnic group into a host culture and society like that of the United States."[60] However, Feagin and Cobas question the idea held by many popular journalists, political pundits, and even some academics that Latinos are simply the next immigrant group that will progress along toward a misguided conceptualization of assimilation.

Early assimilation theorists such as Robert Parks believed assimilation was an ongoing cycle that included initial contact between immigrants and citizens, then competition between them, followed by accommodation, and eventually assimilation. Others such as Milton Gordon focused on a melting-pot conception of assimilation. However, this unidirectional and universal view of assimilation is false; the assimilation of people of color has always included additional racial barriers, and the concept of assimilation itself is immersed in systemic racism. As Feagin and Cobas note, this means that assimilation theory encompasses a hierarchy of racialized groups in this country that is directly connected to resources and rewards, which they refer to as racial capital. These barriers notwithstanding, these early assimilation theorists optimistically believed in the eventual incorporation of non-European groups, especially those from the middle class. Even modern assimilation theorists such as Richard Alba hold an optimistic view of assimilation. Alba believes that racial and ethnic identities are weakening, while at the same time demographic changes in the United States are providing greater opportunities for the incorporation and assimilation of people of color into mainstream US institutions. But these perceptions have many flaws. First, the focus is placed far too readily on individuals rather than on larger societal institutional structures and barriers for immigrants of color. Furthermore, the unidirectional process of assimilation has a bias toward white Anglo culture leading to the exclusion of many ethnic and racial groups. These notions of assimilation hide important power dynamics. Feagin and Cobas state,

> Yet another very serious flaw in most mainstream assimilation analysis is that it *hides* [emphasis in original] the principal white agents who control major societal processes of adaptation by immigrants of color and others coming into the society. These white agents, who are often agents of substantial discrimination, are not called out and analyzed in the mainstream conceptual tradition. Historically, elite whites, and their white and other acolytes, are the ones who shape and control most of the employment, educational, and political access in society, along with the discriminatory barriers (periodically including violence) that restrict and limit societal access for immigrants and their descendants, most especially for those who are racially subordinated.[61]

This racial hierarchy is taught to children in public schools, and underlies the access to public education that has been offered to children of color and immigrants over time. Ron Schmidt notes,

> Each of the racialized peoples of color was subjected to educational discrimination in several ways. First, each group was extended the benefits of public education more slowly and more grudgingly than were European Americans. Second, when education was extended to them, it was within segregated and inferior schools. Third, the groups' cultures and languages were disparaged and suppressed by public educators and other community leaders, and the public schools accordingly denied them the opportunity to maintain and perpetuate their cultural heritages. And fourth, even in the face of these visible forms of rejection and exclusion by the dominant groups in the society, the curriculum that *was* offered was exclusively assimilationist or Anglo-conformist in orientation.[62]

There is a robust scholarship by many other scholars that supports the notion that assimilation ideology does not apply to ethnoracial immigrants.[63] These scholars demonstrate that certain groups are marked by different physical ethnoracial characteristics, "foreign" names, and/or non-English language barriers. Thus, immigrants from nonwhite racial groups have historically experienced and currently continue to experience living in the United States very differently than most white ethnic groups have, and this experience has adversely affected their ability as well as their desire to assimilate.

Despite this body of research, which problematizes past and current views of assimilation, the United States is still largely viewed as a melting pot, with the strongly held idea that immigrant groups from all around the globe come to the United States and blend together to form a new people. However, for a mutually respectful melting pot to occur, the unidirectional Anglo-conformist conceptualization of assimilation must change, particularly considering demographic projections that indicate half the population in the United States will be nonwhite by 2043. The assumption that assimilation is a one-way street is highly problematic and harmful to immigrant communities; it often strips them of their roots, while denying them full acceptance and inclusion in mainstream society. It is imperative that we expand our currently held notions of assimilation if we hope to create a more inclusive notion of what it means to be an American. However, this would require a major shift in US society at the institutional and individual levels, one that would include an end to systemic racism in US society, which Feagin and Cobas define as

> [T]he persisting racial hierarchy, the discriminatory practices, and the racist institutions integral to the long-term white domination of Americans of color. This group domination involves not only racialized institutions, the macro level of oppression, but also the micro-level reality of a great many whites repeatedly discriminating in blatant, subtle, and covert ways against people of color in everyday settings.[64]

Ending racial oppression is a necessary first step in making the United States a multiracial democracy. In other words, until individuals and institutions in the United States treat members of all ethnoracial groups as socially and politically equal, then we cannot as a nation live up to our democratic ideals. Latinos cannot continue to occupy a subordinated location in society. Yet, as we describe in the next section, the treatment of Latinos in general and Latino immigrants in particular (and especially of undocumented Latino immigrants) has been one of racialized framing that underscores and emphasizes our continued adherence to the white racial frame.

Immigration and the White Racial Frame

The white racial frame is embedded personally, structurally, historically, and politically as the foundation of racial inequality in the United States; it originated in the 1600s when slavery was a legal institution, and it has persisted and evolved for centuries. Not only is it foundational to American society, but it has influenced all aspects of society—including the media, schools, politics, and popular culture.[65] Generations of Americans, especially youth, have been aggressively taught the white racial frame.[66] As Nobel laureate Toni Morrison notes, "In this country American means white. Everybody else has to hyphenate." Not only does everybody else require a hyphen as Toni Morrison so aptly notes, but language used to describe immigrants, especially undocumented immigrants, such as "alien" and "illegal" dehumanizes an entire ethnoracial and over time equates all Latinos as always "un-American." This has led to an understanding of white equaling American, which turns up time and again in the stories told by the young Latino undocumented youth that we interviewed for this book. As law professor Bill Ong Hing states,

> The discussion of who is and who is not American, who can and cannot become American, goes beyond the technicalities of citizenship and residency requirements; it strikes at the very heart of our nation's long and troubled legacy of race relations.[67]

This has led to a situation where millions of young people who have lived in the United States for the majority of their lives are trapped in a society that, until President Obama's DACA, would not allow them to live their lives in the open without fear of deportation. What does it say about how democratic the United States is when kids who very much believe themselves to be Americans are considered foreigners? When kids raised in this country just want to be kids, but cannot be? One major root of these policies and this situation is the popular understanding in the United States that "American" means white: the white racial frame embedded in American society that considers white to be superior and other ethnoracial groups inferior.

This white racial frame has legitimized and maintained racism against anyone in the United States who is not of white, Anglo-Saxon, Protestant background. Originally created to justify the enslavement of indigenous populations, and Africans and African Americans, the white racial frame has evolved to apply to each new immigrant group—including white ethnic immigrants such as the Irish and Italians, but particularly to immigrants of color.

> [T]he concept of the white racial frame is an "ideal type," a composite whole with a large array of elements that in everyday practice are drawn on *selectively* [emphasis added] by white individuals acting to impose or maintain racial identity, privilege, and dominance vis-à-vis people of color in recurring interactions. People use what they need from the overarching frame's major elements to deal with specific situations.[68]

How did the United States get to the place where the notion of an American is white? Rogers Smith's analysis of our multiple-traditions perspective mentioned above helps us to understand this; however, understanding the racialization of certain immigrants in the United States today requires further historical analysis of the experiences of the different groups of immigrants, and particularly immigrants of color. According to Bill Ong Hing, rather ironically we are a nation of immigrants with a strong history of anti-immigrant sentiments.[69] This nativism has extended to Russians, Chinese, Germans, Mexicans, and many other groups. This sentiment even extended to some Native American tribes whose children were forcibly removed from their parents and were not allowed to return home to see them again for eight years or more.[70] Mae M. Ngai provides a comprehensive overview and analysis of how immigration has evolved from the European model of assimilation to providing a more accurate, comprehensive, and inclusive discussion of our immigrant past. Ngai accomplishes this by discussing the major issues surrounding groups that did not enjoy the opportunity to assimilate into American society because of exclusionary laws and the actions of an often openly xenophobic citizenry.[71] Through the utilization of firsthand accounts by immigrants and primary legal documents, combined with critical academic essays, Ngai provides a counternarrative to the broadly shared belief that the United States was a homogeneous Anglo-Saxon, Protestant nation for most of its early history.

In every Naturalization Act spanning the period 1790 to 1952, Congress included "white person" as a *prerequisite* for naturalization. Thus, up until the 1950s, basic laws of citizenship *did not* apply to racialized groups. While many European immigrant groups have also confronted hostility, particularly Southern and Eastern Europeans, they have never faced the kind of *legal* racial restrictions on naturalization experienced by people of color. For example, the Immigration Act of 1924 "[C]omprised a constellation of reconstructed racial categories.... At one level, the new immigration law differentiated Europeans according to nationality and ranked them in a hierarchy of desirability. At another level, the law constructed a white American race, in which persons of European descent shared a common whiteness that made them distinct from those deemed to be not white."[72] Ngai argues, "This distinction gave all Euro-Americans a stake in what Matthew Jacobson has called a *'consanguine white race'* [emphasis added] and facilitated their Americanization ... [while the] racialization of the latter groups' [Japanese, Chinese, Mexicans, etc.] national origins rendered them unalterably foreign and unassimilable to the nation."[73] The consequences of these exclusionary laws remain with us today in the form of whom we see as deserving of entry into the American community, and whom we do not, including undocumented Latino youth.

Latinos and Immigration

Numerous studies have documented "the formation and development of a long-standing Latino presence in the United States."[74] A brief review of this history helps us to understand why we have a situation where there are approximately 11 million undocumented Latinos in the country. For example, Sierra et al. provide an overview of specific immigration policies and patterns relevant to Latino immigration, arguing that Latinos have both a long-standing history "of conquest and settlement"[75] in the United States, as well as being recent immigrants. Specifically, to understand how Mexicans have come to be the largest immigrant group in the United States it is helpful to examine briefly the historical patterns of Mexican immigration to the United States, which fall into three general time periods: (1) Mexican citizenship after annexation, (2) mass Mexican migration to the United States, and (3) Mexican settlement in the twentieth century.[76] The presence of Mexicans in what is now the southwest United States predates the arrival of whites to the Americas and the conquest of the region by the United States during the Mexican-American War. The foundation of Mexican-origin American citizens in the United States officially began with the Treaty of Guadalupe Hidalgo of 1848, which ended the Mexican-American War. The treaty mandated the secession to the United States of a large geographical area of Mexico corresponding to what are now the states of New Mexico, Arizona, Nevada, Utah, and parts of Wyoming and Colorado. While the treaty technically granted Mexicans equal rights as citizens and full protection of their property under the US Constitution, in reality they lost many of their fundamental and basic rights including their property rights, political and legal rights including formal voting rights, and the right to testify in court against whites and to serve on juries.[77]

The Mexican Revolution of 1910–1920 generated mass Mexican migration to the United States, as hundreds of thousands of Mexicans sought to escape the economic, social, and political instability of their home country, while at the same time they were drawn to the United States by southwestern industries seeking low-wage labor. Opponents pressured Congress and President Woodrow Wilson to pass immigration laws to restrict the flow of non-English speakers, resulting in the 1917 Immigration Act, which required immigrants to pass a literacy test. Massive lobbying by the agriculture, railroad, and mining industries led Congress to suspend the literacy requirement just six months later, rebooting the continued flow of Mexicans across the border.[78] The flow of workers was repressed during the Great Depression and massive deportation programs were instituted,[79] but when the United States entered World War II in 1942 the country again turned to Mexico for immigrants and their labor. Between 1942 and 1965, 5 million Mexican laborers were brought to the United States under the *bracero* (strong arm) program.[80] Many Mexicans settled in the United States with their families after coming here to work.

This historical basis for the US dependence on Mexican labor continues today. Some scholars argue that the United States is on the one hand addicted to undocumented Mexican labor, while on the other hand, scapegoating them for the many real public policy problems found in the country.[81] Throughout US history Mexicans and Mexican Americans were not accepted, facing both individual and institutional discrimination and violence. Today's wave of anti-Mexican immigration sentiment has a long history in the United States. Indeed, as Schmidt et al. argue, "The new [Latino] immigrants find themselves in an old ethnoracial order."[82]

The 1965 amendments to the Immigration and Nationality Act are important developments for examining patterns of Mexican migration especially because they prioritized family unification and they focused on the labor needs of the country.[83] The combination of these policy priority changes created an increase in immigration, caused a major shift in where immigrants came from, and contributed to the increases experienced in undocumented immigration. These unintended consequences of the 1965 amendments led Congress to enact the 1986 Immigration Reform and Control Act (IRCA), which imposed employer sanctions for hiring undocumented workers and legalized 3 million immigrants, mostly of Latino background. IRCA was supposed to reduce the flow of undocumented immigrants to the United States, but the compromises of the final legislation created mixed status families and a cottage industry of false documents with which individuals could subvert the employment eligibility rules due to weak enforcement of employer sanctions and increased deportations over time.

Massey, Durand, and Malone contend that we have created the "worst of all possible worlds" with our post-1986 immigration policy. IRCA and the North American Free Trade Agreement (NAFTA) in combination have resulted in increased undocumented immigration, lower wages, increased taxes for a less effective border system, and an increased amount of danger for migrants on the border—all of which have resulted in violence and deaths for people making the journey to the United States and made the immigration situation worse in multiple respects. Increasingly dangerous experiences taking place along the border made the cost of returning home and recrossing too high, thus forcing migrants to stay longer, and creating geographic diversification in their settlement patterns in the process. IRCA and NAFTA pushed "migrants decisively away from seasonal, circular migration toward permanent settlement and transformed Mexican immigration from a regional phenomenon affecting a handful of U.S. states into a broad social movement touching every region of the country."[84]

More recently, in 1996, Congress imposed stricter requirements for permanent residents, specifically increasing deportations of those who committed felonies or misdemeanors while in the United States. Congress also passed legislation that would deny permanent residents access to social welfare programs. Finally, Congress made the immigrant sponsorship requirements more difficult to meet. In addition, the continued and extensive militarization of the border has created a situation whereby "circular migration" is no longer possible for most immigrants. For example, in Texas there is a push for southbound security checks, which would substantially increase the risk of detainment and deportation for those returning to Mexico and other Latin American countries. Thus, immigration policy, fueled by fears and myths more than by empirical evidence, continues to be punitive and xenophobic.

Schmidt provides a critical examination of current immigration exclusionists' arguments and the structural impacts of their public policy preferences on the racialization of the undocumented immigration debate.[85] Schmidt details the arguments found on the two main sides of the immigration debate—namely, exclusionists contend that core values of state sovereignty and rule of law are violated with undocumented immigration resulting in the corruption of American economic, cultural, and political ways of life. On the other side of the debate, inclusionists argue that communitarian inclusiveness and egalitarian universalism are long-held, central American values that we violate when undocumented immigrants are kept living in a permanent state of fear and intimidation. Inclusionists further charge exclusionists with racist motives, which exclusionists strongly deny. Schmidt contends that the racializing effects of the contemporary immigration debate are ultimately of greater significance than personal racial prejudices or possibly xenophobic sentiments. He notes,

> In this author's understanding, "racism" and "racialization" do not so much signify people's conscious attitudes, likes and dislikes, as they signify collective behaviors that operate to maintain the dominance and privileged position of one racial group in relation to another group or multiple other groups. These collective behaviors may well operate without the conscious knowledge of those who participate in them as either beneficiaries or as subaltern targets (e.g., through hegemony). And these collective behaviors include both discursive and material actions that affect the social standing and wellbeing of groups in a wide variety of ways.[86]

According to Schmidt, the important question to ask from a public policy perspective is not whether exclusionist proponents of hard-line policies against undocumented immigrants that encourage "self-deportation" are motivated by racist sentiments, but rather "*to what extent does the political agenda of immigration exclusionists operate to construct and/or maintain racial hierarchy in the United States?*" (emphasis in original).[87] To address this question properly, scholars must "understand the role of racialization in the political and policy conflicts over unauthorized immigration in the United States."[88]

Public policy at the state and local levels has also perpetuated anti-Latino stereotypes and racial hierarchies, such as California's Proposition 187, Arizona's SB 1070,[89] and Alabama's HB 56.[90] Schmidt details the historical inaccuracy of an American monoculture and concludes, "to the extent that unauthorized immigrants represent a handy social construction that reinforces the continued stigmatization and marginalization of U.S. Latinos, the cultural narratives employed by immigration exclusionists work to maintain and reinforce racial hierarchy in the United States."[91] Schmidt argues that ultimately it is not racist motives that matter the most, but rather structural outcomes as found in public policies that reinforce racist inequality.

This overview of Latinos and immigration underscores the fact that xenophobia is nothing new in the United States, especially during economic hard times. Politicians and other civic leaders historically have succeeded in redirecting the public's attention to symbolic policy issues that target the most vulnerable, the voiceless, and those who are marginalized. To an American of Asian, African, Middle Eastern, Jewish, Irish, or Southern or Eastern European ancestry, this isn't news. Immigrants from these groups know all too well what it is like to be needed for one's labor, but despised for one's presence. We've been down this road before. Recall the 1882 Chinese Exclusion Act and the Gentlemen's Agreement of 1907, halting new Japanese immigration in exchange for nondiscrimination against those of Japanese descent already in the United States, as examples of racist immigration practices in this country's past. Arizona's SB 1070 is not unique in our history. What is new is that this treatment is now being directed to children who have been raised in the United States.

Generally speaking, the current immigration debate focusing on Latinos is no different from previous debates. Whether one is a proponent of earned citizenship through some type of amnesty, tougher border enforcement either by building fences or militarizing the border, or another guest worker program, or one is engaged in the ongoing debate about whether immigrants cost or benefit society, Latinos in the United States are experiencing prejudice, discrimination, cruelty, and mistreatment from this latest round of scapegoating. The result of this racialization and exclusion of Latinos is that the 50 million Latinos in this country—16.3 percent of the population—are not accepted or seen as real Americans. Racialization and exclusion occur regardless of one's legal or professional status, as one of the authors of this study has documented extensively based on her research on Latino professionals.[92] The current debate on immigration underscores this fact.[93]

CURRENT IMMIGRATION REFORM

Just one week after being sworn in for his second term, President Obama gave a speech in Las Vegas outlining his ideas for comprehensive immigration reform.[94] During his first term, many said that immigration reform was derailed by health care reform, and the slow economic recovery is threatening to derail immigration reform during his second term.[95] Thus, immigration was not a policy priority during President Obama's first term in office. As of this writing, the president has not been successful at getting Congress to pass comprehensive immigration reform during his second term, and the odds of a sudden change of heart among opponents in Congress are very unlikely. However, Obama has repeatedly argued that the time to act is now:

> [M]ost Americans agree that it's time to fix a system that's been broken for way too long ... business leaders, faith leaders, labor leaders, law enforcement and leaders from both parties are coming together to say now is the time to find a better way to welcome the striving, hopeful immigrants who still see America as the land of opportunity. Now's the time to do this so we can strengthen our economy and strengthen our country's future.[96]

President Obama's priorities for immigration reform include (1) a focus on enforcement, (2) a pathway to citizenship for the 11 million people who are undocumented, and (3) modernizing and streamlining immigration so that it does not take years to process applications.[97] President Obama concluded his remarks by stating, "So that's what comprehensive immigration reform looks like—smarter enforcement, a pathway to earn citizenship, improvements in the legal immigration system so that we continue to be a magnet for the best and the brightest all around the world. It's pretty straightforward."[98]

Meanwhile, on June 27, 2013, the Senate passed S 744, the Border Security, Economic Opportunity, and Immigration Modernization Act.[99] Some of the items that this bipartisan legislation proposes include emphasis on border security, a thirteen-year pathway to citizenship, and the passage of the main provisions of the DREAM Act. The Senate bill has been criticized by liberals for its tough border enforcement provisions, which include 24/7 "unmanned aerial vehicles" (drones), 700 additional miles of fencing along the southern but not the northern border, and 18,000 more Border Patrol agents. These provisions are unacceptable to many Latino advocacy organizations including Presente.org, which issued a statement quoted in the *New York Times* that asserted the militarization of the border was "guaranteed to increase death and destruction."[100] Conservatives, however, are against providing any type of pathway to citizenship to undocumented immigrants, including to the DREAMers. David Damore, senior analyst at Latino Decisions, predicted that the Republican-controlled House would not be discussing immigration reform during the August 2013 recess despite the fact that immigration reform is an important issue to Latinos and non-Latinos alike.[101] Damore believes House Republicans are seriously miscalculating and this could cost them control of the House in the midterm elections.[102] He debunks the conventional argument that House Republicans are in districts without enough Latino voters to sway the election and argues,

> [A] consistent finding in Latino Decisions' polling conducted throughout 2012 and 2013 is that the Republican Party has much to lose when it comes to immigration if it chooses to play an obstructionist role. However, by playing a constructive role in passing immigration reform that includes a pathway to citizenship, the GOP would be able to get beyond an issue that makes it nearly impossible for the party to make in-roads with Latino voters, while at the same time providing valuable political coverage for its most vulnerable House incumbents. If the party instead pushes legislation that focuses only on enforcement, or that proposes to make an already cumbersome path to citizenship even more arduous, then Mitt Romney's 2012 performance among Latino voters may be the GOP's high watermark for quite some time.[103]

Given that the House is unwilling to consider or advance an immigration bill, it is unclear whether comprehensive immigration reform legislation will pass any time soon. The sentiments expressed by Representative Lamar Smith (R-TX), who serves on the immigration subcommittee, are illustrative of the huge divide that separates House Republicans from the provisions passed in S 744: "We should not reward those who have broken our laws with amnesty. Even if we did, there is no guarantee that the border or interior would become more secure."[104] Representative Smith makes many of the arguments other Republicans in the House are making about immigration reform. Below is a verbatim bullet point list of ideas Smith and fellow Republicans believe are required actions to "fix" immigration:

- Require employers to only hire legal workers. This will reduce the magnet of the easy availability of jobs that entices many to enter illegally. And it will reduce the competition for scarce jobs that hurts legal workers. More than 425,000 employers have signed up voluntarily for E-Verify that ensures that prospective hires are legally authorized to work in the United States. And 99.5% of legal workers are confirmed immediately.
- Increase work-site investigations by Immigration and Customs Enforcement to make sure employers are hiring legal workers. This will protect jobs for unemployed or underemployed Americans. Unfortunately, work-site enforcement is down 70% under the Obama administration.
- Implement an entry-exit system using biometrics (such as fingerprints) to identify those who entered on a temporary visa and overstayed their visit. They comprise almost half of all illegal immigrants. This administration has ignored the law requiring them to set up this system.
- Increase border resources and personnel so that fewer illegal immigrants will enter undetected. For every person apprehended today, others escape notice. The Government Accountability Office has determined that only 6.5% of the southern border is under "full control" of the Border Patrol.
- Refuse to issue visas to residents of countries that won't allow their citizens to be returned home after they have committed crimes in the United States. Many of these individuals are now released back into our communities where they often commit additional crimes.
- Expand the Secure Communities program, which identifies illegal immigrants who have been arrested for crimes. These offenders should be detained and then sent home, not released. The Obama administration allows some cities to ignore this law.
- Stop giving automatic citizenship to children born to illegal immigrant parents, which represents about 10% of all births in the United States today. At least one parent should be in the country legally. Automatic citizenship rewards illegal parents and often tempts them to enter the United States just to give birth.[105]

Although S 744 includes $40 billion in border security measures that address many of the concerns Smith details above, there are still aspects of the conservative House members' positions that are non-negotiable to many Democrats such as changing the birthright clause of the 14th Amendment, which affirms that all persons born or naturalized in the United States and subject to its jurisdiction are, in fact, US citizens. The bipartisan Senate bill remains miles away from the conservative House Republican position. Shortly after passage of S 744, House Speaker John Boehner stated, "I issued a statement that I thought was pretty clear, but apparently some haven't gotten the message: the House is not going to take up and vote on whatever the Senate passes. . . . We're going to do our own bill."[106] As of this writing, the House has not done its own bill. In sum, immigration reform during President Obama's second administration is unlikely to occur in Congress, as it is their lack of political will that has created the de facto system of immigration we have today. Because Congress has failed to make immigration policy reforms through the political process via deliberation, compromise, political courage, and leadership, the editorial board of the *New York Times* argues that President Obama must act even if such action is limited in scope.[107] The Board states, "If President Obama means what he says about wanting an immigration system that reflects American values, helps the economy and taps the yearnings of the millions of Americans-in-waiting, he is going to have to do something about it—soon and on his own."[108] While the Board acknowledges that the president cannot pass comprehensive immigration reform without Congress, they argue that he can and must make changes to "push a failing system toward sanity and justice."[109] Meanwhile, those who most acutely suffer the consequences of Congress's and President Obama's inability to pass comprehensive immigration reform are the DREAMers.

OUR RESEARCH METHODS

To document the experiences and attitudes of DREAMers we employ new data collected from 101 interviews of undocumented Latino youth carried out in the summer of 2012 immediately following President Obama's DACA policy announcement. Trained research assistants who are all native Spanish speakers carried out these interviews in California, Oregon, Texas, and Washington. We used a snowball sampling design to recruit participants. A first round of respondents was identified by our research assistants, all of whom are Latino and half of whom are undocumented. This field research team composition provided an advantage in attaining candid and reliable responses from undocumented youth who otherwise might understandably be cautious about what they reveal to conventional social science researchers. As we proceeded we had our research assistants ask the respondents to suggest other potential persons to interview. In these in-depth, face-to-face interviews study participants were asked both open-ended and fixed-response questions focusing on the following topics of interest: political trust and social capital, political values and partisanship, educational background, immigrant background and experiences, ethnic identity, and political attitudes focused on their views regarding President Obama's decision to order federal agencies to stop deporting people in their circumstances. We also explored the circumstances under which they discovered their undocumented status and asked where they see themselves in five years and again in ten years. Many of these topics are understudied; most existing studies of DREAMers have focused on their educational experiences and limitations, with less emphasis on their political values and socialization (see Appendix for the interview questionnaire).

We focused on undocumented Latino youth because their experiences allow for a fuller theoretical and empirical understanding of the political and social incorporation of Latinos into US society. The fact that they typically have been raised and socialized in the United States but cannot participate in many of the main political, educational, and in some cases social institutions allows us to ask important questions about how democratic theories account for their experience. How do they balance their sense of identity as undocumented Latinos simultaneously with their identity as members of the broader American public? Drawing on our empirical interview data, the findings presented in this book provide a much-needed analysis of political socialization, identity formation, and incorporation of undocumented Latino youth who are trying to pursue the American Dream despite the many obstacles and limitations placed in their way.

CONCLUSION

In this study we discovered that for undocumented young people the experience of growing up in the United States *sin papeles* (without legal papers) has an extensive and lasting impact on the way they see the US political system as well as the way they see themselves within that system. In the most significant ways, it does not matter whether one is living in El Paso, Texas; Los Angeles, California; Portland, Oregon; or Tacoma, Washington. In other ways, as we show in later chapters, geographic context matters to political activism and socialization. The experiences of those in our sample locations are complex and insightful. It becomes clear that the sense of feeling "unwanted" held by many respondents does not go away with DACA and they question whether it will go away entirely should Congress pass a DREAM Act. Still, and perhaps surprisingly given the vulnerable status of our study participants, we found that the impact on their political socialization and political consciousness includes high levels of political activism, high levels of focused political knowledge, but also high levels of political cynicism. We also found noteworthy gender differences among our respondents regarding future goals and aspirations, with males focused on personal security and protecting their families and females more focused on giving back to their communities. While DACA has led to feelings of personal optimism and greater hope for the future, growing up in vulnerable circumstances and uncertainty has forever marked the lives of our respondents.

In subsequent chapters we examine the demographic and immigrant background of our participants. We provide a historical and economic argument for passage of the DREAM Act. We examine the complexities of social and political incorporation of mostly Mexican-born but American-raised DREAMers who have always considered the United States to be their home but who remain legally deportable undocumented Latino immigrants. This includes the political values and personal identities of our participants. In this book we question how well President Obama's "classic immigrant story" applies to undocumented youth and see if it is indeed a "story of ambition and adaptation, hard work and education, assimilation and upward mobility."[110] This study provides a better understanding of undocumented Latino youth's lives in political, material, and symbolic ways as they attempt to live the dream in America.

Chapter 2

"We Asked for Workers, but Human Beings Came"

History and Economic Argument for the DREAM Act

> As students with an undocumented status we continuously and always, regardless of paperwork or an attorney that you have, there is always fear of deportation. The fear of being ripped away from your family, your school, or your friends, everything that you've ever known—especially if you've been here at such a young age—is really daunting and quite terrifying.
>
> —*Sebastian, twenty-four-year-old male college student, in the United States since three years of age*

President Obama's deferred action announcement was the culmination, however imperfect and incomplete, of a long history of political discussion and (in)action. Various sessions of Congress and state legislatures had previously attempted to find a way to allow undocumented children brought to the United States by their parents to come out of the shadows and achieve their educational and occupational goals. Many of those proposals noted the economic benefit of this kind of policy change, as opposed to the economic cost of leaving undocumented youth living in constant fear of deportation and unable to pursue their dreams. Texas Governor Rick Perry famously alluded to these arguments during the 2012 Republican presidential nomination contest debates, setting him apart from his Republican rivals. When the other GOP candidates criticized the Texas DREAM Act, Perry quipped, "If you say that we should not educate children who have come into our state for no other reason than they've been brought there by no fault of their own, I don't think you have a heart."[1]

This chapter reviews the principal sources of the young undocumented Latinos in the United States; the history of previous efforts to regularize their status, both successful (at the state level) and unsuccessful (notably, at the federal level); and also the economic arguments put forward by advocates of both sides of the debate. While in some instances members of Congress came close to a deal, particularly in 2006 when senators Ted Kennedy (D-MA) and John McCain (R-AZ) joined in support of a bipartisan comprehensive immigration bill, in later years Republican support dwindled. Reviewing this history clarifies why President Obama felt it necessary to take unilateral executive action in the summer of 2012 when he announced the Deferred Action for Childhood Arrivals (DACA) program, rather than waiting for Congress to come to an agreement on a comprehensive legislative solution.

ROOTS OF THE UNROOTED: WHY WE HAVE AN IMMIGRATION "PROBLEM"

Numerous scholars have investigated the sources of the flows of undocumented immigrants to the United States, including those who bring their young children along for the journey. As pointed out by advocates on both sides of the immigration and DREAM Act debates, these youth often have not been given a choice. They become undocumented immigrants because of decisions made by their parents and often do not even know their status until they face a life event that requires them to present a Social Security number (such as applying for a driver's license or for financial aid for college). Substantial scholarship documents the reality that many of those adults also have limited control over their decisions to migrate to the North. The economic and cultural hegemony that the United States exercises over most of its southern neighbors is directly linked to the fact that these countries supply much of the low-skill labor needed for its farms and many of its service industries.

Between 1942 and 1965, the United States issued nearly 5 million contracts for temporary workers from Mexico, generally for men to work in agriculture, under the *bracero* program. The *bracero* program ended in 1964 and was followed by the Hart-Cellar Immigration Act of 1965, which gave preference to labor certification and family reunification. Many former *braceros* and their family members became legal permanent residents, and the new family reunification preference system allowed many of them to sponsor their close family members to join them. Even with the change in legal status for former *braceros* the demand for Mexican workers continued; however, the government set a cap of 20,000 legal visas per year—clearly much too low to accommodate demand. The decades of legal migration had activated a social network that then aided future flows of undocumented immigrants seeking to fill the new insatiable demand. In the 1970s, as economic woes in Mexico continued, US employers in sectors beyond agriculture such as construction, services, and manufacturing also began hiring large numbers of Mexican workers.[2] In 2005, undocumented immigrants made up a significant portion of the workforce in a variety of US industries: 24 percent of farm workers, 26 percent of landscapers, 27 percent of food processors and butchers, 29 percent of roofers, and 36 percent of insulation workers.[3] The demand for unskilled labor has been increasing over time, but the supply of such unskilled labor from native-born households has been decreasing. Because the cap on visas to fill these jobs was set so low, undocumented immigrants naturally filled the gap.[4]

The 1994 North American Free Trade Agreement (NAFTA) with Mexico eliminated protections for many Mexican industries and farmers; the increased competition from US businesses led to significant job losses, pushing many young Mexicans north in search of employment. As predicted by Philip L. Martin, NAFTA caused the loss of jobs in Mexican small-scale agriculture, now forced into competition with US agriculture and cut off from government subsidies.[5] Mexican immigration to the United States thus soared after 1994. Between 1994 and 2002, Mexico's agricultural sector lost 1.3 million jobs, and more jobs were lost in the industrial sector as native businesses found themselves unable to compete. These displaced farmers, in particular, became a major part of the flow of undocumented workers to the United States.[6]

Industry and politicians have resisted policies that might curb the flow of undocumented workers, such as the strict employer sanctions enforced in much of Western Europe since the mid-1970s.[7] The Immigration Reform and Control Act (IRCA) signed into law by President Ronald Reagan in 1986 obligated new hires to provide documentation of legal eligibility for employment, documents prescribed by the attorney general and listed on a form called the I-9. The Immigration and Naturalization Service (INS), charged with enforcing the law, was directed to educate employers about the I-9 requirement and impose penalties on all known violators. At the same time, Congress encouraged the INS to not enforce sanctions too harshly, to phase them in over a year and a half, and focus on voluntary employer compliance, thereby "avoiding the harassment of business."[8] Not surprisingly, this approach to enforcement, combined with the ease of acquiring fraudulent documents and the steady demand for low-skill workers, meant that the new I-9 requirement had only a negligible effect on the widespread recruitment and employment of undocumented immigrants.[9]

Combined with the IRCA amnesty and I-9 requirement was a new push to secure the border and decrease the flow of undocumented immigrants into the United States. Subsequent federal legislation, particularly after the 9/11 terrorist attacks, has also emphasized border control. Yet, the push and pull factors that bring undocumented immigrants to the United States to fill low-wage jobs are so powerful that would-be migrants are willing to put themselves at considerable personal risk to come north, even as increased border enforcement has increased those risks. According to DeVivo and Fernández: "Each year more people die attempting to cross the U.S.-Mexico border than in the entire twenty-eight-year history of Germany's Berlin wall."[10] At the same time, the rising personal and financial costs of crossing the border mean that the old pattern of circular migration has been replaced by one of permanent residency. Instead of traveling home periodically to visit their families, workers have instead brought their families to the United States to join them. This is true even for those here with green cards and working legally. Because the number of visas is capped severely below demand, immediate relatives (spouses, minor children, and parents) often have to wait as long as ten years for such a visa; not surprisingly, many do not wait. Instead, they cross the border illegally or overstay a visitor visa.[11] As Swiss novelist Max Frisch said of the European guest worker situation in 1965, "We asked for workers, but human beings came."[12]

THE ORIGIN OF THE DREAMERS

As noted in Chapter 1, undocumented children in the United States have certain rights. *Plyler v. Doe* (1982), in particular, established their right to a free public K–12 education.[13] Often, they learn of their undocumented status only as teenagers, when they seek to obtain a driver's license and find that they do not have a Social Security number, or when they begin to consider going to college and learn that they are ineligible for most scholarships and financial aid and either must pay out-of-state or international tuition rates. While their peers with citizenship or legal residency may have visited Mexico for holidays over the years, due to strict border enforcement they are unlikely to have ever visited the country they left as a young child. They are more "American" than their native-born Mexican American friends, often having no memory of their legal homeland. They are thus unlikely to return "home." Periodically over the past decade policymakers have attempted to rectify this situation with legislation by giving these youth a path to regularization of their status, or at least granting access to an affordable college education.

Recognizing that what many of these youth hope for is to achieve the American Dream, that legislation is often entitled the Development, Relief, and Education for Alien Minors (DREAM) Act. The federal DREAM Act would provide a pathway to regularization of the immigration status of undocumented youth who graduate from college or serve in the military; the exact list of eligibility requirements has shifted over time as various concerns about the original DREAM Act have been addressed. Yet, the federal government has thus far failed to pass a DREAM Act. Despite over a decade of legislative debate and widespread public support, the DREAM Act remains but a dream for its many supporters.[14]

STATE DREAM ACTS

Federal law prohibits states from charging in-state tuition rates to undocumented students. The Illegal Immigration Reform and Immigration Responsibility Act of 1996 (IIRIRA) requires that states not provide any postsecondary education benefit to undocumented students who are residents of the state unless that benefit is also made available to other citizens and nationals of the United States without regard to whether they are state residents.[15] Although no state has ever been compelled to enforce the law, two governors cited it when vetoing measures that would have given in-state tuition to undocumented students, and the State University of New York changed its tuition policy to avoid violating the statute. Governor Gray Davis of California cited the need to comply with IIRIRA in his veto message of AB 1197 in 2000, noting, "I believe the State's priorities and funding must be focused on higher education attainment for California legal residents, both present and future."[16] Wisconsin governor Scott McCallum used his line-item veto to eliminate a similar provision approved by the Wisconsin legislature in August 2001. Just over a year later, however, in October 2001, Governor Davis signed AB 540, which allows certain types of undocumented students to pay in-state tuition. That California statute allows individuals who attended high school in California for three years or more and graduated from a California high school to pay in-state tuition rates at California State University and California Community Colleges, but does not include the same privileges for the highest tier of the state university system, the University of California system. AB 540 students, as they are popularly known, are also required to file an affidavit stating that they have or will file an application for legal immigrant status as soon as legally permitted. Because the law uses attendance at and graduation from in-state high schools to define eligibility rather than residency, it does not violate federal law.

The intent of the IIRIRA is "to remove the incentive for illegal immigration provided by the availability of public benefits." As noted in a recent *Harvard Law Review* article, AB 540 does not threaten this interest because immigrants overwhelmingly come to the United States for employment, not for college. This point was made by Supreme Court Justice Brennan in the *Plyler v. Doe* decision, when he noted, "The dominant incentive for illegal entry into the [United States] is the availability of employment; few if any illegal immigrants come to this country . . . in order to avail themselves of a free education."[17]

Many states have taken action on their own to encourage the continued education of undocumented students that graduate from in-state high schools. State DREAM Acts allow undocumented residents who have graduated from high school to pay in-state tuition. Such assistance is usually of major significance to undocumented students, as they are not eligible for federal financial aid and are more likely than the general population to live in poverty.[18] Texas was the first state to pass a DREAM Act back in 2001; the latest to join the list was Maryland, in November 2012, bringing the total to twelve (California, Connecticut, Illinois, Kansas, Maryland, New York, Oklahoma, Rhode Island, Texas, Utah, Washington, and Wisconsin). Oklahoma repealed its DREAM Act in 2007, but the Oklahoma Board of Regents nonetheless allows undocumented students to pay in-state rates by virtue of board action. Undocumented students in Texas, New

Mexico, and California are also eligible for state financial aid, and Illinois has a private scholarship fund for DREAM Act students.[19] In Massachusetts, under a policy announced by Governor Duval Patrick in November 2012, undocumented youth who have obtained a federal work permit under President Obama's deferred deportation plan are now eligible for in-state tuition.

When California governor Jerry Brown signed the California DREAM Act that extended financial aid to undocumented students—a bill that had been vetoed four times by previous Republican governors—he said in a statement, "Going to college is a dream that promises intellectual excitement and creative thinking. The Dream Act benefits us all by giving top students a chance to improve their lives and the lives of all of us." Similarly, Illinois governor Pat Quinn, signing the bill creating a privately funded Illinois Dream Fund and opening the state's college savings fund to parents with a taxpayer identification number (but not necessarily a Social Security number), said, "Today we are showing what democracy is all about. We say to all the people in our country and in our state that we want everyone in and nobody out. All children have the right to a first-class education."

The impact of these state laws goes beyond lowering the tuition costs for existing students; allowing undocumented youth to pay in-state tuition continues active encouragement for them to enroll.[20] In many instances, the ability to complete a college degree still blocks these youth from achieving their dreams and aspirations. As noted by Bhattacharjee, before DACA an undocumented immigrant with a college degree still could not be legally employed.[21] The hope of DREAMers and state legislators was that when the federal government eventually took action to allow these young immigrants to work legally in the United States, they would be ready. Obama's deferred action program means that hope is now a reality for some DREAMers. Many of the youth we interviewed for this book spoke of their desire, and the desire of other DREAMers, to use the degrees they had worked so hard to earn, to pursue careers in science, engineering, medicine, and other fields rather than working dead-end, low-paying jobs. Ximena, a twenty-six-year-old woman who came to the United States at age fourteen, noted, "I already have two master's degrees. I mean, I'm just waiting to work in the United States lawfully and to be able to execute the knowledge that I have in a positive manner." Ricardo, a twenty-year-old man who came to the United States with his parents at age eight, described the same thought, but with more vivid imagery:

A: The passage of the DREAM Act allows you to exercise your degree. You are able to exercise your degree in the field that you study. If you're a Political Science major now you can go into politics. If you are a Biology major, now you can go into Biology. Same with medical fields … it will help people pursue whatever they're dreaming of doing.

Q: What about your own personal decisions concerning work and career choices, how would the passage of the DREAM Act affect that?

> A: Motivate me to work harder, even harder, because now I know that once I reach that light at the end of the tunnel, I'll be able to like, burst, kinda like a volcano—you're building up, you're building up, and as you go up and reach up the crater, once you reach the crater and you realize that there's nothing on top of it holding you down, you're just going to erupt. And that's what the DREAM Act is, actually.

Other respondents noted that for many undocumented youth, the *lack* of a light at the end of the tunnel means that they give up on their dreams. Frida, a twenty-year-old woman who came to the United States when she was three, commented, "I feel like some people have already given up, especially when—the job where I work at, it's a fast food restaurant and I see older people ... and it makes me sad that they feel like even though they are in this situation, they feel like that's the only thing that they can do."

In contrast, other states have taken the opposite approach, passing legislation to bar undocumented students from paying the same tuition rates as legal residents (Arizona, Colorado, Georgia, Indiana, Ohio, and South Carolina). Legislators in Alabama have gone even further, completely barring undocumented students from the state's colleges and universities. Many provisions of the Alabama law containing this ban, the Hammon-Beason Alabama Taxpayer and Citizen Protection Act, were immediately stayed by court order, and many were eventually nullified. Left untouched by the legal battles, however, was the provision barring undocumented immigrants from attending state colleges and universities.[22]

THE FEDERAL DREAM ACT

The precursor to the modern federal DREAM Act was introduced on April 25, 2001, by Chicago Democrat Luis Gutiérrez and thirty-four cosponsors. The Immigrant Children's Educational Advancement and Dropout Prevention Act of 2001 (HR 1582) aimed to allow undocumented youth "of good moral character" to regularize their status. Eligibility was limited to youth who were in the United States for at least five continuous years before turning twenty-one, were younger than twenty-five, and who were attending high school or an accredited two- or four-year college or had applied to attend college. The bill was immediately referred to the Subcommittee on Education Reform, where it died. Yet, the spirit of the bill has lived on and inspired continuing efforts to address the DREAMers' barriers to access to higher education. As Gutiérrez noted in the original bill's list of findings and purposes,

> (a) FINDINGS—Congress makes the following findings:
> (1) Undocumented children come to the United States for a variety of reasons. Most are brought to the United States by adults and have no ability to

make an independent decision about whether or not to migrate to the United States. Some come with their parents. Others are brought by smugglers and traffickers intent on exploiting them.

(2) It is the policy of the United States Government, supported both by acts of Congress and Supreme Court precedent, to permit undocumented children to attend public schools in the United States. This policy is rooted in recognition of the fact that such children often are not in a position to make an independent decision about where they will live, of the vulnerability of children, and by the desire to ensure that such children have an opportunity to become educated while in the United States.

(3) Each year, 50,000 to 75,000 such undocumented children graduate from United States public schools after having resided in the United States for 5 or more years.

(4) Young children who have resided in the United States for a substantial period of their lives often are acculturated as Americans, including learning to speak English. Often, they consider themselves Americans and have little or no knowledge or ties to the country in which they were born.

(5) Current law provides little avenue for long-staying alien children to regularize their immigration status. This, in turn, prevents them from continuing their education past high school, making it less likely that they will succeed in life and encouraging many to drop out of high school before graduating.

(6) While current law requires State and local governments to provide elementary and secondary education to undocumented alien children, the law effectively precludes State and local governments from providing in-State tuition to these same alien children once they have graduated from high school.

(b) PURPOSES—The purposes of this Act are—

(1) to provide an opportunity to certain alien children who were brought to the United States at a young age and have since been acculturated in the United States to adjust their status to lawful permanent residency and become contributing members of United States society;

(2) to restore to each State the flexibility to provide in-State tuition to all children residing in the State, including to undocumented alien children; and

(3) to permit and encourage alien children who were brought to the United States at a young age and have been educated in United States elementary and secondary schools to continue their education through high school graduation and into college.

On May 21, 2001, Utah representative Chris Cannon (R-UT) introduced a different proposal to regularize the status of undocumented youth, but limited its benefits to those younger than twenty-one (though retaining the other provisions of the Gutiérrez bill). This proposal garnered sixty-two cosponsors, but nevertheless met a similar fate—namely, it was referred to subcommittee, never to be seen again.

In the other chamber of Congress, Senator Orrin Hatch (R-UT) and eighteen cosponsors introduced the Development, Relief, and Education for Alien Minors Act (S 1291), which paralleled Cannon's proposal but limited eligibility to youth currently enrolled in school. The bill was reported out of the Judiciary Committee in June 2002, but was never scheduled for floor consideration. Subsequent attempts to regularize the status of undocumented students at the federal level have retained the title from Hatch's bill, but each time Congress has failed to send a DREAM Act to the president for consideration. In 2003, Senator Hatch again introduced a DREAM Act (S 1545, on July 31), with forty-seven cosponsors, but the bill met the same fate—it never made it to the floor.

In the next session of Congress, on November 11, 2005, a DREAM Act was introduced by Senator Dick Durbin (D-IL) (S 2075, with twenty-seven cosponsors) and subsequently included in the 2006 Comprehensive Immigration Reform Act (S 2611), which was approved by the Senate on May 25, 2006. As revised in this measure, eligibility would have been limited to those who entered the United States aged younger than sixteen and who had lived here continuously for at least five years, were of good moral character, and had earned a high school or equivalent diploma or been admitted to an institution of higher education. The Senate measure included a variety of enforcement enhancements, including increased border security and enforcement of work eligibility requirements, and it also included a path to regularization for up to 10 million undocumented immigrants already in the United States, paralleling the amnesty provision of the 1986 Immigration Reform and Control Act (IRCA).

In the House, in contrast, members approved HR 4437, The Border Protection, Anti-Terrorism, and Illegal Immigration Control Act of 2005, also known as the Sensenbrenner Bill for its sponsor, Jim Sensenbrenner (R-WI). HR 4437 focused on border control, including building a 700-mile fence between the United States and Mexico, and criminalizing those providing aid to undocumented immigrants (i.e., their friends and families, churches, and aid organizations). The bill is widely recognized as inspiring millions of undocumented immigrants and their supporters to take to the streets for the famous immigration marches of March, April, and May 2006. Given the striking difference in tone between the House and Senate versions of immigration bills that year, it should come as no surprise that members of the Congressional Conference Committee were unable to come to consensus, and neither immigration reform bill was approved.

In the 110th Congress (2007–2008), Senator Durbin tried again, introducing the DREAM Act on March 6, 2007 (S 774, twenty-six cosponsors). On the House side, Congressman Gutiérrez on March 22, 2007, introduced HR 1645, the Security Through Regularized Immigration and a Vibrant Economy Act of 2007 (STRIVE Act), with seventy-nine cosponsors. The latter included the DREAM Act, but within the context of a broader immigration reform package. The DREAM Act was also included in the 2007 Comprehensive Immigration Reform Act (S 1348); despite strong support from Republican president George

W. Bush, Republican opposition in the Senate in the form of a filibuster prevented the bill from passing.

The Comprehensive Immigration Reform Act of 2006 was approved by the Senate in no small part due to the combined efforts of Senators Ted Kennedy (D-MA) and John McCain (R-AZ), a bipartisan powerhouse that shepherded the bill through despite the desire by colleagues in both parties to make immigration an election issue for 2008. A year later, however, Senator McCain was running for president and thus was attentive to the anti-immigrant sentiments of the core of the Republican Party. Without his partner across the aisle, Senator Kennedy was unable to garner enough Republican support for the 2007 Act despite pressure from the president and support from Senate Republican Jon Kyl (R-AZ).[23]

After the Comprehensive Immigration Reform Act of 2007 was killed by a Republican filibuster, Senator Durbin in late 2008 moved to attach a DREAM Act to the 2008 Department of Defense Authorization Bill. This version of the measure included an age cap of thirty and extended eligibility to obtain citizenship to those who graduated from high school and either completed two years of college or served in the military. According to Durbin, the military supported the measure as a means of broadening the pool of potential recruits and overcoming recent challenges in meeting recruitment quotas.[24] In his remarks about the amendment, Durbin emphasized the addition of the path to citizenship via military service:

> Some people might ask why the Senate should revisit immigration again and whether an immigration amendment should be included in the Defense authorization bill. The answer is simple: The DREAM Act would address a very serious recruitment crisis that faces our military.
>
> Under the DREAM Act, tens of thousands of well-qualified potential recruits would become eligible for military service for the first time. They are eager to serve in the Armed Forces during a time of war. And under the DREAM Act they would have a very strong incentive to enlist because it would give them a path to permanent legal status.[25]

The amendment was never considered. In October 2007 Senator Durbin tried again to garner support for a freestanding DREAM Act (S 2205). In an attempt to garner bipartisan support, the bill was introduced with three cosponsors, including two leading Republicans, Richard Lugar (R-IN) and Chuck Hagel (R-NE), as well as Democrat Patrick Leahy (D-VT). Hoping to end a Republican filibuster, Senator Leahy spoke on the Senate floor in favor of the bill. He noted that DREAMers had been brought to the United States by their parents, through no choice of their own. Leahy continued,

> Those who would benefit from the DREAM Act are young people we should be encouraging to follow their dreams. The status quo, in which our policies create barriers to advancement for so many young people who yearn to achieve

and contribute, works to the disadvantage of the United States. Rather than barring young people from entering the American mainstream, we should strengthen our Nation's future through increased participation in higher education and in the military.[26]

A number of other senators rose to speak to the DREAM Act before the cloture vote. Senate Majority Leader Harry Reid (D-NV), noted,

> We should vote for this legislation because the DREAM Act recognizes that children should not be penalized for the actions of their parents. Many of the children this bill addresses came here when they were very young. Many don't even remember their home countries—in fact, most of them don't—or speak the language of their home countries. They are as loyal and devoted to our country as any American.[27]

These arguments notwithstanding, the vote for cloture failed, killing the bill. Republicans argued that the bill was an amnesty for those who had come into the country illegally, regardless of their age. Senator James Inhofe (R-OK) remarked, "this or any other type of an amnesty bill would be a slap in the face to all those who came here legally." Republican Minority Leader Senator Mitch McConnell (R-KY) noted, "Though I recognize and appreciate the tremendous contributions to our country made by generations of immigrants, I do not believe we should reward illegal behavior. It is our duty to promote respect for America's immigration laws and fairness for U.S. citizens and lawful immigrants."[28] But other Republican senators spoke in favor of the bill. Senator Kay Bailey Hutchison (R-TX), commented,

> [T]here are young people who have been brought to this country as minors, not of their own doing, who have gone to American high schools, graduated, and who want to go to American colleges. They are in a limbo situation. I believe we should deal with this issue. We should do it in a way that helps assimilate these young people with a college education into our country. They have lived here most of their lives. If we sent them home, they wouldn't know what home is. There is a compassionate reason for us to try to work this out.[29]

Durbin agreed that if the cloture motion was successful he would work with Hutchison to amend the DREAM Act to make it more palatable to Republicans. In a passionate appeal to his colleagues just before the final vote, he said, "We are talking about children. We are talking about children who are brought to this country by their parents. Since when in America do we visit the sins and crimes of parents on children?"[30] Yet, in the end, the cloture vote failed by a wide margin, 52–44, killing the DREAM Act's chances for the 110th Congress.

Proponents of the DREAM Act continued their work in the next session. On March 26, 2009, the act was reintroduced in both chambers of Congress, with forty cosponsors for the Durbin bill (S 729) and 139 cosponsors of the House version (HR 1751), introduced by Representative Howard Berman (D-CA). Reflecting previous debate and Republican objections, the bill included further limits and adjustments compared to previous DREAM Acts. Eligibility for conditional permanent residency was limited to those aged twelve to thirty-five, with no access to federal educational grants, and undocumented immigrants could lose their eligibility and be deported if they failed to meet the educational or military service requirement within six years.

During the course of the 111th Congress, various amendments to the bill were made to garner additional support, including reducing the age cap to twenty-nine, requiring criminal background checks and the payment of significant application fees, and limiting the ability of DREAMers to sponsor family members for citizenship.[31] Each time it was brought to a vote, however, the bill was killed with a Republican filibuster. On September 21, 2010, Senate Majority Leader Harry Reid (D-NV) brought the DREAM Act to a vote as an amendment to a Department of Defense spending bill, noting its support from the Pentagon. The move was criticized as election-year politics by Republicans, including McCain, who called out Reid for holding up the nation's military budget in order to reach out to Latino voters in advance of the November 2010 election. In a written statement, Reid responded to McCain directly, noting, "Senator McCain and anyone else who thinks the DREAM Act is not directly related to our national security should talk to the brave young men and women who want to defend our country but are turned away."[32]

Nevertheless, the DREAM Act appended to the defense bill was defeated by a cloture vote of 56–43 (with 60 needed to end the filibuster). Every Republican senator voted against the amendment, as did the two Democrats from Arkansas, Blanche Lincoln and Mark Pryor.[33] The outcome of the vote was not a surprise: Republican opposition to the DREAM Act combined with Republican opposition to ending the military ban on openly gay service members (Don't Ask, Don't Tell), which was also appended to the defense bill, guaranteed defeat. Yet, the outcome still came as a blow to supporters:

> Several young people who would have benefited from the legislation watched the vote from the gallery, some wearing graduation caps and gowns. Many sat stone-faced when the vote tally was read. A young woman dressed in a gold cap and gown wiped away tears.[34]

Durbin reintroduced the bill the next day, September 22, 2010, with two cosponsors (Leahy and Lugar); it did not come to the floor for a vote during the rest of the regular session.

Supporters tried one more time during the lame-duck December 2010 session, appending the DREAM Act to another, unrelated piece of legislation.[35] Hoping to build momentum for the measure, supporters first brought it up for a vote in the House of Representatives, where it was approved by a vote of 216–198.

But the proposal died in the Senate, killed by another Republican filibuster and a 55–41 cloture vote (again falling short of the 60-vote supermajority needed).

During House floor debate, proponents were careful to focus on the limited eligibility of the act, and the very strict requirements and limitations for beneficiaries. Opponents focused on the threat to American jobs, on the possibility that fraud would inflate the number of eligible participants, and the concern that passage of the bill would encourage future flows of additional undocumented immigrants. As with many controversial measures, a reading of the text of the House floor debate might give the reader the impression that supporters and opponents were not debating the same piece of legislation, given how differently they portrayed its components and probable effects. In general, Democrats were supportive while Republicans were opposed. Representative Chet Edwards (D-TX) noted, "[M]y faith and my values teach me we do not punish children for decisions made by their parents. That's why I rise in support of the DREAM Act."[36] Representative Rush Holt (D-NJ) noted the new version's delay of ten years until a beneficiary could apply for legal permanent resident status and the substantial fees ($525 upon filing and $2,000 to extend at year five): "Thus, this bill provides no amnesty and is most definitely not a 'free ride' for illegal immigrants."[37] Representative John Conyers Jr. (D-MI) noted, "the bill is very popular. Most Americans support the DREAM Act. Poll after poll, the majority of Americans approve of the DREAM Act." Conyers also cited the "voluminous" conditions for eligibility in the bill, including residency and educational requirements and the need to submit biometric information and undergo law enforcement background checks.[38]

On the other side of the aisle, Representative Lamar Smith (R-TX) called the DREAM Act "a nightmare for the American people." In his floor remarks during the December 8, 2010, debate, he claimed the DREAM Act would cost Americans their jobs, as they would be forced to compete with millions of newly eligible workers, that the DREAMers would use their new positions to petition for their parents, brothers, and sisters to join them, creating an "endless chain" of new immigrants, and that it was sure to be abused by those not truly eligible.[39] Smith continued,

> We all know that the point of this bill is to give amnesty to almost everyone who is in the country illegally and who is under 30. Illegal immigrants get amnesty if they can show hardship if they are sent home. Illegal immigrants can stay if they just claim to be eligible under this legislation. Illegal immigrants get amnesty if they use fraudulent documents because the Federal Government has no way to check millions of claims. Illegal immigrants get amnesty even if they have committed crimes like DUI, document fraud, and visa fraud. This is a bill that gives amnesty to more than 2 million people who are in the country illegally. It encourages fraud and even more illegal immigration.[40]

Representative Tom Graves (R-GA) quipped, "[T]his bill is not the American Dream. This bill is the amnesty dream."

This is no dream. This is a nightmare. This is a nightmare for the taxpayers of our country. This is a nightmare for America itself. Besides the fundamental problem of rewarding and incentivizing illegal behavior, this bill worsens our debt and puts a further strain on American families. Simply put, an open-door amnesty policy, with no spending cap, no limit in scope and a free invitation to all the Federal benefits of this country, adds up to a cost that our taxpayers cannot afford. I urge my colleagues tonight to vote for the American Dream by rejecting the amnesty dream.[41]

Representative Elton Gallegly (R-CA) argued that the bill would encourage future flows of undocumented youth by parents hoping for another, similar amnesty bill.[42] Representative Steve King (R-IA) argued, "If you support this nightmare DREAM Act, you are actually supporting an 'affirmative action amnesty act' that rewards people for breaking the law and punishes those who defend America."[43]

Comments on the Senate floor the next day, December 9, 2010, were similarly bifurcated. For example, Senator Robert Menendez (D-NJ) commented,

This is not amnesty. Amnesty—which I have heard some of my colleagues use, and they will use it on anything that is immigration related. Right away they roll out the word "amnesty." Amnesty is when you get something for nothing; when you did something wrong and you have to pay no consequence. In this case I believe wearing the uniform of the U.S. Armed Forces, risking your life for your country, maybe losing that life before you achieve your goal and your dream, is not amnesty. I believe working hard and being educated so you can help fuel the Nation's prosperity and meet its economic challenge, that is not amnesty. That is paying your dues on behalf of the country. For if you do all of that, you still have to wait a decade before your status can be adjusted to permanent residency. So you have to be an exemplary citizen, you have to do everything that is right, everything we cherish in America. That is what the DREAM Act is all about.[44]

On the other side of the aisle, Jeff Sessions (R-AL) argued,

[D]o not continue to reward illegality. Do not continue to provide benefits for people who violated our law, please. The first thing you do is don't reward it. The second thing you want to do is to end the mass illegality that is occurring in our country—600,000 people were arrested last year trying to enter our country illegally at the border—600,000. This is a huge problem.... [This bill] is not set up for military, it is not set up for valedictorians and salutatorians, it is not set up for people going to Harvard. It is set up for people who have come into the country, can be brought in illegally as a teenager, they go to high school—they have to be accepted. They get a GED or get a high school degree, and they apply and have a safe harbor in our country indefinitely. I introduced yesterday a chart showing a Google page with a whole long list of places you can order false high school diplomas, false transcripts, false GED certificates. There are no people funded to investigate any of this. People are going to walk in and say: I am 30 years old and I came at age 16. I'm in. Who is going to go out and investigate that? Nobody is. There is no funding to do it, and there is no plan to do it. It is a major loophole.[45]

Senator David Vitter (R-VT) argued that the bill would put at least 2.1 million undocumented immigrants on a path toward citizenship, "which will also allow them to have their family members put in legal status." He added,

> [W]e are in the middle of a serious recession. The American people are hurting. Things such as slots at public colleges and universities, things such as financial aid for those positions are very scarce and very sought after, more than ever before, because of the horrible state of the economy. These young illegals who would be granted amnesty would be put in direct competition with American citizens for those scarce resources.[46]

Three Republicans crossed the aisle to vote for passage, but the effort to pass the DREAM Act failed once again, garnering only fifty-five of the sixty votes needed to end the Republican filibuster.

Repeated attempts to win Senate approval of a DREAM Act during the 112th Congress were similarly unsuccessful, particularly as the field heated up in advance of the 2012 presidential election. Widespread belief that the Latino vote would be crucial to the outcome meant that Democrats wanted to pass a DREAM Act in order to help ensure President Obama's reelection, while Republicans were similarly committed to blocking the president from any ability to claim victory on immigration. Introduced in both chambers on May 11, 2011 (HR 1842, S 952), this version had 115 cosponsors in the House and 35 cosponsors in the Senate. Just the day before, President Obama visited the border and acknowledged the political gridlock that continued to prevent legislative action on the immigration issue. In remarks in El Paso, President Obama noted that Democrats had already increased border security as Republicans had requested. He quipped,

> Even though we've answered these concerns, I've got to say I suspect there's still some who are trying to move the goal posts on us one more time. You know, they said "we needed to triple the border patrol." Well, now they're going to say we need to quadruple the border patrol, or they'll want a higher fence. Maybe they'll need a moat. Maybe they'll want alligators in the moat. They'll never be satisfied.[47]

Activists at the El Paso, Texas, event pressured President Obama to take unilateral action. Angelica Salas, executive director of the Coalition for Humane Immigrant Rights of Los Angeles (CHIRLA), commented, "We will continue to remind the president: yes, you can stop students' deportations; yes, you can stop splitting families apart; yes, you can do your part now."[48]

Reintroducing the bill on the floor of the Senate, Senator Durbin outlined the major points of the bill, told stories of individual DREAMers, and made a plea for support:

> When we debated that bill on the floor of the Senate last December, the galleries were filled with students wearing graduation gowns and caps, waiting, praying for the vote, and it failed. They left, many of them crying. They went downstairs, and I met with them. They couldn't have felt worse. They just don't know where to turn. They are being rejected by the only country they have ever known, the only place they have ever called home. I said to them: I am not giving up on you. Don't give up on me. We are going to keep working on this. We reintroduced the bill today. I thank my colleagues who have already cosponsored it. I urge and plead with others who have not for simple justice and fairness. Give these young people a chance. That is all they are asking for.[49]

Referred to relevant subcommittees, the only action taken was hearings in the Senate Judiciary Subcommittee on Immigration, Refugees, and Border Security. At those hearings, on June 28, 2011, Senator Durbin again made a passionate introduction, calling the DREAM Act "one of the most compelling human rights issues of our time" and noting, "These Dreamers would happily go to the back of the line and wait their turn for citizenship, but there is no line for them to get into."[50]

Margaret Stock, a retired military officer, attorney, and political science professor, testified that the DREAM Act "would enhance America's future ability to obtain high-quality recruits for the United States Armed Forces."[51] In contrast, Steven Camarota, director of research for the Institute for Immigration Studies, criticized the bill for having no provision to discourage future flows of undocumented immigrants; and because it would allow participants to sponsor their parents for green cards, increasing competition for scarce American jobs; and for being vulnerable to fraud. Hitting yet another theme of DREAM Act opponents, he argued, "if we give legal status to people who live here illegally, it is necessarily a slap in the face to legal immigrants. It makes those who play by the rules look like dupes for having taken our immigration laws seriously."[52]

No further action was taken, despite increasing numbers of DREAMer actions. As in 2010, Republicans did not want to give Democrats or the president a victory on which to campaign. Instead, several Republican senators who had previously supported versions of the DREAM Act, including John Cornyn of Texas, Jon Kyl of Arizona, John McCain of Arizona, and Lindsey Graham of South Carolina, now became opponents, citing the need to focus on border security and only pass a DREAM Act as part of a larger, comprehensive immigration package. At the hearing, Senator Cornyn noted that while he had been a supporter of the DREAM Act for many years, the current measure was too susceptible to fraud and to generating "chain migration" of relatives, issues that could only be resolved by including the DREAM Act in a broader immigration bill.[53] In this extremely heated partisan context, overcoming a Senate filibuster was impossible. Pressure mounted on President Obama to take unilateral executive action, which he finally did in June 2012 with his announcement of the DACA program.

ECONOMIC IMPACT

Throughout the years of debate, various projections of the cost of the DREAM Act were calculated and debated, both from the nonpartisan Congressional Budget Office as well as nongovernmental organizations and research centers on either side of the immigration debate. The estimates differ, both because there were so many different versions of the DREAM Act from which to begin and because each required making assumptions about the number of eligible undocumented immigrants who would take advantage of their ability to regularize their status, either through military service or by attending college.

The December 2010 report by the Congressional Budget Office (CBO) used as the basis of its report the 2010 Senate version of the bill, S 3992. Overall, the CBO estimated increased costs from 2010 to 2020 of $912 million, increased revenues of $2.3 billion, and an overall reduction in the federal budget deficit of $1.4 billion. However, the CBO also noted that costs would increase after 2020 due to the eventual conversion of DREAMers into legal permanent residents, thus eligible for federal health insurance exchanges, Medicaid, and the Supplemental Nutrition Assistance Program. "CBO estimates that the bill would increase projected deficits by more than $5 billion in at least one of the four consecutive 10-year periods starting in 2021."[54]

Estimates of increased revenues were based on a number of considerations. One such assumption was that some undocumented workers would become authorized workers, thus leading to increased reporting of employment income and thus increased collection of social insurance and personal income taxes. Bringing workers out of the shadows would also lead to decreases in revenue, including larger tax deductions by businesses for their labor compensation and also because legal workers would be entitled to file tax returns and claim refunds, but these decreases would be heavily outweighed by the tax increases. Costs of the DREAM Act from 2011 to 2020 would include $961 million for refundable tax credits, $77 million for Social Security, and $29 million for Medicare, with a small additional amount for federal student loans. Costs incurred by the Department of Homeland Security to implement the law would be more than offset by the estimated $700 per case that the DHS was expected to collect from affected individuals, actually reducing their expected outlays due to the lag between the collection of fees and spending that revenue.[55]

Taking an even longer-term view, out to 2030 instead of 2020, the Center for American Progress, a progressive think tank, projected that passage of the

DREAM Act would add $329 billion to the US economy and create 1.4 million new jobs. DREAMers themselves would benefit, of course, due to their ability to obtain legal employment and by moving them into higher educational levels. Overall, their aggregate earnings would have increased by 19 percent, to $148 billion by 2030. In addition, non-DREAMers would benefit from $181 billion in induced economic activity, the creation of 1.4 million new jobs, and the collection of more than $12.2 billion in additional state and federal tax revenues.

Put simply, higher earnings for DREAMers translate into more money flowing into our economy through greater consumption of goods and services. This added consumption ripples through the entire economy as businesses increase in size to meet the demands of the DREAMers' consumption. This increase generates additional earnings for workers, creates new jobs, and raises additional tax revenue.[56] The DREAMers we spoke to for this book often articulated the benefit to the US economy that their labor could potentially provide. Allison, a twenty-three-year-old woman who came to the United States as an infant, commented,

> [N]ot only will we be able to contribute to the economy even more but we'll be able to work in jobs that will help society: teachers, social workers, doctors, you know, all these jobs that we will be able to come in and be a part of society and be included and not be excluded after graduating.

Along similar lines, Daniel, a twenty-two-year-old male who came to the United States when he was two, said the DREAM Act would mean the ability to use his degree after graduating. "I feel that I have a lot of skills and the passage of the DREAM Act—I'd be able to put those skills to use and actually give back to the community." Alessandra, an eighteen-year-old who came to the United States at age six, said the DREAM Act would allow her to pursue her goal of becoming a lawyer. She commented,

> [I]t's really saddening to see, like, that there are many qualified people, not only for lawyers but any profession out there, but they're just simply denied because they don't have a Social Security number. And, you know, given that opportunity, I think, you know, America would be better off having the most qualified people, even if, you know, they aren't Americans. As long as they're qualified, I think that it would definitely give America better opportunity to, you know, survive.

Vicente, a twenty-seven-year-old who came to the United States at age fourteen, saw benefits for the economy and his community:

> I mean, it's gonna affect our communities tremendously, right? Like, I live in Los Angeles and Los Angeles has the largest undocumented immigrant community in the nation, and obviously also the largest immigrant youth community in the nation, and by folks being able to enter, you know, the formal economy and

then, and continuing with their educational careers, have professional careers, they'll be able to contribute back to the economy and to the community and make it stronger.

Additional details from the Center for American Progress report are shown in Table 2.1 and Figure 2.1. Benefits of the DREAM Act were predicted to increase over time as more eligible immigrants became old enough to join the workforce and contribute to the economy. Labor income represents the aggregate total of the increase in earnings combined with earnings from new jobs generated. Value added is the total earnings, profits, and business taxes added to the economy. This total also represents the amount by which the nation's Gross Domestic Product (GDP) will increase. Total production represents the total increase in economic activity.

Even larger estimates of economic benefits were generated by a 2010 study from the North American Integration and Development Center at the University of California, Los Angeles. In this study, the authors generated two sets of economic impact predictions: one for a scenario in which only 825,000 individuals took advantage of the DREAM Act, the Migration Policy Institute's lower-bound estimate of the number of eligible immigrants who would apply for and receive benefits, and a second scenario, called "No DREAMers Left Behind," which estimated the effect of extending benefits to all 2.1 million potential beneficiaries. The study also noted that the DREAM Act would allow taxpayers to increase their return on prior investment in the K–12 education of undocumented youth, and that increased educational attainment of DREAMers "would also advance the U.S. global competitive position in science, technology, medicine, education and many other endeavors."[57]

The UCLA study estimated how much income the DREAMers would generate, assuming a forty-year work life (from age twenty-five to sixty-five), as $1.4 trillion assuming the lower-bound estimate and $3.6 trillion under the No DREAMers Left Behind scenario.

Table 2.1 The Induced Benefits of Passing the DREAM Act

Category	2010–2020	2020–2025	2025–2030	Total
Jobs generated	356,000	416,000	602,000	1,375,000
Labor income	$16 billion	$19 billion	$27 billion	$62 billion
Value added	$27 billion	$34 billion	$50 billion	$112 billion
Total production	$46 billion	$55 billion	$80 billion	$181 billion
Federal business taxes	$1.2 billion	$1.4 billion	$2.0 billion	$4.6 billion
Personal income taxes	$1.4 billion	$1.7 billion	$2.5 billion	$5.6 billion

Source: Juan Carlos Guzmán and Raúl C. Jara, *The Economic Benefits of Passing the DREAM Act* (Washington, DC: Center for American Progress, October 2012), 11.

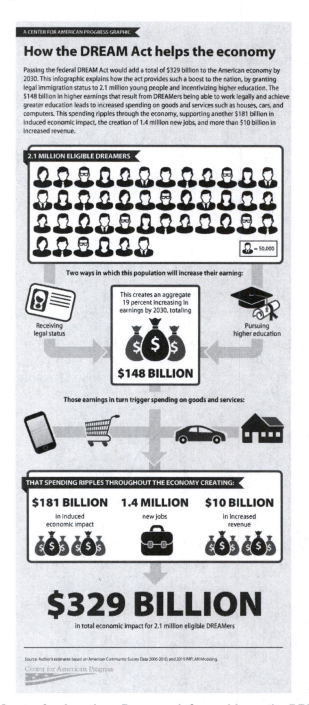

Figure 2.1 Center for American Progress Infographic on the DREAM Act[58]

Table 2.2 North American Integration and Development Center Forty-Year Income Estimates for DREAMers

	Average Income (current dollars)	Lower-Bound Scenario (825,000 beneficiaries)		No DREAMer Left Behind Scenario (1.2 million beneficiaries)	
		Estimated Number of Beneficiaries	Total over 40 years	Estimated Number of Beneficiaries	Total over 40 years
PhD/doctoral degree	$85,000	4,383	$14.9 billion	11,846	$40.3 billion
Master's degree	$60,250	12,585	$30.3 billion	34,011	$81.9 billion
Bachelor's degree	$45,000	421,392	$758.5 billion	1,138,793	$2,049.8 billion
Associate's degree	$37,250	317,640	$473.3 billion	857,850	$1,278.1 billion
Military service	$36,799	71,000	$104.5 billion	107,500	$158.2 billion
Total			$1.38 trillion		$3.6 trillion

Source: Raul Hinojosa Ojeda and Paule Cruz Takash, *No DREAMers Left Behind: The Economic Potential of DREAM Act Beneficiaries* (Los Angeles: North American Integration and Development Center, University of California, Los Angeles, October 2010), 10.

Opponents of the DREAM Act also generated economic impact reports. The Center for Immigration Studies looked specifically at the cost of providing in-state tuition to DREAMers, at an average cost of $5,970 per student per year. Given the possibility that as many as 1.038 million undocumented immigrants would take advantage of the bill to attend community colleges and state universities, this would mean an additional possible tuition cost to taxpayers at the state level of $6.2 billion per year.[59] Perhaps in response to this criticism, later versions of the bill removed the requirement that states offer in-state tuition to beneficiaries, leaving that decision to the states. Opponents also tended to call attention to the long-term negative impact projected for the federal deficit in the CBO report, as noted above. Opponents frequently expressed concern that more legal employees would increase job market competition, to the detriment of US citizens seeking work, but despite the vehement claims to this effect often expressed on the floors of the House and Senate, published studies have consistently concluded the opposite, as noted above.

SUMMARY

US immigration policies, past and present, have generated push and pull forces that send undocumented immigrants to this country in search of employment.

Recent efforts to stem the flow via increased border security have merely interrupted the previous circular patterns of migration, encouraging undocumented workers to stay permanently in the United States rather than risking repeated crossings, and in many cases to bring their families to the United States to join them. Undocumented youth are eligible for K–12 education, based on the 1982 *Plyler v. Doe* decision, but they generally find their paths toward educational and occupational success blocked after high school. They cannot obtain driver's licenses, they cannot apply for federal financial aid, and in most states they are not eligible to pay in-state college tuition rates. These children have grown up as Americans, saluting the American flag, dreaming the American Dream, but they cannot achieve that dream because of their legal status.

Various state legislators and governors have taken action to allow these DREAMers to pay in-state college tuition, easing their path toward their higher educational goals. But until the federal government took action, they were unable to work legally in this country and often still cannot afford to go to college; those eligible under DACA can now apply for two-year work permits, but for most DREAMers institutional barriers to their dreams remain in place. Over the past decade, proponents of a federal DREAM Act, mostly Democrats, have continued to push for such a bill, tinkering with the eligibility requirements and restrictions in response to Republican opposition. Yet, each time the bill has come to a vote it has been blocked by a Republican filibuster. Despite support from a majority of members of the House and Senate, proponents have thus far been unable to reach the supermajority of sixty votes to end Senate debate. In fact, the last few years have seen a reduction in Republican support, even as a series of academic and think tank studies have predicted generally positive economic impacts. As this book went to press, media reports confirmed that an immigration reform bill was unlikely to emerge from Congress during Obama's presidency, despite his renewed calls for action in the 2014 State of the Union address. The issue has become yet another victim of the increasingly bifurcated world of partisan Washington politics. In this political environment, and seeking to reach out to Latino voters in advance of the November 2012 presidential election, President Obama announced on June 15, 2012, that his administration would stop deporting DREAMers, creating the Deferred Action for Childhood Arrivals program.

Chapter 3

Flying under the Radar

The Racialization of Immigration and the DREAMers

> [B]eing an illegal immigrant shapes who you are, ... when you're growing up, like what you become and ... how you act and whatnot.
>
> —*Jorge, twenty-one-year-old male*

Hugo is a Latino male in his early twenties who came to the United States with his mother—after spending his young life separated from his father—at the age of four. He sits down with our interviewer at a Starbucks in East Los Angeles, signs the consent form to participate in the interview, and begins to talk about his life as an undocumented Latino raised in southern California. Growing up in Monterey Park, initially his greatest obstacle was learning English when he began kindergarten. However, he soon discovered that there would be many more barriers he would have to face, ones that would make not knowing his father until he was four, or having to quickly learn English, easy in comparison. The oldest of three, Hugo was held up as an example for his twin siblings. His parents would say to the twins, both of whom are US citizens, "Look at your brother. Your brother doesn't have any papers, but look at what he's been able to accomplish ... if he could do it, you guys could do that, and more." As an honor roll student and a star football player in high school, Hugo was given many scholarship offers from universities only to have to turn them down because of his status. His cautious nature about his status stayed with him until his senior year of high school. He says, "I understood that I wasn't gonna be, like ... they require your Social Security and whatnot." Hugo had always been private about his undocumented status. "I was one of those guys that ... I always did well. I excelled in everything. But

49

I never wanted anyone to know about my status because I didn't want anyone to feel, you know, pity for me or feel like I was any different. I didn't want to be categorized as an 'other.'" Thinking about the decisions he had to make after high school that were impacted by his undocumented status, Hugo states, "I applied to the UCs ... UCLA, UC Berkeley, UC Davis, UC Irvine, and UC Riverside.... I got into every school. I got into *every* school, but none of the schools gave me any scholarships.... I didn't get anything. They said, 'Congratulations, you've been accepted' ... but I knew, like, I couldn't afford it." Despite the bitter disappointment he felt about not being able to attend any of these institutions, he was in time offered a full scholarship closer to home at California State University, Los Angeles. Graduating from CSU, LA in two and a half years with a 3.95 GPA, he now works two jobs as a waiter while continuing on with his education. Now at twenty-three years of age, Hugo reflects on the decisions he had to make and how he does not let his status stop him. Hugo says, "So, it affects my decisions. Yeah. So I just keep on going to school. And I'm just gonna keep on going to school until, like, I understand that, you know, I have a long road ahead of me, but I'm just gonna keep going." His undocumented status does not deter him from pursuing his dreams.

The experiences that Hugo describes about his life as an undocumented youth are not unique. Most of the DREAMers interviewed for this book shared similar stories of starting school in the United States, often as early as kindergarten, and participating in all the activities and events that their friends did. They were just kids being kids. Then one day, usually in high school, they were faced with the reality of how their undocumented status sets them apart. It often came as a crushing blow that not only stopped them from obtaining scholarships or the right to drive, but made them feel like they simply did not count. As Hugo states, "I didn't exist. I didn't have a number."

When asked about how deferred action was going to change his immediate circumstances, he observes, "Oh man, you know what's going to change? I'm actually gonna be able to apply for a work permit." He continues, "And when I get a work permit, I'm gonna go straight to the DMV and apply for my driver's license." The importance of this seemingly minor act comes out when Hugo adds, "[G]et my driver's license ... I feel like a part of my life is gonna be real, you know."

Similar to Hugo, study participants' experiences as undocumented youth have affected many areas of their lives, from not being able to obtain a driver's license, to being cautious about revealing their status to potential friends and romantic partners, to not being able to accept offers of acceptance from some of the top universities in the country. In the next three chapters we tell the stories of 101 undocumented Latino youth who often felt as though they "didn't exist" because they "didn't have a number." We show how despite being good students and civically engaged citizens, they often are blocked at many of life's turns. Like Hugo, most of them know no other country besides the United States, yet they are excluded from many important American political, educational, and social institutions. In significant ways their lives and destinies are not in their own hands, but in the hands of a Congress that is incapable of governing. Having lost the ability to compromise, Congress has lost the capacity to pass much-needed legislation such as tax reform, infrastructure renewal, gun safety, and immigration reform; not even the popular (and once bipartisan) DREAM Act is able to make it into law in the contemporary Congress.[1]

In the next three chapters we look at US politics and practices from the eyes of the DREAMers. In addition to examining their personal experiences we also discuss representative responses to open-ended questions regarding immigrant background and experiences. This sets the stage to discuss their political views, political socialization, and ethnic identity. Based on these interviews, we go beyond highlighting the experiences of undocumented youth from various states across the country in the post–deferred action period to demonstrating how their experiences have affected their views of themselves, their life choices, and their political perspectives. We will come to understand why many of our respondents consider deferred action "too little, too late" as a public policy.

We begin in this chapter by laying out the demographic and immigration background of our sample of DREAMers. Next we highlight some of the most common ways our respondents discovered they were undocumented. We move on to discuss how living in mixed–legal status households has affected them. Finally, we examine their perceptions about treatment from others who know about their undocumented status. We conclude this chapter by looking at how their undocumented status has affected their decisions and choices about their future. In each of these sections we provide numerous interview vignettes and comments because we want to, as much as possible, present their stories and experiences through their own words as opposed to our filtering of their experiences through our collective lens. Their stories are about how living as a racialized immigrant group means living "under the radar" in a state of vulnerability where they or their parents could be deported at any time, and how these circumstances have permanently shaped their identities as well as their views about the United States. Our interviews show that growing up as an undocumented Latino has been a heavy burden for our study respondents. The stories we highlight in the next three chapters are life tales from those who have been excluded from American society legally, politically, and often, also socially. Every single DREAMer we recruited for this study in four US western states believed that their situation as an unauthorized person affected their life in significant and often detrimental ways. These detrimental consequences include personal and professional decisions, choices about whether to go to college and where, what to do with their lives after college graduation, how to secure decent employment, and even deeply personal decisions such as whether to tell boyfriends or girlfriends about their undocumented status. Their stories demonstrate in concrete ways the racialization of Latinos discussed in Chapter 1, including their counterframes and acts of resistance to their legal status. Their words are examples of how the white racial frame has negatively impacted all areas of their lives.

DEMOGRAPHIC INFORMATION

In order to begin to understand the experiences of our sample of DREAMers we must first provide some information about their demographic backgrounds. Most existing scholarship on undocumented youth was published prior to President Obama's announcement of the deferred action program. Therefore, what we know about the lives and experiences of undocumented youth is primarily focused on those undocumented youth who have overcome great odds and are held up as examples of American meritocracy. Fewer studies focus on the "wasted lives," as Abrego and Gonzales describe them.[2] Abrego and Gonzales focus on the struggles faced by those who *do not* attend a four-year university, arguing that focusing on the exceptional undocumented youth perpetuates the myth of an American meritocracy while ignoring the experiences of the majority of Latino youth. They argue that it is important for scholars to focus on the experiences of undocumented youth who are not in college because those are the ones who will be stuck in poverty and thus held back from reaching their full potential, both educationally and economically. Without the legal protections that the passage of comprehensive legislation such as the DREAM Act provides, for fear of being deported these undocumented youth do not even utilize existing social services that for generations have assisted immigrants. Because only about half of undocumented youth graduate from high school, the primary path policy needs to take is to increase the educational pipeline. They note,

> These young people can legally attend school, but they cannot work, vote, receive financial aid, or drive in most states. Furthermore, routine tasks and social events, such as buying cell phones, establishing credit, applying for library or movie rental cards, and even going to R-rated movies or bars, become extremely complicated. Most important, at any time, these young men and women can be deported to countries they barely know. Therefore, although they have legal access to K–12 schooling, they are unable to make full use of their education. Their situation provides a stark example of just how out of step current immigration policies are with contemporary realities.[3]

As Table 3.1 demonstrates, our sample of study participants falls squarely in line with what Abrego and Gonzales call exceptional undocumented Latino youth: 97 percent of our respondents have a high school diploma, 70 percent are currently enrolled in college, and almost 17 percent have already graduated from college. Although we agree with Abrego and Gonzales that it is important to study the most vulnerable among the undocumented youth—those without even a high school diploma—we contend that there is also much that can be learned from focusing on the "exceptions." These are the future leaders in the Latino immigrant community, individuals who have faced obstacles despite evidence of great individual promise, and thus who exemplify the image of "wasted lives." These are Latino youth who often have been forced to relinquish awards, scholarships, and acceptances to top universities simply because of their undocumented legal status. Despite their educational achievements, many work as nannies, in fast food restaurants, or as laborers. Their educational attainment is truly "wasted": they cannot contribute to society in their chosen professions because they lack a Social Security number.

As shown in Table 3.1, we spoke to forty-six men and fifty-five women, and can thus speak to the experiences of youth of both genders. Mirroring the demographics of the US DREAMer population, our sample is overwhelmingly of Mexican origin (97 percent). Virtually all of our respondents have a high school diploma or equivalent, and 70 percent are currently enrolled in college or university. These figures are considerably higher than the figures from the broader Latino population, with the high school graduation rate currently at an all-time high at 78 percent[4] and the college enrollment rate at 56 percent.[5] While the educational achievements of our respondents are quite high, clearly our sample did not come from families with high levels of formal education, or what is known as inherited intellectual capital.[6] Table 3.2 details the levels of education attained by the parents of our sample.

As shown in Table 3.2, an overwhelming majority of our sample of DREAMers are first-generation college students: only half of their parents had completed a grade school education and less than 20 percent of them have high

Table 3.1 Undocumented Youth Background Information (*N* = 101)

Gender	
Male	46
Female	55
Immigration status	
US citizen	0.0%
Permanent resident	5.0%
Other	95.0%
Family's status	
Same as participant's	28.7%
Mix	71.3%
Place of birth	
Mexico	97.0%
United States	0.0%
Other	3.0%
Educational status	
High school diploma or equivalent	97.0%
Currently enrolled in college	70.3%
Graduated from college	16.8%
Age	
Average age of participants	21.9
Age range of participants	18–30
Average age of arrival to US	7.2
Average age of finding out about status	11.4

Table 3.2 Parents' Educational Attainment (in Percentages)

Highest Grade Completed by Parent	Mothers	Fathers
Grade school	54.0	50.0
Some high school	9.0	7.4
High school diploma/GED	18.0	14.9
Some college	7.0	9.6
Associate's degree	4.0	3.2
Bachelor's degree or higher	8.0	14.9

school diplomas. Only 8 percent of the mothers and 15 percent of the fathers had a bachelor's degree.

HOW THE RESPONDENTS DISCOVERED THEIR UNDOCUMENTED STATUS

As we document in Table 3.1, the average age upon arrival of our sample of DREAMers into the United States was only seven years old, the age of most first- or second-grade children, who are, as one of our study participants described, "still playing with dolls and watching Dora." This is the age when most children are learning to read, ride their bikes, and lose their baby teeth. They are years away from contemplating driving, applying for scholarships, going to college, or getting their first jobs. In fact, as we show in this section many of our respondents first discovered their undocumented status during their preteen and young adult years, usually as they tried to participate in an extracurricular activity or when it came time to apply for scholarships and university admission. Because most of our respondents arrived at such a young age the news of their undocumented status often came as a complete shock. We asked our respondents the following questions: "How did you find out about your immigration status? How old were you?" While the specific details and circumstances varied among the answers we received to these two questions, the majority of the DREAMers we interviewed responded with stories of being denied access to experiences and opportunities. Below is an example of a typical answer to this question by Ricardo, who has lived in the United States since he was in the third grade:

A: When I went to apply for a job … I was 15 and that's when I found out; I couldn't get the job because of that same status that I had.

Q: Wow, 'cause you didn't have a Social Security number?

A: 'Cause I didn't have a Social Security so I couldn't go out to work.… Yeah, that's when it hits you that you realize that you're in a system that doesn't really want you to contribute to it 'cause you don't have that number and you feel discouraged, thrown out, segregated … like a leftover.

Ricardo, who had lived in the United States since he was eight years of age, felt as though he was a "leftover," and "thrown out"—as though he doesn't count and cannot contribute to society.

In addition, we discovered that while most of the respondents did not know they were undocumented until they were much older, even the ones that knew from a young age that they were not *Americanos* did not understand the full implications of what it would mean to their lives until they were much older. Below is a lengthy but important exchange that demonstrates this gap between growing up knowing one was undocumented and learning as a young adult how much it mattered. This is the story of Allison, a twenty-three-year-old college student at California State University, Los Angeles, majoring in social work, who arrived in the United States from Mexico as a baby.

> A: In the 8th grade, I was offered a scholarship.... I was an honor student so ... they were able to award three scholarships and because of my GPA, they gave me one of those and basically that money was going to be available once I was able to give proof of what college I was going to go to. So the money was going to be put in a safe fund for me. However, my counselor did not know that I was undocumented, and I wasn't aware either because as a child, we don't see, you know, whether you're undocumented or not. It's not like, "Mom, let me have my Social [Security number] to, I don't know, play bank," or something. So when she told me if I have a Social Security number it's like, I don't know, I was gonna put my phone number because it basically fit.
>
> Q: Oh, you thought it was your phone number?
>
> A: I thought it was my phone number [laughing] 'cause it did just kind of fit so she said to go home and give a letter to my mom which she's saying that she's congratulating me for a scholarship, but she needs for my mom to sign the consent form and to provide me with the following information. One of those was a Social Security number.

Allison describes what happens next. She recalls her mom sitting down and starting to cry as she tried to explain what lacking a Social Security number would mean to her.

> A: [S]he sat me down, and I was like, "what's going on?," you know, 'cause, "let me have that Social Security number, whatever they're asking for," and she compared me to my sister who is a US-born citizen and she said, "you were born in Mexico," which I knew, "so because of that you don't have papers, and your sister was born here in the US, so she has papers," and I grabbed her paper and I was, like, "What do you mean? I *have* papers." I'm like a child, so I don't even understand what she's saying, and she's like, "No, you don't have this number that your sister has because she was born in the US." And that's when I understood and I'm like, "oh, but why can't you just go

get it?" Like, in my mind it's not something bad, like "why can't you just go apply" and she says, "You can't, because you were born in Mexico, so you're like a Mexican *citizen.*" And I was like, "Oh!" So she put it into words, in terms so that maybe I would understand, but I'm not thinking that, you know, they're going to take away the scholarship.... I went back to school the next day and my mom actually wrote a letter to the counselor and that's when they were both talking on the phone and I was just sitting there and once she hung up the counselor just said, "You know what, I'm sorry but unfortunately we have to refuse the scholarship to you because you don't have this number, but you will still be invited to the ceremony, you'll still get a medal, you'll still get an award," but I didn't get the scholarship. So we went to the ceremony and everything else but I didn't get the money, basically, and that's when I realized, as an undocumented person, this was taken away from me. What else will be taken away from me?

Allison discovered what her undocumented status meant in the context of losing out on a scholarship that would contribute to a promising future for her. This was only the first of many opportunities that were going to be "taken away" because she was undocumented. The exchange between her and her mother shows how difficult this can be for a young child to grasp. It was not until this respondent lost the scholarship funds that she began to understand the full implications of not having a Social Security number. Brought to the United States when she was a baby of eight months old, she has never known another country, and yet at age twelve she received a message loud and clear that she did not belong to this one.

The following quote from Romina is another typical example of a common situation reported by our sample of DREAMers regarding how they discovered they were undocumented:

I found out I think I was in junior high and I tried to apply for a program and they denied it because I didn't have a Social [Security number].... We were going to go to state level [competition] and I couldn't go. It was already state finals so they told me like I couldn't go because of that.

Romina was only five when she arrived in the United States and similar to Allison's experiences, she grew up thinking she was an American, a member of the land of opportunity. But when she was twelve years old she discovered that many opportunities were not available to her. Ironically, many of our sample of DREAMers discovered their undocumented status so young because they excelled in school and sports and this meant they were offered opportunities of travel and scholarships that were taken from them once they could not produce a Social Security number.

While many of the DREAMers we talked to did not realize they were undocumented until it was time to apply for a driver's license or a job or a scholarship, others learned their status at an early age when they experienced the trauma of separation from their parents or other more drastic circumstances. We did not ask our respondents if they had ever spent time separated from their family because of their legal status; however, many of our respondents discovered they were undocumented because they shared an experience of being separated from their family when their parents were deported. For example, Emily arrived in the United States as a baby at the age of one, but her parents were deported when she was just four years old. In her own words:

Q: How did you find out about your immigration status?
A: Um, I think it was just ... it was never like a huge talk it was just kinda, I was aware I guess, since my parents were like this ... in the same situation as me then I kinda just figured I was in the same situation as them.
Q: Did they ever like tell you, you couldn't do something because of your status?
A: No, but my parents were deported when I was like about four, so ... that's kinda when I realized like what was going on.
Q: Did you go with them or how did they—
A: No, like, I was in school, and like both of my parents worked at a fast food restaurant and they were just deported and I was taken by one of my mom's friends at the time.

Alma, who was only one when she arrived in the United States, also discovered her undocumented status when she became separated from her parents:

Um, I would have to say probably when my parents got deported, both of them, so I kinda figured that I was in the same situation as them and that was when I was around four or three, around that age.

Traumatic as these experiences were, Alma and Emily were some of the lucky ones because both of them were eventually reunited with their parents. Every year, thousands of children who are separated from their parents due to deportations end up in the foster care system.[7] Once in the foster system, it is extremely difficult for parents to regain custody of their children, because of language difficulties, legal status, resources, and more generally a lack of understanding of how to negotiate the complex system. Because of the way we have racialized Latino immigrants, they are caught in a situation where in an effort to provide a better life for their families they lose the most important and precious thing in the world to them—their children—simply because they wanted a life free from destitution and poverty. This is the result of the racialized punitive immigration policy that the United States is enforcing, one where the cost of working without documentation is that you could lose your children. When did separating very young children from their parents become an American value? Most people cannot imagine the destructive long-term consequences these policies are having on immigrant families. It should take an offense far more severe than trying to earn a living or to secure a better future for one's children to justify the government's separating parents from their young children. The act of dividing families, particularly families of color, reveals a dark side of America—one we have seen before with black slave children removed from parents and sold off like they weren't even humans and with Indian children who were removed from their homes and placed in boarding schools to teach them how to be white people. Americans justified these atrocious acts in the past and we are doing it again as part of the racialization of undocumented immigrants. As long as people of color, especially the poor and the most vulnerable, are racialized and treated as subhuman, then we will have these devastating policies.[8]

Other respondents also knew from a relatively young age that they were undocumented, but not due to a traumatic experience such as being separated from their parents due to deportation. Santino, for example, was very aware of his unauthorized status from the beginning, because he arrived in the United States when he was in the sixth grade. However, despite this knowledge, similar to the majority of the DREAMers we interviewed, Santino did not understand the barriers his undocumented status would place on him until he began applying for scholarships and for university admission.

> [A]s a little kid, you know, it was easy for me to just move on, start learning new things. School came about, you know, successful at that, um, when I was—although I didn't start realizing that I was an "illegal" and that my chances of success were little to none, was when I started applying to colleges. And the only college's scholarship that I qualified for because of my GPA and my activities in school, you know they require a Social Security.... You know, it was in my senior year, I had all my friends leaving out for college ... and they were all like, you know, I was voted most likely to succeed in my high school. So it was kinda hard for me to come and stay at PanAm [the University of Texas–Pan American].

EFFECTS OF MIXED LEGAL STATUS IN FAMILY

According to the Migration Policy Institute, which is an independent, nonpartisan think tank focused on the study of worldwide immigration,[9] 82 percent of children of undocumented parents are US citizens resulting in 4.5 million children living in mixed–legal status family households. Paralleling the broader DREAMer population in the United States, approximately 70 percent of the DREAMers interviewed for this study are from mixed–legal status families. This means that some of the members of their families are undocumented and some (usually their younger siblings) are US citizens. This family circumstance of living in "mixed status" households has had a profound effect on their lives in many ways. We asked our respondents the following questions about their family status: "What is your family like—are the other members of your immediate family of the same immigration status as you or is it a mix?" We then asked the follow-up question, "Does this family member's immigration status affect your daily life? If so, in what ways does it affect you?" A number of themes emerged from the responses to these questions, including an increased sense of fear and lack of freedom, a sense of greater limitations and fewer opportunities in comparison to their siblings, and a feeling of resentment toward and disappointment in their siblings and cousins who are US citizens, but who (according to our respondents) are often not taking advantage of the privileges and opportunities that come with US citizenship.

Before discussing each theme in greater detail we want to underscore the heavy burden that living in a mixed status household has had on our study participants and their families. The following remarks by Allison, whose parents are also undocumented but whose younger sister is a US citizen, provide a good example of one of the many ways that living in mixed status households affects the daily lives of DREAMers:

> Q: Does this family member's immigration status affect your daily life?
> A: Um … it does … my mom actually owns her own daycare business at home so she became her own businesswoman. I wasn't really so much afraid of her safety 'cause I was able to educate her as to if ICE [Immigration and Customs Enforcement] came to the house what she's supposed to do, like train her not to open the doors, she knows the lawyer's number, and so forth. My dad on the other hand is kinda tricky because he has two strikes now, so for me it's kinda scary too because if he gets pulled over or if something happens to him; I always have that in my head, "what if I get home and my parents get deported?" *So that's always in my head every single day* [emphasis added], and it's like what if I'm home and I have to … now I'm old enough but I was in high school I am thinking every single day of my life, "I will have to drop everything and take care of my [younger] sister and figure it out from there because both of my parents are undocumented," so that's the reality.

Allison carries the burden of not only losing her parents, but also of trying to figure out how to provide for her younger sister if her parents are deported. This is a heavy burden for a teenager to bear.

Of course, living in mixed–legal status households does not just affect those who are undocumented, but it also affects the siblings who are US citizens in the household. The answer below from Paulina, a twenty-four-year-old student at the University of Texas, San Antonio, who has been in the United States since she was four years of age, illustrates this:

> [I]t impacts my sister who is a citizen because she can't get a driver's license because my mom has her Social [Security number] under that. So, I mean it affects *all of us* [emphasis added], even my sister who is a citizen. I mean, last year was the first year my sister was in college and she actually used all the

financial aid she got to help me and my brother pay for our school. So, instead of, I mean, she could have kept it for herself, but she knew that we needed help paying tuition and she helped us out. And I mean it does affect your daily life because you have to figure out other ways to pay for school or get around. I mean, my parents have always done odd jobs and mowing lawns and cleaning houses and whatever you can do to get by. Um, I paid for all of my Master's, um, by buying books at *ropa usada* [used clothing] and I would go and sell them at the flea market, um, sell them online, and that's how I would save money for rent and for tuition and all that. So, it does affect daily life.

Clearly the impact on the entire family is significant. Paulina's sister who is a US citizen cannot get a driver's license because her mother used her Social Security number to obtain one for herself. In addition, the only sibling in the family who is eligible for federal student aid shares this benefit with her siblings, including Paulina, because the undocumented children in the family do not qualify for financial assistance for college. Living on the margins economically with the instability of providing for one's family through mowing lawns or selling used clothing only adds to the daily burdens. The struggles associated with being undocumented affect everyone in the family.

FEAR AND LACK OF FREEDOM

Another common theme that emerged from our interviews was the sense of fear and lack of freedom that haunt individuals in mixed status households. This affected daily activities ranging from driving to shopping. Jose described an incident where his mom had a panic attack at Walmart because she saw a sheriff and thought he was an immigration agent:

> A: I think that it definitely is affecting my daily life now that I'm not afraid of going out and have that experience of fearing that something might happen and that you might get stopped and that you may get arrested and they will deport you.... Before it was always like watching your back.... You never know.... What if today I have a bad day and ... something happened and I ended up being arrested?
>
> Q: What about your family? I'm assuming that when you went out, because you were undocumented before, they would be worried about you. Driving was an issue, stuff like that, you know, the daily life in general, I mean, is it, is it different? How'd you—how would you say it's changed?
>
> A: Yeah, I think it's definitely different. My mom especially, she would, she was already worried, worried about me and [would] try to protect me, as a mom, you know, every mom does that. But I remember one time that we went to Walmart and they—there was this sheriff shopping and she thought it was immigration.... And at the time it was two years after I came [to

the United States] ... and she saw this man dressed with all this green and she was, oh that's *la migra*, and she started getting, like, a panic attack.

Q: Yeah.

A: Like, "oh my God, oh my God, immigration is over there."

Q: Yeah.

A: [A]nd she started like walking away, away from where the police was and has to look at them really good. And I was like, "No Mom, that's not Immigration, that's just the sheriff." 'Cause you know, that was ... it was a situation like that, that even though she was already legal, she was still fearing Immigration because I was not ...

Q: Oh wow.

A: So every time I would go out ... she would [be] looking out ... so I think that even though she was not undocumented anymore, she had that fear about Immigration and "what if they got—they get my child and we're separated."

This story demonstrates how mixed legal status impacts all levels of life, creating a permanent and heightened sense of anxiety on the part of undocumented immigrant parents and their children. This underlying sense of fear is even present when doing something as simple as shopping at Walmart. Another story, from Mateo, a twenty-two-year-old Portland Community College student, also describes the fear of being separated from one's family through deportation:

[Y]ou know somewhat because we have to be worried about each other, if someone's not home by a certain time, you worry you know like, what happened to 'em, you know, did the cops get 'em? If the cops got 'em are they in ICE holds, or ... because my dad was deported when I was ... seventeen so, I mean ... I was kinda like ... it realized the fears that we had, it's like "hey, this can happen to any of us."

This fear that separation from one's family "can happen to any of us" is understood even by young children. Many of our sample of DREAMers understood from a very early age that they needed to be careful. They learned to grow up with a sense of fear and uncertainty because they could be separated from their families at any time.

The final representative story comes from Nicolas, a twenty-three-year-old student at the University of Washington. It demonstrates how fear and lack of freedom go hand in hand for the majority of our sample of DREAMers:

[T]here's always that fear of going back to the place where you come from and you don't feel, well I mean, you do feel some freedom but not as much as, not full freedom. You can't do this, you can't do that. So, you can't travel, you can't do nothing to do business here. I mean like, I guess you can travel to the states but even some states like Arizona or some of those states are really being tough now with immigration. It's good freedom but *not full freedom* [emphasis added].

The DREAMers that we talked to lived in Texas, California, Washington, and Oregon. Regardless of their geographic location, they all experienced life with a greater sense of fear and lack of freedom from living in mixed status households. It was particularly felt while they were shopping, traveling, or driving. In some cases, it even affected their willingness to call the police if someone had been in a car accident. Living as an undocumented Latino youth in the United States is, as Nicolas stated, "not full freedom." Similar to the experiences of immigrants in the past (described in Chapter 1), our sample of DREAMers is affected by the white racial frame in that they are racialized targets at every turn, not just when they try to get a job or go to college, but during everyday events like shopping or just leaving the house. This racialization places greater limitations on all aspects of their lives.

GREATER LIMITATIONS AND FEWER OPPORTUNITIES THAN US-BORN SIBLINGS

Another theme that came out of the question of how living in mixed status households impacted our sample of DREAMers is that those who were undocumented faced greater limitations and had fewer opportunities compared to their siblings who were US citizens. In one interview, Santiago, a twenty-three-year-old college student at both Pasadena City College and East Los Angeles Community College, who has been in the United States since he was an infant, provides a revealing example of what this has meant for him as a college student:

> A: [L]ike I wish I had done what they did ... like my brother went off to school in New York.... [M]y little sister is now at East Bay, ... or my other sister Carla, who just did the study abroad thing at Pasadena, so she studied abroad in England, ya know, spending a whole semester in England, ya know, studying what she wanted to do ... yeah, it would have been cool if I could have done something like that, so ya know it's kinda like I don't get to experience as much ...
> Q: So, if you had the opportunity that they had ...?
> A: Yeah, I would have totally done the same thing ...
> Q: You would have had those experiences so you feel like you don't have that opportunity.
> A: Yeah, like as much as I try I am still kinda *stuck in this bubble* [emphasis added] where I can't really push myself to really get out there much ...

Instead of studying abroad in England as his sister Carla had been able to do, or attending university in another state as his brother, Santiago struggled at two local community colleges. This story is representative of how mixed legal status makes a profound difference in the educational experiences and opportunities of DREAMers, from access to financial aid, to travel overseas, to education-promoting work opportunities. This had a great impact on their lives, often leaving a bitter feeling about the terrible consequences their undocumented status has on their opportunities in life. The consequences are significant and concrete, and at the same time unrelated to their merit as individuals.

RESENTMENT AND DISAPPOINTMENT

It is not surprising that faced with greater obstacles and limitations than their US-born siblings who are living in the same households, our DREAMers would express resentment and disappointment. There was also a sense that their American-born siblings or cousins could be doing so much more with their lives because of the privileges that come with US citizenship. Many DREAMers we interviewed criticized these family members for not utilizing their citizenship to full benefit. The following conversation with Juan Diego, a twenty-four-year-old engineering major at California State University, Northridge, hits upon these themes:

Q: Does your mixed status affect your life in any way?
A: [T]he situations that we are in—that my parents and my sister and me . . . we do struggle, but it doesn't mean that because we're here or anything that we're not going to struggle. And even though we're not citizens . . . everyone struggles; undocumented people struggle the most.
Q: So you said that undocumented people struggle the most, um, do you see yourself as struggling more than your brothers and sisters who are citizens?
A: Yeah, I do 'cause they're young, they don't even have to work, they don't have to go to school. I mean, they have to go to school, but they're not working on their BA or . . . right now they don't, but as they get older, they're going to struggle and have to go to school and get a career. But as much as we do, I don't think they have so much struggle. *They have everything. As a citizen I believe that they can have everything.* [emphasis added]

Juan Diego's comment that he will have to struggle more than his US-born siblings who, in his words, "can have everything," reflects a painful reality for him, particularly since he has been in the United States since he was a toddler of three years old. These unfair circumstances are familiar to the majority of our respondents. The following exchange shows the frustration felt by Rafael, a twenty-four-year-old UCLA student who has been in the United States since he was one:

A: [W]hen my brother graduated from high school—it wasn't so long ago—it was like a year ago, last June, and when he was applying and trying to go to college, he didn't really apply to a four-year school, which I wanted him to, but he was never really into his studies as much as me, but still saw that he saw like a goal towards his life, but it wasn't clarified in his mind yet. So you know, I would always tell him, "You have your papers, why can't you put your goals together? You are able to do all this where I can't."

Q: So it was a point of frustration between the two of you?

A: It was a point of frustration because I always saw him being not too into school and it frustrated me that he had all these things laid before him and he wasn't taking advantage of them.

Similar sentiments were shared by many of our sample of DREAMers, especially those who have been in the United States since infancy. Our sample of DREAMers often expressed US citizenship as a "gift" that their siblings had and they did not have. In addition, sometimes parents, whether intentionally or not, added to the tension between siblings in mixed–legal status households. As Allison noted, "My mom ... always tells me, 'the one that needs the most care doesn't have the resources and doesn't have the papers but the one that has the papers doesn't want to do anything with it and doesn't need it.' [Laughing] So, it's like FAFSA too, 'you go to college and you need the money but the one that has everything doesn't want to go to college.'" Time and again our sample of DREAMers shared stories of how they felt the bitter sting of living in families where their US-born siblings had greater opportunities and lived with different rules, laws, and expectations.

VULNERABILITY WHEN OTHER PEOPLE DISCOVER THEIR UNAUTHORIZED STATUS

Next we examine some of the issues pertaining to people knowing about our study respondents' legal status. We asked our sample of DREAMers a series of questions concerning this situation: "Do any friends or teachers/staff at school know about your status?" "Have you had to 'come out' to some people?" "Did this change how they perceived you?" "Have you ever been 'outed' without your permission?" "Did you suffer any negative consequences as a result?" "Have you found that those who know about your status treat you differently than those who don't know?" In this section we explore the issues raised in their answers.

The vast majority of our respondents indicated that most friends and teachers did know about their undocumented status. Nevertheless, they still experienced stress, discomfort, and a sense of vulnerability about how others would respond to the information, especially when they felt compelled to tell people that they were undocumented. For example, Carlos, a twenty-one-year-old student at Portland Community College, stated, "It's uncomfortable because you don't know if that person is gonna accept you or is against your status, I guess, and take advantage of it." Carlos captured the vulnerability of being undocumented when he shared how people could "take advantage" of his status. Romina, a twenty-year-old biology student at the University of Texas–Pan American provides another example of how difficult it can be to explain one's legal status. She admitted, "I do feel shy when I tell them. I don't consider myself Mexican because I've lived my whole life here, and having to explain to them is kind of hard." Romina has been in the United States since she was only five years old and clearly indicates that she does not consider herself to be Mexican. Yet, legally she is not American either. The awkward situations that Carlos and Romina describe are yet another consequence of the white racial frame. They are both racialized as outsiders. They feel uncomfortable and don't know whether they will be accepted once people know that they are undocumented: Carlos wonders if his status will be used against him and Romina feels shy—those are their words. Underlying those words, and those of others we spoke to, is a sense of not belonging, a sense of otherness that they cannot overcome and that they fear revealing to others.

One of the areas of greatest difficulty for our sample of DREAMers regarding others' knowing about their undocumented status was in the area of intimate and personal relationships. Dating can be difficult enough for young adults, but adding legal status to the mix makes dating even tougher. As Alejandra commented, "[M]y boyfriends, like people I date, I find it very difficult to tell them, because it's a very personal relationship, so I really struggle telling boyfriends what my current immigration status is and I try to leave it off for as long as possible." Alejandra is a twenty-year-old student at the University of Washington who has been in the United States since she was four years old. She prefers to put off addressing the issue of her status in her romantic relationships as it can be a source of shame and discomfort. Santiago shared a similar sentiment:

A: Oh ... well ... yeah!... It's a big problem when you date.

Q: When you're dating ...? [laugh]

A: Dating ... [laugh] ... it's a big problem!

Q: Tell me about that ...

A: 'Cause like ... it's something you don't want to mention [right] off the bat, right. Especially when you start talking about where you [are] from.

Q: What do you think it's such a bad thing? Like why? Why is this such a bad thing?

A: I always get the same joke ... ya know ... "you just want me for my papers" ... "you just want me to get you papers."

Although he felt comfortable joking about it during the interview, the fact that Santiago has been teased about his motivations in relationships, that he's just dating women in order to regularize his status, makes for discomfort in his relationships and also potentially puts him in a disadvantaged position. This is not unlike an intimate relationship where one person comes from a much higher socioeconomic status than the other person. This imbalance in social (or economic) status can create an atmosphere of suspicion and distrust about the intent of the person in the disadvantaged position. Adding to the stress is the very real vulnerability on the part of the undocumented person of being exposed to authorities if the relationship ends badly, as in the following story shared by Paulina:

> [M]y ex-boyfriend made it seem like it was no big deal, but when he broke up with me he told me later, like, "Oh yeah, I thought about calling border patrol or ICE and telling them to go pick you up." So, I mean, you really don't know how people will treat you, I mean, especially if you get on their bad side. So that's why I'm really choosy about who I tell and it's always scary 'cause you don't know.

In these and many other stories shared by the DREAMers we spoke to, the sense of vulnerability about their undocumented status, and having it revealed, was overwhelming. Some have taken this position and used it as a source of political activism, while others are nearly immobilized by fear. We return to this topic in more detail in Chapter 5.

"COMING OUT"

We heard a variety of themes when we asked our respondents whether they had ever had to reveal their immigration status to other people. For some it was a source of pride and identity, especially around political events such as "coming out" days and walkouts in their communities and schools. For example, Mateo, the Portland Community College student we introduced earlier, stated, "I guess it feels like you're being true to yourself. It's like I don't want to say I'm something that I'm not because I'm proud of my heritage, I'm proud of my struggles." Many of our respondents expressed similar sentiments, embracing their undocumented status and taking pride in it rather than continuing to hide in the shadows. This decision to come out and share with others their immigration status parallels the struggle faced by many youth from the lesbian, gay, bisexual, transsexual, queer (LGBTQ) community in coming out of the closet about their sexual identity and orientation. And, in fact, a number of our respondents also found themselves coming out in that respect, as the following discussion with Antonio demonstrates:

> A: Oh yeah, I tell them all the time.
> Q: Yeah. How—how does that work? How do you, um …
> A: I think, like, in terms of how—'cause I organize with undocumented folks, what I always do, is when I introduce myself, I always say, my name, and I say that I'm "undocuqueer," right?
> Q: "Undocuqueer." That's—that's cool.
> A: Yeah. And so, like, I reveal my statuses …

Antonio has been in the United States since he was three years old and didn't find out about his undocumented status until he was in ninth grade, when his brother told him he was not going to be able to attend college as a consequence of being undocumented. It came as a huge blow to him and for a time, he says, he just "gave up." He describes feeling a definite sense of shame about his undocumented status. After a few years, however, Antonio recovered. He had to work hard just to graduate from high school, but eventually he became involved in political activism around his multiple identities, including being undocumented and being gay. Nineteen-year-old Joshua, who has been in the United States since the age of seven, directly compared the two coming out experiences, noting that coming out about his immigration status was easier than coming out about his sexual orientation.

> Q: Have you had to come out to some people?
> A: Yeah, I have ... a lot of people actually.
> Q: What was that like?
> A: Uh, easier than coming out as a gay male, that's for sure. But um, most people were like shocked because they didn't expect it, especially me going to college and getting good grades and everything, being a school athlete and all of that, they broke the stereotype that they have in their heads.

This theme was repeated by many of our respondents. Perceived by others to be successful Americans, their coming out about their immigration status challenged the negative stereotypes perpetuated by society about undocumented immigrants. These stereotypes, and the very real threat that knowledge of their status could be used by others to hurt them and their families, generated significant trepidation about whether to come out, and to whom. And yet, repeatedly, they did so, reaffirming their individual identities and, often, leading to positive results.

POSITIVE TREATMENT

After some initial feelings of trepidation about being perceived "differently," many of the Latino youth in our study were surprised to discover that once others knew about their unauthorized status, the treatment they received was quite positive. For example, Alessandra, an eighteen-year-old Whitworth University student originally from Cuernavaca had this to say:

> I guess, you know, in my high school setting, it just made teachers help me, wanna help me more you know, so that I can have a better future, you know, so I can, you know, kind of open doors for the next generation.

Opening the doors for the next generation is what Alessandra will most likely be doing once she completes her college education. As Chávez discovered in her study of Latino professionals, the benefits of a university education go far beyond private gains of individual Latinos, especially among first-generation Latino college graduates.[10] Chávez found that the benefits of having Latino professionals are wide ranging, including benefits for the Latino community as well as for the community at large, through increased levels of civic participation and community leadership commitments by Latino professionals.[11] Although neither of Alessandra's parents went beyond a grade-school level of education, Alessandra is now attending one of the best private liberal arts universities in the state of Washington. She will be poised to benefit the "next generation" with her entry into the professional and educated classes. Up to this point, she has not let her undocumented status stop her from achieving her dreams.

Many of our respondents stated that once teachers discovered they were undocumented they were given increased respect and support. Some of our respondents have even had offers of financial assistance from high school teachers and professors, as this exchange with Allison demonstrates:

> A: I would just say, "I'm in this situation; this is what happened, what can I do, or what they can do." A lot of teachers offered to pay for my vacations for Cal State [LA], for my vacations to USC [University of Southern California] in high school. Here [CSU, LA] it's a whole different thing. When I tell them my situation and allow professors to understand me and know that I'm telling them for this reason. I've had so many professors—one who bought my books and who gave me half of the payment to pay for school.
> Q: Wow, you're kidding.
> A: Just so much; it's not even me asking them for the money it's like, "I'm doing this and that," and they're like, "well how much do you need," and they're like, "I'll write the check, don't worry about it." It's kind of like, wow! They really not only trusted me, but really they see something in me.
> Q: They see potential.
> A: They see potential yeah, and so they're willing to invest in me and not just saying, "I'm going to give money."

That Allison's professors could see something in her and even offer to support her with tuition and travel support is an unusual level of assistance, but many of the DREAMers we spoke to shared similar stories of how they experienced support and positive treatment after sharing their immigration status. As Allison notes, there are those who see "the potential" in these undocumented youth, and who understand that assisting them in whatever way they can to reach their dreams is an investment in both their futures and the future of the country.

NEGATIVE TREATMENT

Of course, not all DREAMers experienced positive treatment when others found out about their legal status. Many described receiving negative treatment in work settings, where those who are undocumented and working under the table cannot easily speak out against workplace abuses. As Miranda, a twenty-seven-year-old woman from Texas who has been in the United States since she was six years old, observed, "When you work in a restaurant I guess sometimes they kind of treat you bad, like, 'she isn't going to say anything anyway. She doesn't have her papers.' ... I guess like being racist kind of thing." Ashley, a twenty-three-year-old female student at the University of Texas–Pan American shared a similar experience:

> I work at a restaurant, and the owner, he perceives that not all of the people that work there might have a Social Security number and, I don't know, sometimes he's kind of like just talking to people in a mean way.... [H]e says, "Oh you're working here because I'm giving you a job because you cannot work somewhere else 'cause you don't have a Social Security number."

The white racial frame is evident in the way both Miranda and Ashley are treated at work. As noted in Chapter 1, the white racial frame includes the idea of superiority. It legitimizes and maintains racism against those in the United States who are not white, Anglo-Saxon Protestants. Miranda understands what is going on in the treatment she receives while working at the restaurant. She knows all too well that what she is experiencing is a "racist kind of thing."

The negative treatment our respondents reported experiencing often included perceptions that as undocumented students they were receiving benefits they did not deserve. This comment from Romina, the twenty-year-old DREAMer from Texas, describes this perception well:

> [Y]es ... and that makes me feel uncomfortable and it kind of brings me down. Like I was in migrant services in high school. Well, some students would always say that we had it easy because they would give us everything, which is not true because having to be in my situation sometimes you have to work in the fields, being a waitress, any little job that I could find to support myself or help my mom in some ways, but it did affect my life in some ways. I think of what would my life have been if I did have one [Social Security number] all these years. I wouldn't have to go through all this. Or I wouldn't have to be denied some scholarships that I applied to in high school. There's only certain amount of scholarships that you can apply if you don't have that status.

Romina knows that because of her status, she is "denied some scholarships." Yet the common perception is that Latinos and other ethnic and racial minorities receive more scholarships than do white Americans. Cybelle Fox documents how the perception and reality about benefits received by racialized groups have a long history in the United States. Fox finds that white immigrants actually received welfare assistance and benefits in far greater numbers than did blacks or Mexican immigrants during the Progressive Era and the New Deal.[12] However, this does not change widespread perceptions and misconceptions to the contrary.

The notion that undocumented immigrants are unfairly competing with US citizens for benefits and opportunities is held even by other Latinos, as the story

of a conversation between one of our respondents and her Latina college room-
mate reveals. The story is from Linda, who was first introduced in Chapter 1. It
illustrates the tension between undocumented Latinos and Mexican Americans or
Chicanos. Linda is describing a conversation she had with one of her best friends
in Iowa, another Latina. Linda's friend did not know of her undocumented status
and Linda was careful about telling her:

> A: When I was in Iowa, and I learned to be cautious about coming out because
> one of my current best friends, when I met her, you know, we were in classes,
> we were friends and then I started organizing a DREAM Act panel on
> campus that was open to the community. And then she was like, "Why are
> you doing this?" And I was like, "Well, because I think everyone deserves
> a chance to higher education, especially if they're willing to contribute
> back to the place where they're already living and most of them are already
> contributing." But I really kept it in the third person.
>
> Q: Oh, wow.
>
> A: And she was: "Well, I don't agree with that because they're just stealing my
> opportunities. It's already hard enough for people of color," Um, 'cause she's
> Mexicana, or Mexican parents, and you know, "they're stealing my oppor-
> tunities." ... And I [responded], "Well, you should still come anyway, maybe
> it'll change your opinion." And then, she [replied], "Well, I don't know." I
> said, "Come on, just go." And she [said], "Okay, I'll go." ... And then ... [a]
> month later, I [said], "I have a question for you," 'cause it was really bother-
> ing me.... "What do you think of me?" She [said], "What do you mean?" I
> was [asked], "Yeah, what do you think of me? I'm your friend, why am I your
> friend? Why did you decide to push that boundary and become my friend
> versus just my classmate? Because, you know, we're more than classmates.
> You want me to be your roommate next year, so we're obviously friends."
> And she [said], "Well, because you're smart, and you're funny and we get
> along well," and this and that and I [replied], "Well, you don't think I'm
> like bad or something? What if we're interviewing for a job? I would be your
> competition, like, I would be, I'm, like a threat to steal your opportunities."
> And then she [said], "Why are you being so weird? Like, shut up, you're
> being dumb." And I [said], "Well ... 'cause I have something to tell you....
> I'm undocumented and your words was exactly were that we're a threat and
> we're competition and that we're stealing your opportunities."
>
> Q: Yeah.
>
> A: And she was like, "What! ... No, that's not what I think about you." And
> I'm like, "Well, that's what you think about undocumented people." And
> she was like, "Oh my God, like I need time to think about this." And then
> she completely changed. Like, now, she's one of my strongest supporters.

In this vignette there are two Latina college students—one a US citizen
and one an undocumented DREAMer. It is another clear example of the power
of the white racial frame. The Latina who is a US citizen had clearly bought

into the white racial framing of undocumented immigrants in that she believed undocumented immigrants "steal her opportunities."

This negative treatment and animosity from other Latinos, especially those who are citizens, is not uncommon. Research by Chávez, Wampler, and Burkhart discovered that most undocumented Mexican farmworkers in Idaho were distrustful of the Mexican Americans in the area because of similar treatment and experiences.[13] Although it might be a difficult reality for Latinos to grapple with, the differences between those who are citizens and those who are undocumented can create a situation where there is resentment on both sides. As Martina, a twenty-year-old Pierce Community College student who has been in the United States since the age of three, commented, "In that case, I think that they [Mexican Americans] felt a little bit superior and they felt like, 'oh, well, I have papers so I'm cool, I'm justified.'" Martina has also experienced the negative consequences of being "outed" in the workplace: once, one of her coworkers brought up her unauthorized status and as a consequence she was fired. Similar stories are shared in the next section, which describes the stories our sample of DREAMers shared of being outed without permission and the consequences that followed.

"OUTED WITHOUT PERMISSION"

We asked the DREAMers we spoke to if they had ever been outed without their permission and if they had suffered negative consequences as a result. Forty-two of the 101 respondents shared stories of having their immigration status shared without their consent. For example, Fernanda, a twenty-year-old nursing student at Portland Community College originally from Chiapas, said,

> [I]n my workplace, one of my co-workers and that actually caused my job to end. I know she didn't do it on purpose, but she did harm because the next day she's like, "well I'm sorry, you're a good employee but you gotta go." Not even that but they actually didn't pay me like the last three weeks of my work.

Fernanda not only lost her job, but she was also denied three weeks of pay for her work. As this story illustrates, being outed can have negative financial consequences. The denial of wages earned to undocumented workers is a pervasive problem, one well known to the immigrant community.[14] Fernanda knew very well that she was not in a position to demand the wages owed to her.

The following vignette describes an unusual circumstance where one of the DREAMers we interviewed was outed during his tenure as the student body president at California State University, Fresno. Francisco, a twenty-three-year-old male originally from Jalisco, Mexico, had been in the country since the age of three. Like most of our respondents, he only discovered his undocumented status when he was making plans to apply to college. He eventually became student body president, but because of his undocumented status could not receive the traditional payment for his services in student government and served as a volunteer. This created a controversial situation that ended up attracting the attention of the national and international media. Francisco's story is longer than most of the stories shared in this book, but it is well worth reading in its entirety because it is illustrative of the extreme stress and turmoil some DREAMers undergo when they are outed without their permission.

Q: So it's not so much you coming out; it was you being ...

A: What ended up happening was that the student body and the student newspaper picked up a tip; somebody I guess there was a leak. The reason why it came out was the fact that I wasn't getting paid 'cause I didn't receive that stipend and I couldn't get my paycheck for being student [body president]; I was being student body president voluntarily, I worked it and somebody found that very fishy ... I guess they either might have done a public records request or maybe somebody internally from the administrative staff—I don't know—just released that information. They contacted me saying, "We have this tip that you're not getting paid 'cause you're undocumented, is this true?" And then the local newspaper, the *Fresno Bee* also got that word, "I keep getting that you're blah, blah, blah, is this true?" So I was faced with the choice of, I can come out or I can just say, "No, it's all lies," I could have easily done that ... I could have easily just told the newspapers, "It's not true. Don't believe it." There's no way they can verify or not 'cause it's FERPA laws and it's all student confidential. I just decided you know what, I don't know where they got this information, but it's going to come out sooner or later.

Q: So your coming out was more of a forced "outing" in a way so to speak and you decided to go a step ahead and come out yourself?

Francisco became national and international news. He was interviewed by Katie Couric, CNN, the *Los Angeles Times*, the BBC, and by newspapers in Japan, Mexico, and Colombia. Many people who heard his story lashed out at him, calling for Francisco to step down as student body president and even demanding that he leave the university to open up a spot for a "legal" student. Francisco continued,

A: Yeah and these people had really limited or no connection to the university; their main thing was, "you're not supposed to be here, you're taking a spot of another student, you're costing taxpayers money," that was their basic arguments.

Q: These were directed at you?

A: Yeah.

Q: How were they directed at you? Were there like picket lines or something?

A: Yeah ... our meetings, our student body council meetings, they would come during public comment and they would come and have at me for the past year they would do that; for the full year they did that.

Q: Wow, were these like weekly or bi-monthly meetings?

A: Bi-monthly; every other week. And there was also a lot of allegations of other things and I was under investigation by like the Secretary of State and they even got the CIA and FBI on me.

Q: For what? What were the allegations?

A: Voter registration fraud, that I was registered, that I was buying houses, I was impersonating other people. The thing was is that they had mistaken me for another Francisco Ramirez that lives in Tulare and Fresno.

Q: No kidding.

A: Some Francisco Ramirez Morales I believe or something like that ... like some 40-something year old man. So it got pretty intense.

Q: Okay and tell us about, what was the website ... Stop Francisco or something?

A: No there was one that; they had a couple: DeportFrancisco.org and then TheRealFrancisco.com.

Q: Tell us about the founder of that last one, TheRealFrancisco? Who was behind these websites? What were some of the things that were on those?

A: I don't know who was the founder of the DeportFrancisco.org. All I know is that the objective was to get people to call the Department of Homeland Security and Immigration and Customs Enforcement to do their job and deport me; that was their thing, they were just getting people to call. TheRealFrancisco was just one of those blogs and tabloid things where you can find information about my life and what I've done, all the crimes I committed, or didn't commit and things like that ... just allegations.

Q: And who was the ...?

A: The person running [it] was a student.

Q: So it was a student ...?

A: Very passionate, angry student.

Q: Were there any other negative consequences associated with your "outing"?

A: Personally I literally *lived in a bubble* [emphasis added] for that year or even to this day I kinda still do. I couldn't do much of what I used to do or go out; you know, basically what college students do, have much of a social life and the little social life that I had.

While Francisco's story is different and more extreme than those shared by other DREAMers in our sample, it clearly demonstrates the way society racializes, harasses, and targets Latinos, especially those who are undocumented. Francisco became the target of investigations by the FBI and the CIA. The fact that he had a similar name to someone who had allegedly committed crimes does not justify the harassment Francisco endured while serving as student body president at Fresno State. Many Latinos have names that are similar, but proper investigations can determine when there is a case of misidentification. Instead, stories of Customs and Border Protection agents harassing and detaining individuals of color, regardless of citizenship status, are common, according to the American Civil Liberties Union.[15]

Francisco has since earned his bachelor's degree and is completing a master's in Public Policy and Administration at California State University, Long Beach. It bears repeating that he has lived in the United States since he was three years old. Yet because of his undocumented status he experienced so much turmoil as an undergraduate who was voluntarily serving the university as student body president that he basically had to check out for a year until the attacks against him died down. The fact that a person of exceptional character such as Francisco can be demonized because of his status as an undocumented immigrant, despite being raised in the United States since he was a toddler, and whose status is no fault of his own, speaks volumes about the strength of the white racial frame.

DECISIONS BASED ON IMMIGRATION STATUS

The final question we address in this chapter is whether our sample of DREAMers made decisions about their futures based on their immigration status. Almost universally, *98 percent* said that they did, and the answers from the remaining two DREAMers suggest that they did as well, even if they don't recognize having done so. One described her decision to not go to college because of financial reasons; another asserted that she just takes life "one day at a time." Overwhelmingly, time and again, the lack of financial aid available to our sample of DREAMers made going to college extremely difficult. Others felt discouraged by the fact that they had such a high mountain to climb to go to college, which might include working three jobs to afford tuition, commuting for hours on the bus because they couldn't legally drive, or giving up because they saw only a future where they had graduated from college and could still not work legally. That said, recall (Table 3.1) that 70.3 percent of our sample of DREAMers are currently enrolled in college, these concerns notwithstanding.

When our sample of DREAMers was asked how their immigration status had shaped their major life decisions, the most common answer was that not having their "Social" forced them to make difficult decisions and give up or put on hold parts of their dreams. Some expressed great sadness and regret about being accepted to elite universities, but, because of their ineligibility for financial aid, choosing instead to turn away those acceptances, go to work, and struggle to afford to attend a community college. Below is a representative statement from Samuel, a nineteen-year-old Portland Community College student who has been in the United States since he was five years old:

> I got accepted [to university], it was the financial aid paying for college that really, that really was a hindrance and so PCC [Portland Community College] was not my first choice, but it's something and so, but I definitely feel like my immigration status definitely affected where I could and couldn't go and how I could pay for that schooling and so that's why I took a year off so I could raise some money.

Similar to most of the DREAMers we talked to, Samuel's immigration status has affected his educational opportunities. For some of our respondents this included not only choosing between a university or a community college after high school, but also choosing where to attend geographically. This was especially true for the youth we spoke to in Texas, who were geographically trapped in the Rio Grande Valley because of checkpoints both to the south and to the north of them. Ana Paula was one of many of our respondents from Texas who expressed the experience of being "stuck":

> We—we're stuck in the border between Mexico and you can't go. You're stuck between the checkpoints and you can't go up North. Even though I can—you can—like, obviously able to go anywhere in Texas, I couldn't cross that stupid little checkpoint without risking it all. Leaving my mom, leaving my brother, leaving my dad. I was applying to University of Denton. I got in, but I could not go.... And I went to PanAm [the University of Texas–Pan American].

Another powerful story was shared by Damian, who was accepted into four different institutions in the University of California system, but could not afford to attend them. His experience is noteworthy in that it demonstrates the enormous barriers and constraints our sample of DREAMers faces when attempting to attend a university where they have been accepted. Similar to most of our respondents, Damian was determined not to let his undocumented status stop him from realizing his goals. However, when he went to see what his options were at the financial aid office at UCLA, he was given some eye-opening advice by one of the financial aid officers. This left a lasting impression on Damian. He states,

> That, the person in charge of financial aid at UCLA at that time ... I approached him and I said, "Look, I'm undocumented, I want to go to college." The guy said, "Don't waste your time. Go get a job and get, get your ass to work. You won't be able to go to college, you won't be able to pay tuition at a, at a university. Don't waste your time."

The advice to "get your ass to work" that Damian received is instructive in that Latinos, even Latino professionals, are often viewed as "laborers" who should "work their asses off" but not as part of the professional and educated classes in America. It is yet another powerful example of the white racial frame. This is a common experience faced by Latino lawyers who are often mistaken for the "defendant" in a court of law or the "gardener" in the nice neighborhoods in which their newfound economic status allows them to live.[16] It is even an experience shared by the one Latino on the US Supreme Court, Sonya Soto-mayor, as she describes in her recent autobiography.[17] One can only speculate as to how many Latinos this financial aid officer advised to "not waste their time" trying to get an education at UCLA, how common it is for Latino students to hear such advice. We suspect that it comes as a blow to many such students, perhaps deterring them from attending college and certainly damaging them psychologically.

But Damian was not deterred. After graduating from California State University, Los Angeles in 2009, Damian saw this financial aid counselor at a reception for the speaker of the Assembly of the House of California. Damian recognized him and confronted him in a clear example of a counterframe. After confirming that the financial aid officer remembered him, Damian told him, "[Y]ou told me seven years ago that I was not gonna be able to make it. So get my ass to work, to get a, a job and forget about college. Well, here I am with my degree. . . ." Confronting this person took a lot of courage on Damian's part, but it also demonstrates the power that these racialized comments have on young people who are just trying to find their way. Even after Damian successfully graduated, the financial aid counselor's comments were still with him. And they probably always will be. And yet, he graduated. Damian credits his family, especially his father, for the tenacity and courage to continue to pursue his dreams despite the many obstacles placed before him: "I have to mention that in my family, my dad always said, it's not our—it's not an option but it's an obligation. You have to graduate from college." This explanation about the role Damian's father played in his success underscores the importance of home-frames and counterframes among people of color.[18]

When we conducted our interviews in the summer of 2012, 70 percent of our sample of DREAMers were attending college. Dylan demonstrates the tenacity they must have in order to graduate from university, despite their undocumented status. He states,

> Well, whatever is within my reach I'm going to do it. After I finish my bachelor's and continue my master's, and if possible go into the PhD program; if not, I'll set up a business as I have a business already, so keep going and make it bigger. I won't stop. If there's something in my way I'll just go another way.

CONCLUSION

In this chapter we provided the background demographic circumstances of our sample of DREAMers and discussed how their undocumented status has impacted their lives, both within their families of origin as well as outside their families—with their friends, teachers, and significant others. We've also discussed how their undocumented status has affected the decisions they have made about their futures. We have whenever possible let their stories and their words describe their experiences.

Their testimonies point not only to the arbitrariness of US citizenship, but they also show that the United States has a very long way to go when it comes to reaching our ideals of equality, justice, and freedom. Insights from their life experiences have given them knowledge and strength beyond their years. These experiences debunk many of the stereotypes about undocumented immigrants so common in American society today. They also underscore the power of the white racial frame in contemporary American society. Indeed, the experiences described by our sample of DREAMers also call into question the commonly held belief that the United States, as a nation of immigrants, has readily welcomed and successfully incorporated newcomers into society. As Aristide R. Zolberg argues, "From the moment they managed their own affairs, well before political independence, Americans were determined to select who might join them, and they have remained so ever since."[19]

Our findings underscore what some other scholars have found—namely, that individuals living in a society with limited social, professional, or political incorporation are more likely to become isolated from and disenchanted with the broader society.[20] As we have seen from the stories shared by the DREAMers interviewed for this study, this can lead to very real consequences, from having a boyfriend threaten to turn you in to ICE or being separated from your family because of deportation or having to work three jobs to afford to attend a community college instead of accepting the offer of admission you received from an elite university. In other words, the life experience of our sample of DREAMers has been one of continually adapting and adjusting to being treated as outsiders in the United States as well as often having to adjust their goals. As Nicole, a twenty-four-year-old woman, stated about living in a mixed status household,

> Yeah, the mixed status … well, I think my parents have always engrained it in my head that it doesn't matter, so I can do whatever it is that I want and everything is gonna be fine. *When in reality it … you know that's not true.* So like, I … I could have had a BA, been in a Master's program currently, and not being able to find a job in the field that I wanted to …, because I have a lot of friends that are undocumented that have BAs that are working jobs that aren't necessarily in the field that they studied, or they want … they are working for minimum wage or whatnot. So, I think that's a clashing reality that I have with my parents. And, that's a constant one … um … because they feel that's irrelevant, that my [undocumented] status is irrelevant … and it's all about hard work ethics.

Nicole knows all too well the very real limitations her undocumented status imposes on her. So does Linda. And Francisco. And Damian. All of the DREAMers we spoke to recognized that their immigration status had had powerful impacts on their lives. And yet, they keep dreaming.

Chapter 4

Living in Limbo

Neither Here nor There and the Concept of Citizenship

It is a gamble we are taking. We are already letting the system know we're here, letting them know you're undocumented and they're not giving you any status. I mean, they're just giving you a work permit. They are suspending your illegality. You're in this country for a period of two years, right, but they are not giving you a [permanent] status that will allow you to freely integrate into the country, to be seen … as a legal, documented individual. So we're pretty much asked to be in limbo for two years and then at the end of those two years, we might be at their mercy and then can ask for another two years. I guess the good thing is that they allow us to work. The bad thing is they don't give us any [permanent] status. I definitely think this is a political move. So I hope that if the president gets re-elected he truly pushes for the DREAM Act. But again, at the end of the day, its politics and we are at the mercy of congressmen.

—Ximena, female, age twenty-six,
responding to the ways her circumstances will change
as a result of President Obama's executive order on deferred action

Ximena, a graduate student in South Texas, has been in the United States since she was fourteen years old and was just wrapping up her second master's degree when she spoke with us. She has always known about her status, given her age when her parents decided to stay here and let her visa expire. A year after their arrival, her brother died; three years after their arrival her parents went home to Veracruz, Mexico, leaving Ximena alone in the United States. Despite the uncertainty of her future here, she has been active in her community and on her university campus, and she has achieved noteworthy academic success. However, as is the case for most of the young people we interviewed, she has struggled greatly in her pursuit of the American Dream. Like many of her counterparts she has been disappointed by the lack of action by Congress in the area of immigration reform. As illustrated in this chapter's epigraph, she expressed a kind of skeptical optimism about deferred action that was common among the DREAMers we spoke to.

Ximena has been engaged politically, but still sees herself as acting primarily outside the system—even with the inception of President Obama's Deferred Action for Childhood Arrivals (DACA) executive order. As Ximena points out, deferred action is only a temporary fix, and major questions remain about her long-term status—along with that of over 5 million others with the same undocumented status. While the United States is a country of immigrants and one where the rule of law is the norm, the burning question for undocumented residents has been how the country, its leaders, and citizens will negotiate inclusion of the ideal of the American Dream into immigration law. There have been conflicting visions of citizenship in the United States since its inception, and a story (myth) of willing acceptance of immigrants emerged as a result.[1]

According to that fanciful story, now part of the national mythology, the United States has long opened its doors to people from across the globe, providing opportunity for all those who seek it and are willing to work. However, as documented in previous chapters, significant scholarship demonstrates that this story does not match up well with the sociopolitical reality of US immigration policy and its outcomes. This myth is particularly problematic for DREAMer youth, who have been raised and socialized into the American social fabric. Many of the DREAMers to whom we spoke cling tightly to the ideals of the American Dream, which has been carefully woven into the national mythology about immigration. Contrary to what we are taught in schools across the country, immigration policy was not crafted to maximize opportunity for immigrants, but rather has been quite precisely crafted to achieve specific national goals and address particular needs of the moment.[2] According to Massey, US immigration policies over the course of the nation's history

> were not founded on any rational, evidence-based understanding of international migration. Instead, they were enacted for domestic political purposes and reveal more about America's hopes and aspirations—and its fears and apprehensions—than anything having to do with immigrants or immigration per se. When policies are implemented for symbolic political purposes, and massive interventions are undertaken with no real understanding of how they might affect a complex social system such as immigration, the results are not only likely to be unanticipated, but counterproductive.[3]

This is the public policy and domestic politics nexus at which DREAMers find themselves today. The American Dream, a set of ideals in which freedom includes the opportunity to achieve prosperity and success and upward social mobility through hard work, has motivated millions of immigrants to come to the United States. The concept captures the hope for a better life—the idea that anything is possible if you work hard for it.[4] Despite the recent economic downturn and the nativist environment existing in many parts of the country over the course of the last decade,[5] immigrants have a continued belief in the American Dream and in a governmental commitment to the ideals of a pluralistic society.[6] Undocumented youth have accepted the label of DREAMers, and in so doing they pay homage to this ideal. In this chapter we examine DREAMers' reactions to deferred action and President Obama's immigration reform strategy. The qualitative nature of our data enables us to move beyond superficial analyses of immigrants' desire to realize the American Dream toward a more nuanced understanding of how undocumented youth reconcile the national mythology with their lived experiences. We find that despite President Obama's decision regarding deferred action, most DREAMers feel they are living in limbo as they continue to reside in the United States without a clear path to becoming legal, permanent residents or citizens. Many DREAMers are cynical about the intent behind DACA and feel manipulated by the nature of the symbolic politics so often associated with the public debate regarding comprehensive immigration reform.

Historical conceptualizations of citizenship color the contemporary immigration debate. Citizenship rights have been restricted since the earliest days of the nation.[7] The concept of citizenship has been highly contested and politically constructed throughout US history. Understanding this concept is important because it allows us to talk about what types of people are defined as being a "legitimate" part of society in the United States. In 1790, at the very dawn of the nation, Congress established the first naturalization law authorizing free white persons who had lived in the United States for two years to become citizens; entry into the British colonies that came to be the United States was virtually unlimited before that time. Since then, immigration policy has vacillated between open access and increasingly restricted entry as the nation alternated between relatively open and nativist periods in its domestic politics. Most of the DREAMers in our study migrated to the United States in the 1990s, a clearly nativist period in our political history.

CONCEPTIONS OF US CITIZENSHIP

While the US Constitution does not contain a definition of citizenship, three distinct conceptions of US citizenship have arisen through legislation and federal administrative codes. The first is *jus soli*, where a person is a citizen because she or he was born on US soil. The second is *jus sanguinis*—literally translated, "citizenship by blood." In this case, a person is a citizen because at least one of her or his parents is a US citizen. Finally, a person who does not qualify under *jus soli* or *jus sanguinis* can go through the process of naturalization to become a US citizen. Naturalization is the act whereby a person voluntarily and actively acquires a nationality that is not her or his nationality at birth. The first two concepts are fairly straightforward since they are determined entirely by birthright. In the case of the DREAMers, the most immediate questions are, how has the US government decided who can come to the US without a birthright, and why?

Some theories about these questions have been developed in the literature on citizenship. For example, Smith's analysis, which spans the period from the colonial era through the Progressive Era, shows that throughout this time most adults were legally denied access to full citizenship, including political rights, solely because of their race, ethnicity, or gender. Smith argues that basic conflicts over these denials have driven much political development and greatly influenced civic membership in the United States. He further posits that these conflicts are what truly define US civic identity even today, and that in the politics of nation building, the cardinal principles of democracy and liberty have often failed to foster a sense of shared "peoplehood." Smith concludes his analysis by noting that the United States is currently in a period of reaction against the egalitarian civic reforms of the last "civil rights" generation—a set of reactionary, nativist, racist, and sexist beliefs regaining their prior influence.

Zolberg takes Smith's argument even further, effectively demonstrating that the United States never had an entirely "open door" immigration policy toward immigrants. In fact, the US government has been utilizing immigration policy to shape US national identity since colonial British America. Lawmakers selectively chose those immigrants considered to be desirable to the nation and deliberately excluded those they deemed unfit for civic and economic life. The United States is accordingly a nation by design, whose immigration policy has been and continues to be used as a tool for nation building. The same kind of rationale is being used to guide contemporary immigration policy debates.[8]

As noted in Chapter 1, the landmark immigration reforms of 1965 were broadly claimed to represent a sincere attempt to eliminate the nativist and racist tone of previous US immigration laws. The removal of national origin quotas was the most noteworthy policy change in this regard. However, notwithstanding those claims, immigration and border security policies in the United States have since become increasingly restrictive. For the first time, hard numerical limits were imposed on immigration from the Western Hemisphere, and these limits were tightened in subsequent years. This restrictive policy turn resulted in drastically reduced opportunities for legal entry from Mexico, and sent a message that immigrants coming from countries south of the border were undesirable.[9] Inevitably, these numerical limits were far below historical patterns of migration and quite predictably gave rise to mass undocumented migration.[10] In response, US policymakers decided to increase border enforcement exponentially, scaling up deportations to record levels during President Obama's first term in office. The immigration enforcement "industry" presently deports an unprecedented 400,000 undocumented migrants per year.[11] This is the broader context—namely, restrictive immigration policy climate and record-setting deportations—in which about 5 million undocumented youths find themselves in the contemporary

United States. It is in this context, too, that DACA was enacted. We asked the DREAMers in our study if they were aware of DACA, their perceptions about it and the leaders involved in its development, and the impact this policy change would likely have on their lives in the immediate, mid-, and long terms.

Before turning to the content of the interviews, it is worth clarifying the differences between Deferred Action for Childhood Arrivals (DACA) and the Development, Relief, and Education for Alien Minors (DREAM) Act, which we also discussed with DREAMers during our interviews. DACA is a kind of administrative relief, a temporary remedy—one that does not provide a path to lawful permanent resident status or US citizenship, and will only be granted on a case-by-case basis. Individuals who submit requests with United States Citizenship and Immigration Services (USCIS) must demonstrate that they meet the threshold guidelines; if they do so, removal action in their case may be deferred for a period of two years, subject to renewal (if not terminated), based on an individualized assessment. In contrast, the DREAM Act would permit certain immigrant students who have grown up in the United States to apply for temporary legal status and to eventually obtain permanent legal status and even eligibility for US citizenship. Qualifying youth would then have six years of conditional permanent resident status to complete at least two years of college or military service. Only after meeting these requirements would they be granted full permanent residence (a green card). A DREAM Act would create new rights under law, and thus requires passage of legislation by Congress. DACA, however, is a form of prosecutorial discretion that neither confers lawful permanent resident status nor provides a path to citizenship.

This chapter encapsulates DREAMers' reactions to DACA and the DREAM Act. Our respondents predicted changes in their lives that will come to pass as a result of DACA, but at the same time noted that they will continue to live in a perpetual state of limbo given the temporary nature of deferred action. We now turn to the interviews with the DREAMers.

NEWS TRAVELS FAST

The DREAMers we spoke with were asked a series of questions about whether they were familiar with DACA and how they thought their lives might be impacted in the immediate future as a result of the policy change. The extant literature about low levels of political knowledge among youth populations would lead us to expect relatively low levels of familiarity with public policy and politics generally speaking, particularly among Latino immigrant youth. However, all 101 of the DREAMers interviewed indicated that they had heard of deferred action. This finding can be explained by the high level of salience DACA has for the lives of the youths with whom we spoke. An illustrative response comes from Alejandra, a twenty-year-old sociology and education major who has been in the United States since infancy:

Q: Are you familiar with President Obama's Executive Order directing the Department of Homeland Security to end the deportation of school-aged undocumented youth?

A: Oh yeah, absolutely. Actually funny you mention that. I'm having a couple girlfriends come over tonight. I got trained by a lawyer to help somewhat understand the forms … so we are going to be filling it out over at my apartment today. Um, yeah, so I'm absolutely aware of the deferred action plan.

Many of the youth interviewed in our study had already spoken with an attorney or nonprofit organization about DACA before speaking with us, despite the fact that DACA was announced just weeks prior to our interviews. Even those who indicated a lack of any knowledge about the details of DACA had, indeed, heard of deferred action.

DEFERRED ACTION AND LIFE CHANGES?

There was considerable variation in responses to the question about how DACA would immediately change the lives of our respondents. Some of the DREAMers said they would expect no change at all while others talked about how their lives would likely change in many ways. The research literature suggests that Latinos tend to be more trusting than other ethnoracial groups,[12] and that noncitizens of Mexican origin are generally less cynical than Mexican American citizens.[13] This previous work would lead us to expect that responses to deferred action among the young people featured in our study would be relatively positive. It is important to keep in mind that many of the DREAMers we interviewed have been thoroughly socialized in this country, and, in fact, many of them believed until recently that they were US citizens. So perhaps the responses we document here were relatively critical regarding deferred action because Mexican Americans who are both highly acculturated and are aware of discrimination against Latinos tend to be more cynical than those who are not as aware.[14]

Despite the overall sense that DACA falls short of a substantive solution to address the broken immigration system, respondents provided a laundry list of both major and minor life changes they thought would likely result from the executive order. A few examples of such life changes include being able to get a driver's license and car insurance; being able to drive without fear of deportation; going to college, and then being able to work in their field of study; feeling equal and/or safer; being able to travel freely, both domestically and internationally; being able to work legally and for fair wages; the opportunity to build credit; eligibility for internships; ability to lease an apartment; ability to apply for some academic scholarships; ability to marry for love (not papers); capacity to have a full social life and contribute to family and society; ability to be able to volunteer for nonprofit organizations; and freedom from fear of background checks.

Next we explore these responses in more depth, beginning with responses that are most cynical about the opportunity for change as a result of DACA. For example, Angel, a twenty-two-year-old from Central Mexico living in Oregon since he was six, said his immediate circumstances would not change with the passage of DACA:

> They generally won't. First of all, that's on a case-by-case basis so, not everyone's guaranteed for the most part. If you qualify, yes they won't deport you but you should, probably would, still need a lawyer.... My future circumstances won't be any different until they grant amnesty or something ... until it's like 100% fact that I can get permanent residency or citizenship.

Jimena, another twenty-two-year-old in Oregon living in the United States for over a dozen years, gave a similar answer:

> [I]t will change, but very slim I think. I think it still won't provide a pathway to plan out my future or resolve my immigration status. I think it's a short-term solution to my personal status.... I think it will allow me to feel more motivated towards my future, towards my education. And I'll be a step further towards planning out my educational goals.

A final example of the cynicism we observed comes from Juan Diego, a twenty-four-year-old from Mexico City who has been living in the United States since he was three:

> I think that the whole pressure is off; it does take it off but at the same time you know we're still struggling. It doesn't matter if they do that, if they give citizenship or if they give residency, more opportunities you know, we're still going to struggle. It doesn't mean that the struggle [for comprehensive immigration reform] is over.

The cynicism displayed in these comments reflects the fact that DACA does not authorize a change in immigration status or allow DREAMers to become full-fledged members of society.

It is important to bear in mind that many of these youth have real concerns about being deported, based in part on their knowledge of the high rate of deportations under the Obama administration. For example, Allison, a twenty-three-year-old from Guadalajara living in Los Angeles since infancy, said in response to this question,

> I don't think they will change at all ... there's still thousands of students, thousands of people being deported every 2.5 minutes ..., and more so here in California. More people are being deported here than in Arizona. So, I'm just hoping that those numbers have been decreased and if those who are getting deported are those who have a criminal record.

Another illustrative example comes from Santiago, a linguistics student living in the United States since infancy, who recounted a conversation he had with a classmate who had suddenly disappeared from class. He described how he thought his classmate just took "a little break from school" but then discovered that his classmate was deported after being pulled over and fined for driving without a license. Santiago notes, "I think he wasn't wearing a seat belt ... he got deported and ... and he's like, 'Yeah, I actually just came in [back to the United States] like two weeks ago.'"

The DREAMers we interviewed know that deportations are not an abstraction, an imaginary threat. It is real. They know people—friends, classmates, and often family—who have been deported and/or are in deportation proceedings. The uncertainty and fear expressed by some of the youth interviewed in our study do not reflect a lack of support for US culture or American identity. The cynicism and doubt documented here are not simply the results of being exposed to the harsh reality of racism and discrimination in this country, or to the frequent political attacks made on immigrants. Rather, it is a reflection of a lack of a sense of belonging.[15] The constant and real threat of deportation serves as a perpetual reminder that DREAMers do not belong. Again, this explains why so many of our study participants are paying close attention to political developments in the area of immigration reform; the stakes are so high for them and the anxieties involved are so palpable.

A GLIMMER OF HOPE IN THE MIDST OF UNCERTAINTY

Francisco, the undocumented former student body president at Fresno State whom we met in Chapter 3, nevertheless sees promise in DACA. Now twenty-three years old, this young man was born in Jalisco but has lived in Long Beach since he was three. He grew up believing himself to belong here, that he was a US citizen, but as a college student faced a harsh, racist backlash against his student leadership, and was repeatedly told by society that he did not belong here. Responding to our question about how DACA would change his future, he speaks directly to the idea of belonging, and says that he sees some potential in this policy shift:

> For the most part it doesn't change my status—I'm still an undocumented person. What it does is ... it integrates me and the students that qualify under this program into society ... and they're going to be integrated into their respective communities more than ever. It essentially shifts us from what a lot of us call ourselves, we're in the shadows. We live in the shadows. We work, but nobody knows that we're here. Nobody complains generally ... nobody knows who is and who isn't. We have a general profile, I guess, of what an immigrant looks like but nobody knows who is one.... So what you'll see is you're going to start seeing students that are going to get working as teachers. Students that are going to be more in their churches like

pastors, possibly even lawyers, firemen, police officers and things like that. So it literally changes the topic of immigration. What are you going to do with these students now that they have an avenue to exercise their potential? You're going to start seeing a lot of these students become active, start being involved in community more hopefully and able to be more active ... and it gives ammo to our movement when it comes to political engagement and removes a lot of the arguments that most of anti-immigrant groups tend to use like, "they don't pay their taxes, they're a burden on society." So now the momentum's on our side, politically.

This hopefulness was a common theme among the DREAMers we interviewed who were active in political activities related to immigration reform; these individuals will be discussed more fully in Chapter 5.

Other respondents were not so much cynical as they were cautious. Paulina, a twenty-four-year-old born in Coahuila who has been living in Texas for the last two decades responded to the DACA consequences question this way:

> Honestly, I'm not sure it will change a lot.... But I consulted with lots of people: other DREAMers, other lawyers, and I mean big name lawyers. And a lot of people didn't know how they'd react. They were like "I think they could still—they can't deport you, but you could easily be brought in detention center and forgotten for a long time."

This theme of fear and risk-taking associated with the executive order was revisited when study participants were asked about whether they planned to apply for DACA, as we discuss below. In part, this fear and uncertainty reflect the complexity of the regulations derived from DACA (see Chapter 1) and the leap of faith being asked of DREAMers considering submitting an application to the program. These young people must trust the government enough to be willing to provide their personal information while still living in the United States with undocumented status. They must trust the government because they are desperate and have no other option.

MORE UNCERTAINTY THAN HOPE?

Many DREAMers in our study were confused and/or fearful about what this kind of policy shift meant for them and their communities, beyond issues of deportation. A comment made by Ximena, whom we introduced at the beginning of this chapter, represents this subgroup well:

> There's mixed messages at this point. USCIS [United States Citizenship and Immigration Services] is saying if you left the country for something ... for humanitarian reasons or the like, then you should be okay. But then it also says

that if you entered the country with an inspection then you wouldn't qualify. Or if your visa is still valid you wouldn't qualify, but the tourist visa is only valid for you to stay here for up to 30 days, which I have always violated but my visa is still valid and so those are the sticky situations that I don't know where I fall.

In addition, many of the youth we spoke to are still living with undocumented family members who may not qualify under DACA, and they expressed concern about their respective fates. An illustrative example of this concern for other undocumented individuals comes from Claudia, a twenty-one-year-old from Veracruz, who has lived in Oregon since she was eight:

> To some of us it's going to help, but it's … I don't know, just students though. Like there's no other people … there's other people that just come here to work, you know, and like they don't get that chance because of their status so he's [Obama] just helping students to like grow…. It's a help and it's a start, but how is that going to help everybody else?

These concerns notwithstanding, most of the DREAMers we interviewed saw DACA as bringing positive change to their lives. For example, Esteban, a twenty-three-year-old who came to California from Mexico at age eleven, commented,

> I'm going to be able to get a Social Security number, a work permit; I think that's going to open a lot of doors for me because in the past I have applied to several scholarships and they have told me many times that I can't get those scholarships because I don't have a Social Security number, so that's one thing. The second thing is I'm going to be able to apply my knowledge and be working in a job where I can use my skills. And the third thing is being able to drive legally and travel across the states; it's not that I haven't done it, but I guess traveling without the fear.

The feelings of relief, opportunity, and an increased sense of freedom are clearly linked; together they construct a sense of increased possibilities. This sentiment was also expressed by Joaquin, a twenty-one-year-old Monterrey, Nuevo León native living in Texas since the age of six who said, plainly, "I wouldn't feel persecuted all the time."

Amalia, a twenty-one-year-old student majoring in public relations at the University of Texas–Pan American, came to the United States at age ten and has since then found herself trapped in the Rio Grande Valley: unable to travel back to Mexico, but also unable to travel north farther into the United States due to internal checkpoints. For her, the major immediate impact of DACA would be the restoration of her freedom to travel: "I can cross the checkpoints and get out of the Valley. I can move somewhere else."

There are seventy-one traffic checkpoints operated by the US Border Patrol, including thirty-two permanent traffic checkpoints near the southern border of the United States; they are located between twenty-five and seventy-five miles of the Mexico-US border along major US highways. There are a number of Border Patrol checkpoints in the northern border states as well, and these are located within 100 miles of the Canadian border. The primary purpose of these interior inspection stations is to deter both undocumented immigration and smuggling activities. According to the US General Accounting Office, agents at these internal checkpoints have legal authority that they do not possess when patrolling areas away from the border. Border Patrol agents may stop a vehicle at fixed checkpoints for brief questioning of its occupants, even if there is no reason to believe that the particular vehicle contains undocumented immigrants.[16] As intended, these checkpoints limit the ability of undocumented people such as Amalia to move within the United States.

The comments from the youth we interviewed focus on the idea of becoming—as individuals and as part of a larger ethnic community—less isolated and a more integrated part of the American social fabric, in particular on how their contribution(s) and increased perception of freedom will strengthen the country. These comments support previous reports that Latinos want to be and consider themselves a part of American society,[17] and rebuffs arguments that Latinos refuse to become part of the American melting pot.[18] In fact, thinking about the possibilities opened up by DACA led the DREAMers we spoke to to reveal contradictory emotions of relief and hope, of cynicism and frustration. They still feel vulnerable, and cautious about the details, but they were also excited by the possibility that deferred action would change their lives for the better and allow them to feel more at home in the only home that many of them have ever known.

BEYOND DEAD-END JOBS

Other respondents identified additional immediate benefits, particularly in the areas of education and career development. For instance, Ashley, who came from Tamaulipas, Mexico, to Texas at age eleven and is now twenty-one, commented, "I think I would be able to work in my school district either as a substitute or a teacher." Romina, a twenty-year-old majoring in biology who has been living in the United States for fifteen years, talked about how her status kept her from pursuing her educational dreams:

> Well, before I had this attitude that I would, I had actually wanted to go for the RN [registered nurse] program. But I found out in my second year ... I had to apply to the program and in order to do that I had to take the state-level exam and I couldn't take it because you have to have your Social [Security number]. So, what would be the point of going through all four years studying for that

and then at the end I can't take the test? So, well, that would benefit me if I could now take the test.

Some scholars refer to education as "Latinos' great hope";[19] without question education has shaped the path to inclusion, social mobility, and the American Dream for generations of Eastern and Southern European immigrants. Quotes like those from Romina illustrate a yearning for a similar trajectory among our respondents, who no longer want to live in limbo—somewhere between undocumented and citizen.

Others, like Sara, responded in a similar vein. Living in the United States since the age of seven, twenty-two-year-old Sara lives in Portland and talks about the possibility of pursuing her chosen career:

> I will no longer have to be stuck in ... "dead end jobs"—so that's a first. I have more options and since I want to be in a medical school I will have more options in the medical field to start somewhere. And then as far as with school I can apply to different schools because I would have a working Social [Security number] so they would be able to accept me and I would qualify for more scholarships.... So in a nutshell: better job, more scholarships, more schools, more opportunities and hopefully get me to where I want to be at the end of the road.... He's [Obama] finally going to give me the opportunity that I've been waiting for—even though it may be temporary but ... you have to take in what you get. So it's gonna, it's really going to make a change in my life.... I will no longer have to be scared anymore. I can feel like I'm part of this country, which has rejected me so much, even though I grew up here; I went to school here, graduated with honors, work here, pay taxes, I can finally feel like I'm going to be part of this country because I have the numbers that apparently, make you a part of this country. So that's the biggest one, I will no longer have to be scared or feel like I'm living under the shadows ...

Sara's response reflects the feelings of many of the youth we interviewed. She sees herself as someone who can contribute to the economic, social, and cultural life of the nation; she wants that type of engagement. This idea that Latino immigrants such as Romina and Sara are valuable assets rather than a threat to the American way of life is not new, and is reflected in previous research.[20] At root, the Latino threat mythology is socially constructed—it is engineered to rationalize the exclusion of Latinos and the restrictive immigration policies of the last half century. This myth can be deconstructed; the comments of the DREAMers we spoke to demonstrate that they have already embarked on that process.

A relatively small portion of the DREAMers we interviewed are excited about the possibilities DACA offers for them. Ana, an eighteen-year-old living in Oregon since the age of five, but born in Puebla, looked forward to being able to drive legally, to help her family financially, and to pay for her education. Julia, born in Veracruz to Costa Rican–born parents, arrived in the United States at the age of four and is now eighteen years old and a student at the University of Texas–Pan American. As had a few of the DREAMers we spoke to, in the summer of 2012 she had already filed a DACA application for a work permit:

> I paid for the lawyer, I paid for the—the actual filing process and I think it's gonna change my life a lot because, those two years would be the two years I'm in grad school. And if—I would, like, if I'm getting job offers or I could potentially get a job, that'd be great and I could get a job here at UTPA as a grad assistant or teaching assistant or whatever they give me. But, I think it's funny because, like, going from zero income to like a hundred dollars would be amazing, so anything is really good.... I just feel like this big door is opened, and I feel a lot better about being open about my status and about, just doing more because I always ... felt like I couldn't do as much because I could be, like, someone was gonna find out that I was illegal or whatever ... so, yeah, it's a big difference. It's a huge difference, yeah.

Whether she would go on to obtain a paying job or a volunteer position or internship, Julia looked forward to not having to fear going through background checks—to not living in fear, and to having the doors of life, of opportunity, opened up to her. Similarly enthusiastic and optimistic feelings were expressed by another DREAMer we spoke to, Adriana, who has lived in Texas since she was eight years old: "Es para lo mejor. Me podría estudiar y darle una mejor vida a mi hija la que yo no tuve. Osea cambiaria mi vida por completo." [It is for the best. I will be able to study and give my daughter a better life, one that I did not have. In other words it would completely change my life.]

Some different patterns in responses were evident across the four states. For instance, respondents in Texas talked more about having mobility within the United States and the need to defend their rights, as well as the ability to help younger siblings and parents. This reflects the fact that all of the Texas DREAMers interviewed live in the area between the US-Mexico border and internal Border Patrol checkpoints. This region has slowly displaced the Tucson enforcement zone in Arizona as the hot spot for illegal crossings, and border security efforts have been stepped up to meet this increase.[21] The youth we spoke with have witnessed these changes, and their responses reflect what they see and directly experience in this area. In California, in contrast, there was a relative emphasis on being able to get a driver's license and not having to fear police and deportation during routine traffic stops. There was also quite a bit of concern expressed for family and friends who do not qualify for deferred action. California respondents tended to be a bit more cynical about seeing immediate, positive changes in comparison to study participants interviewed in the other states. In Washington, respondents tended to talk more about being enabled to serve their communities through being better educated, engaging in military service, joining the Peace Corps, and working for nonprofits or being entrepreneurs. Finally, in Oregon, study participants were comparatively more optimistic that this governmental action would affect them positively and spark additional action on immigration reform, despite being cynical about the motivations behind this shift in policy.

REACTIONS TO PRESIDENT OBAMA

Nationally, there was a marked increase in Latino support for President Obama in response to the DACA announcement. According to polls conducted by Latino Decisions, Obama's support among Latinos increased from 66 percent to 70 percent between June and July 2012.[22] Polls conducted by the *Wall Street Journal* saw President Obama's support among Latinos jump from 58 percent to 67 percent.[23] Thus, we expected the DREAMers we talked to for this book to also have favorable opinions of the president's action. Although most were supportive, they also expressed considerable cynicism about the timing of the announcement and the program's serious limitations.

Some respondents were in fact quite disappointed in the president, and expressed feelings of anger, distrust, and disappointment. Linda is a twenty-five-year-old born in Colombia who came to the United States when she was three years old and now lives in California. She said,

> It's unfavorable because, um, considering what he—what was in his power to do ... legislation that can be, you know, it could be held up in court, you know? ... it's a failure and so, that's—that was my concern and you know I don't trust, like, the Department of Homeland Security because, or Immigration Customs Enforcement because they have a quota that they announced two years ago, deporting 400,000 a year.

Linda's comment showed clear disappointment in the limited nature of the program, as well as a clear lack of trust in immigration authorities. She went on to elaborate that she did not feel comfortable with the level of discretion immigration officials have, even under DACA:

> [T]hey can choose to ignore all these cases of, like, like DREAM-eligible youth that might come their way and because there's no consequences for them. It's based on discretion, case-by-case, so it's still up to them, right? And so, that's one part that we don't agree with, um, and also, it's not a guarantee.

Linda said she felt betrayed by President Obama—he promised comprehensive immigration reform with a path to citizenship and delivered deferred action instead. Like many of the DREAMers we spoke to, she expressed concern about what would happen after the 2012 presidential election—particularly if President Obama failed to be reelected and the next president chose to rescind the program. Jorge, a twenty-one-year-old from Sinaloa living in the Portland area, shared similar concerns. He was clearly angry with President Obama for breaking his promise of immigration reform, and also angry with how Latino immigrants in general were being treated:

> 'Cause it's, I don't want to be used, you know, people say this is a free country, well why not share it? You know like, instead of us Mexicans coming over and using us to work because nobody else wants to do the jobs, you know like, and then after thirty years, after you're thirty, you can't apply—like it's just stupid, that's not what he was promising for one; two, they can take it away at any time, and three, you still have to be approved to get it and it's not guaranteed that you're gonna.

Another California resident, Juan Diego, a twenty-four-year-old engineering major from Mexico City, commented,

> People are fed up and they're going to talk you know and they're gonna say, "this guy [Obama] has made us believe that, he's gonna give us papers even when he was going to become first black President," he said that, "oh we're gonna give you residency." And that didn't happen and so now that's he's deported so many people.... How come he couldn't do that when he was first President? How could he deport so many people?

These DREAMers' comments, like those made by immigrants' rights organizations to the media during this same time period, reflect the urgency with which they believe the government needs to create a better immigration process.[24]

At the same time that they expressed anger and disappointment about DACA, these DREAMers almost all planned to move forward with an application. This speaks volumes about the desire to become a legal part of society, illustrating the persistent desire to feel a sense of belonging.

DISILLUSIONMENT

A few respondents who said the deferred action was unfavorable showed a pattern of disappointment and feelings of being alienated by this policy shift. Consider this comment from Valentino, a twenty-year-old native of Tequila, Mexico, who has lived in Tacoma, Washington, since infancy:

> I think it's like ... kinda like disrespectful that he [Obama] only came out with that, only being like a couple years, only being like a work permit. You know that doesn't change anything at all ... I just think it's kinda like, disrespectful that he promised something so big for so many people that got him the presidency, the Latino vote you know. He promised a big immigration reform and I understand that as the President you have a lot to deal with ... I think,

it kinda feels like slapping us across the face, its like, "okay you know what, I want to deport you guys. I won't grant all of you guys papers or any of that, but here's one permit for two years—meanwhile let the next President, if that's me, try to fix it ..." That's my opinion on that.

There is a strong sense of political alienation in Valentino's statement, a relatively enduring sense of estrangement or rejection from the political system.[25]

A similar sentiment was expressed by Sofia, a twenty-year-old from Michoacán living in Oregon, who has been in the United States since she was seven years old:

> I really hope that it [DACA] helps a lot of people but in some ways I feel like they just, it's temporary and they just did it because everyone's been protesting. They want something to happen and because the DREAM Act hasn't been passed already three times. I feel like they just made something up right now so we can calm down. But there's still a lot of little things that people don't realize that we still don't get to benefit from it. And one of the things that I hate ... if you don't get accepted the first time you won't ever be able to apply again. That's one of the things that I don't agree with.

Some scholars argue that the political nature of policymaking limits the chance for marginalized groups to participate in the democratic system in which they reside. DREAMers, the segment of American society most directly affected by DACA, had little power to influence decisions about the program, and thus are left with severely limited options, all of which involve putting themselves at risk.[26]

One option is to apply for relief via deferred action, which provides the federal government with information about their undocumented status. For instance, Axel, a twenty-three-year-old born in Michoacán, has lived in Washington since he was eleven. He shared his sense of trepidation:

> I'm scared. I mean, what if Obama doesn't win? What's gonna happen after two years, you know? Would I get deported or not? So, that's my biggest fear right now, you know. I'm in the application process, but I'm still thinking should I turn it in or not? I mean, I don't know.

Mauricio, a twenty-three-year-old who has been living in the United States since infancy, expressed similar concerns:

> I know we have to provide information about our family members and I don't know how the information is going to be used ... they could use our information to deport us or they could use that information to deport our families.... I don't know how to take that just yet.

Mauricio's and Axel's comments are illustrative of those made by many of the DREAMers we spoke to. They believe they are taking a significant risk, and some even discussed how their applications might put their entire families at risk. These perceptions are based on their own prior experiences and the on experiences of people they know who have been deported and/or detained. These youth have been made quite aware of their relative standing in American society through the way the media covers immigration, the anti-immigrant/anti-Latino backlash that for decades has set the context of political discourse, and the lack of noteworthy progress on immigration reform. Previous research suggests, for example, that US crime reports in newspapers have constructed a negative representation of Latino migrants, and this has an indirect, negative impact on Latino schoolchildren.[27]

Concern for those left out of DACA because they are ineligible was also a common theme among responses to this question. Rafael, a twenty-four-year-old environmental science student, said, "I feel like a lot of people were not taken into consideration with this action … like the parents of undocumented students you know … those parents are not protected by that law and the many other people that have been here for years."

Several study participants expressed their concern that DACA only allows for two-year work permits, rather than a more long-term resolution of their immigration status. Paulina, a twenty-four-year-old in San Antonio, commented,

> I think that it's a good step and hopefully this step will bring about new immigration reform. But I also don't think it's enough. It doesn't make any sense for you to have people here legally for two years and then just have them renew their status. I mean, you're renewing your status. Are they going to have a limit on how many times you can renew it? How're you—if it's not a path to citizenship. How are they going to determine when you can't get it renewed anymore? I think really it should be more a path to citizenship. I also don't like the DREAM Act because, just because I think it's ridiculous that it would take over ten years to become a citizen when you've been here for double that amount or whatever.

Other DREAMers, such as Ximena, said that they were even considering leaving the United States for their countries of origin—countries that they hardly know— in order to stop living in limbo and make use of their educations and potential:

> I already have two Master's degrees. I mean I'm just waiting to work in the United States lawfully and being able to execute the knowledge that I have in a positive manner. I mean, now that I have it I would actually get compensated for what I know. If the dream lasts only two years it would only last only two years. I know that with the education that the United States has given me I can go make [myself] rich in any other country if the United States no longer wanted me here.

These are powerful statements about the level of frustration DREAMers feel about living in limbo. They raise the question, what does it take to be recognized as an American—as part of the country they have been raised and socialized in? It is noteworthy that some DREAMers are even willing to physically exit a society they feel does not want them.

WHAT ABOUT THE MOVEMENT?

Many of the DREAMers we interviewed expressed concern about how DACA will affect political engagement on issues of immigration reform beyond DACA. How will the momentum that has characterized a growing political movement, particularly protests and marches in California, be affected by deferred action? Symbolic politics and the policies they create have real impacts on the lives of community members.[28] Some respondents believe that DACA will sap this momentum and deter political engagement, leading to decreased pressure for more comprehensive immigration reform. Others see deferred action as the figurative spark for increased sociopolitical change. For example, Mauricio commented, "I feel like because now some undocumented people will have a work permit, I think that they'll see it as enough ... rather than fighting for full rights.... I think that we're still sort of enslaved in this idea that a two-year work permit that's renewable is going to be enough."

Similar concerns were shared by Aaron, a twenty-one-year-old from Baja, California, who came to Los Angeles when he was just three years old:

> In terms of like a movement for people who are undocumented who are trying to stand up for something greater than like ... upward mobility; like the Social [Security number] or license or all of that, it's unfavorable because what it's gonna do is satisfy a lot of DREAMers and they're going to stop fighting for their families, they're gonna stop fighting for liberation, which is much more important than a legislation that ... we're still going to be criminalized by the cops ... you know 90% of people of color are behind bars and in prisons and we're still going to be that; it doesn't matter if you're a citizen or not.... This is far more deep than the DREAM Act or legislation that's not going to empower people to stand up if it fails. I'm empowered to fight no matter what; no matter if they put legislation in my way, fuck it, I'll support it; I'm not going to put all of my efforts into it and forget about these people being deported over here ... in terms of like a movement ... and trying to make some change with like respect and dignity ... it's just a political tool for Obama.

Aaron's comments illustrate the robust tendency of our study participants toward cynicism and a desire for a more substantive policy response. The alternative view, that deferred action is a step in the right direction that can be a building block toward more comprehensive immigration reform, will be addressed later in this chapter.

CAUGHT BETWEEN DONKEYS, ELEPHANTS, AND ELECTIONS

The third theme across responses to this question focuses on the political dimension. A significant proportion of DREAMers we interviewed discussed feeling like pawns, feeling manipulated and used by President Obama for political gain in the November 2012 presidential election. Consider this exchange with Jimena, who has been living in the United States since she was ten years old:

> A: I feel like it's too much of a political move to gain him votes for his administration for the upcoming election and very little to do with solving or even pushing the DREAM Act forward.
> Q: So it's more of a political move than …?
> A: Yeah, I feel like it is. He had already said that he would pass the DREAM Act within a year and that his hands were tied because of Congress, or it not passing … he should have done this executive order, he should have done it before the DREAM Act was up for vote, then the Senate and the Congress could have felt the pressure to find a resolution rather than feel like Obama's taking his executive power too far. The timing is everything and the timing that he decided to do this, for me, reveals that it's more political motive than to actually find a solution to the DREAM Act or thousands of undocumented youth that are present here.

Tomas, a Veracruzano living in Oregon, also highlighted the issue of President Obama's timing: "I just feel like they're playing 'cause he [Obama] promised us this when he was gonna run for President, that he was going to do something about it but in four years he didn't do anything till the end and I was like, 'okay that's a little weird.'" Rafael commented, "because elections are coming … so it's like, 'elect me, look what I'm going to pass.'"

Other participants shared similar responses, adding that they feel even further marginalized by the way Obama went about putting deferred action in place. Romina explained,

> My opinion, I heard that he did it because he wants to get re-elected. That's one thing. Two, I've gone over it in my head. Why didn't he do it before? Why now? So, to me—it benefits me, I don't care the circumstance, but he could have done it earlier and helped other students. I know some people that already graduated and even got their Master's degree … but haven't been able to work in what they want because they don't have the opportunity to do it.

An analogous response comes from a twenty-two-year-old, Mateo, in Oregon:

> I just feel like it shouldn't be about politics, it shouldn't be about Republicans versus Democrats.... We're not just chess pieces that you can just, you know, move around any way you want. We're actually human beings, we have you know, dreams, we have aspirations. So just knowing that they're kind of taking this at a political level, it's really angering to me knowing to me that, you know, even though, you know, "yay for this," it's still like knowing the steps behind it, the reasons behind it—they're not to help us.

These statements reflect intense feelings of marginalization and lack of political voice. They also highlight the feeling of DREAMers that immigration reform is as much about the outcome as it is about the intent and process used to create it.

Some respondents saw President Obama's actions as a response to the immigration reform movement. Jose, a recent permanent resident, explained his thoughts this way:

> I also think that he [Obama] did this because he doesn't want to be bothered with any more protests. Because you know, we have been escalating. We start with, like, civil disobedience, we start doing, getting arrested in different buildings [occupying President Obama's headquarters]. And that's what triggered for him to sign the deferred action.

Hugo, a twenty-three-year-old master's student living in Los Angeles, stated, "I thank the Obama administration ... but ideally I thank the people that are behind the movement."

DREAMers were not the only ones questioning President Obama about the lack of progress on immigration during his first term. For example, in September 2012, just weeks before the election, Univision's Jorge Ramos delivered one of the president's toughest grillings of the 2012 campaign season, with a focus on his broken immigration reform campaign promises. Ramos said, "You promised that, and a promise is a promise. And with all due respect, you didn't keep that promise." Ramos also asked Obama whether his unilateral move to prevent deportations of young illegal immigrants with the DACA program was a political move, and asked what had been his biggest failure as president. The president did not hesitate: "As you remind me, my biggest failure is that we haven't gotten comprehensive immigration reform done, so we're going to be continuing to work on that. But it's not for lack of trying or desire."[29] This pressure to deliver *something* on the issue of immigration reform was recognized by the DREAMers we talked to. For example, Esteban, a twenty-three-year-old born in Zacatecas, had this reaction to Obama's program:

It was definitely favorable. I see it as a political move by the Obama Administration because they knew that we're getting closer to the elections and they failed on delivering a comprehensive immigration reform. They failed on delivering the DREAM Act in 2010, and I guess some of it was a political move but also I guess what pushed him to grant deferred action was the fact that the student movement really reorganized and we launched an actual campaign to pressure him and get other allies and Congress members to also pressure him. So I think it's a combination of things, but it's definitely favorable.

LEANING TOWARD PROGRESS

Many respondents indicated that while they thought DACA was not ideal, it represented progress for the immigration reform movement. Bruno, a twenty-five-year-old from Monterrey, Nuevo León, voiced a timid sense of progress in these words:

To tell you the truth, I mean it's favorable but it's not what we would like, I mean it's not like being on our way to be legally here as a resident or as citizen. It's not the way. I mean President Obama said that it is just a protection. But I think it is better than being completely without any protection. So yeah, it's better. In a way also that we might work legally so that of course is way much better.

Two Washington study participants, one from Jalisco and the second from Mexico City, also expressed a sense of progress. Jesus said, "He's [Obama] actually going through with it so it's not just a promise that he's making for re-election, so it's actually happening." Alonso called deferred action "A step in the right direction. Not ideal, but it's, as it's named a temporary relief in that it's not by any means a be-all, end-all solution it's just the minimum that could have been done." A less cynical response comes from Mateo, a twenty-two-year-old sociology major in Portland:

That's true, but you always have to take it one step at a time. So I think it's good to do and it's a good first step. It's definitely not the end of it. I mean, I'm not gonna sit here like, "you know what, I have a work permit now, I'm happy." It's not how it works, but you have to take it one step at a time. You have to learn to walk before you can run.

Others, like Daniela, a twenty-three-year-old born in San Luis Potosi, shared a sense of relief during their interviews:

It's helping the youth. People that were brought here, we were all kids. We didn't know uh, we were here legally or illegally. We didn't know any better so um, yeah it's for the young people. We want to study; we want to branch out without any fear or always being paranoid.

Dylan responded along similar lines:

[I'm] very happy that finally Barack Obama got it, you know? That after so many years of pressuring for the DREAM Act or just something you know, we just want something. We want a path of legalization that can give us a chance to prove to the United States, prove to the community that we are very educated and that we are ready to work, you know? If they give us a chance, we can work for a—for the better, we are good citizens, and we just want one opportunity and the deferred action will do that for us. And I'm just very happy that that's happening right now and that so many people will get benefits from it.

Words like *hope* and *thankful* were used by others as well. Washington resident Fabiana said,

[W]ell, I think this can be really controversial because like for one, you know that Obama should have done this a long time ago but now, is he just doing it because the elections are coming up? But then again, it's kind of hope and also like, I guess a light at the end of the tunnel. I think it was a right move from him. I think he could have done it sooner, but I think now that it is an action we can take it and like me and many other students and take advantage of the opportunity to be able to be here in the United States and not be afraid of whether one day somebody's gonna come and pick us up or not.

Luna was also optimistic about how DACA would improve her life and the lives of others, and perhaps lead to more comprehensive reform:

I think it's a baby step, it's good, that we're thankful for it, but it's not enough. With the deferred action, I feel like now I can even share with more people my life secret 'cause it's not really a secret, but my life. And not be so afraid you know. I think it's going to help people to be able to speak up and um, it's not enough but now we're going to have a little more of a voice we can share, you know, and more DREAMers come together and show who we are and show that we're there and that we want more.

After twenty-plus years of inaction on the question of undocumented immigration, respondents acknowledge DACA as an advancement in the immigration reform effort. However, it is precisely the decades-long wait that contributes to the perception that DACA is insufficient. These study participants understand the limits of DACA, but they've chosen to interpret the result of this long wait for DACA protections with optimism rather than cynicism.

An even smaller proportion of respondents was outright positive. For example, one young woman living in Deep South Texas, Adriana, stated,

> Fue favorable. Pues pienso que fue una buena acción porque le va a dar—va a hacer realidad sueños de muchos indocumentados que estamos aquí. [It was favorable. Well I think it was a good action because it's going to give—it's going to fulfill (make a reality) dreams of many undocumented immigrants who are here.]

Joshua, a nineteen-year-old graphic design student, said, "It was a very brave thing that Obama did." Daniel, a twenty-two-year-old who has been in the United States since he was two years old, went even further in his comments on DACA:

> Yeah, I think it's something that's so amazing. It's really ... for a lot of students who have no hope, they have it now. I also think that it helps reignite the conversation for the passage of the DREAM Act and comprehensive immigration reform because things were pretty bad for a while. That's the way I felt.

A final, exceptionally favorable comment along these lines comes from Martina, who remembers celebrating her third birthday in the United States: "I think this action is something spectacular. I think it's a great opportunity and it's actually a good gift from God."

PATTERNS, HISTORY, AND CONTEXT

Overwhelmingly, most DREAMers interviewed want more in the way of immigration reform. They want a more permanent policy resolution in the area of immigration, and they want something that will move beyond the current, limited group of young people included. Respondents in California, who are also more heavily male, hold more unfavorable opinions about President Obama's actions and criticize him and the policy more harshly in comparison to respondents in Oregon, Texas, and Washington. The long political history of activism among Chicanos, and Latinos more generally, in California also helps to explain this pattern in our interview data.[30] This history developed a distinctive sociopolitical context that continues to shape political engagement in Latino communities in the state today. This is evidenced by the 2006 immigration marches, and the immigration protests against President Obama over the last few years by California residents.[31]

The history of Mexican-origin populations in Texas can also help explain our findings because the contemporary context in which DREAMers find themselves in Deep South Texas is a legacy of that history. The annexation of Mexican territory in the mid-1800s created what is today recognized as the American Southwest. What is often omitted from the discussion about the development of this region, which includes Texas, is that the appropriation of these lands included the annexation of Mexican people as well.[32] While the Treaty of Guadalupe Hidalgo provided for a path to citizenship for the approximately 100,000 Mexicans living in the area who did not relocate to Mexico, hostilities against those who remained were high. Juan Cortina, who led a rebellion in south Texas in 1859, characterizes the situation of Mexicans living in Texas: "Many of you have been robbed of your property, incarcerated, chased, murdered, and hunted like wild beasts, because your labor was fruitful."[33] In fact, in 1850, 34 percent of the rural Mexican population in Texas comprised ranch or farm owners, 29 percent were skilled labor, and 34 percent were manual laborers. By 1900 the distribution of land changed dramatically: only 16 percent of the rural Mexican population in the state comprised ranch or farm owners, 12 percent were skilled laborers, and the majority, 67 percent, were manual laborers. The transition of Tejanos from landed gentry to laborers was prompted by harsh oppression and frequent use of violence, and it is within this historical context that the relationship between Mexican-origin populations and Texas was fomented.

In 1915, persons of Mexican origin living in Texas orchestrated an uprising comparable in scale to Nat Turner's slave rebellion nearly a century earlier. The revolt was responsible for the killings of dozens of white farmers and ranchers in south Texas and stimulated a bloody reaction that claimed the lives of untold Mexicans—a wave of lynching and vigilantism that swept through south Texas. The number of Mexicans killed in what Walter Prescott Webb called an "orgy of bloodshed" is hard to comprehend. Some estimate the number in the "low thousands."[34] The explicit goal of some of the vigilantes, mobs, and official police forces such as the Texas Rangers, and the sure result of their campaign of terrorism, was the transfer of lands out of Mexican hands. Social and political engagement by Mexicans and Mexican Americans in Texas is deeply colored by this context, and contributes to the environment in which DREAMers now find themselves.

WAITING FOR SUPERMAN ... OR CONGRESS?

President Obama's decision to issue an executive order regarding deferred action, an order that holds the full force of law, occurred after more than two and a half decades of stalled immigration reform in Congress. His action follows a trend of executive action on issues of civil rights that have failed to be addressed through customary legislative and judicial processes. For example, in 1948 President Truman integrated the armed forces with Executive Order 9981, and in 1957 President Eisenhower issued Executive Order 10730 to maintain order during the desegregation of Central High School in Little Rock, Arkansas. In 1961 President Kennedy issued Executive Order 10925, requiring federal contractors to take affirmative action in the hiring of employees, and in 1965 President Johnson signed Executive Order 11246, expanding JFK's order by establishing requirements for nondiscriminatory practices. In contrast to executive orders, laws passed by Congress are relatively permanent; yet, despite concerns expressed by our study participants about the limited nature of the two-year work permits, they almost universally agreed that it was best for President Obama to act using his executive power rather than waiting for Congress. The broad sense was that nothing would have been gained by waiting because the likelihood of congressional action was so slim.

An illustrative comment along these lines comes from Vicente, a twenty-seven-year-old born in Mexico City and living in LA, who looked back on previous inaction as predictive of future inaction. Vicente said, "We've learned that waiting for the perfect solution has gotten us nowhere—more, more deeper in the hole of criminalization. So I feel this approach of having piecemeal policies passed will get us through to the ultimate goal of providing relief for everyone." Similar concern about waiting for congressional action was mentioned by Samuel, nineteen, who was born in Michoacán and brought to the United States when he was five years old:

> [T]he more time you take … it kinda fades into the background you know so the fact that he [Obama] made an executive action definitely put pressure on it … there needs to be a reform, like our immigration system is flawed and … there definitely needs to be some sort of fix and the fact that he made an executive action affected me … beggars can't be choosers.

This last line in Samuel's remark was repeated by several DREAMers and conjures powerful images—when resources are limited, one must accept even substandard offerings. Sofia commented in this regard:

> No. I think that if he wouldn't have done anything we would still be waiting right now and who knows how long we'd be waiting. I definitely think he could have done it sooner, and like I said for me it was a political technique. One of the main reasons why he [Obama] became President is because of Latinos who came out to vote for his presidential election. Um, and so I think he was a little scared that they wouldn't come out again. By doing this he knows that well, he has the Latino vote in his pocket, at least the majority of it.

Similarly, Julia responded to the question on presidential motivation as follows:

> That is a hard question, because we've been waiting for, what, ten years? I don't know how much more waiting people can do. And, um, I think it was a good—executive order was good, but, I mean, I see the holes, not having, like, a—it's sort of like this is what you get, like giving someone a crumb and saying "look, you have this now, so don't bug me for a while." So maybe that's part of it, but maybe it could—it could be like now we could take more because we have this.

Other participants expressed a sense of urgency, linked to ongoing concerns about deportation. Luis, a twenty-four-year-old from the Mexican border city of Reynosa who has been living in Deep South Texas for half his life, said, "I think it was better the action that he [Obama] took because some of us are already in the process of deportation so we cannot wait for the Congress to pass something." The issue of not being deportable was also raised by Patricio who said, "I can't discard the fact that I feel like a pawn in like a chess game with a political agenda or political strategy, but nonetheless this Executive Order will allow myself and a lot of us to find work and then not be deported."

HOLD OUT FOR MORE

Those who preferred that President Obama wait for Congress to craft immigration reform expressed concern that DACA did not go far enough to address the real and pressing needs of immigrant families and communities. There are serious questions raised by what deferred action will mean, ultimately, for the fate of immigration reform, the deportation rate, and the lives of our study participants and their families. For example, one DREAMer from California noted that while many celebrate the arrival of DACA, too many people, noncriminals, are being deported in his community. Another respondent, Miranda, commented, "[W]e have been fighting for permanent residency, not just a work permit."

In general, there are feelings across Washington, Texas, and California that President Obama could have done more and that he waited too long to enact deferred action. In contrast, about a quarter of respondents from Oregon would have preferred he wait for congressional action. This may reflect the fact that Oregon is the only state included in our sample that is not situated on a border; thus, immigrant communities in Oregon have experienced relatively less pressure than have those in border states. As we described earlier in this chapter, the experience of living on the border is different—security is tighter and deportation is more likely. Between 2010 and 2012 nearly 205,000 parents of US-born children were removed from the country;[35] border states were hit the hardest by these deportations.

STILL DREAMING

All of our respondents, save one, were familiar with the DREAM Act and want to see a federal DREAM Act come to fruition. While most acknowledge that the DREAM Act has flaws, they favor it because in most versions (see Chapter 2) it includes a pathway to permanent residency and citizenship. Without question this is what our DREAMers want. While the youth we spoke to are concerned about the length of time the naturalization process could take under the DREAM Act, possibly more than a decade, and others do not like that military service is a pathway toward citizenship, they still hoped that it would soon become law. Asked how his life would change if Congress were to pass a federal DREAM Act, Nicolas, a twenty-three-year-old from Chiapas, Mexico, living in Washington since he was eleven, responded,

> I don't feel like I'll have full freedom. This will change somewhat my perspective on the topic, now I'll feel more safe. I feel more freedom than before. I feel like I don't have to watch behind my back no more. So, I feel like I can … I can have a fair shot of anything. I'll have an equal opportunity.

Similarly, Nicole, a twenty-four-year-old female living in California, said the DREAM Act would allow her to "plan out my life" far more than one year at a time. She observed in this regard:

> You know like have some type of certainty of … not that I don't plan my life in more than year increments but like set particular goals in my life. You know this is realistically what I can achieve in this amount of time. I can aspire to what I want to do five years from now. I can aspire to be in a place five to ten years from now but because my circumstance/situation—things can change very much for me at any given point so this sort of gives me an assurance that for the next two years of my life, if I do get this work permit, I can like find a job, have a job, you know.

These comments demonstrate the desire of DREAMers to move out of limbo and into safety and stability, essential building blocks for social and political integration and the fulfillment of the American Dream.[36]

There is also a strong sense that the United States is home. Santino, who came to the United States from Honduras at the age of eleven, explains as follows:

> You have thousands of students like myself that try every day to do the best they can, not to go back to their home country because there's no future for them over there. And, they—this government has raised us, they have educated us, they have given us every single—every single thing that every American has here. So why should we be thrown back to our countries where we don't know nothing of? You know, we don't know how the economy is, we don't know how they are. We don't know nothing about them.

The DREAMers we spoke to want the concrete benefits of citizenship: the right to vote and access to financial aid to complete their studies. But most of all they want to feel a sense of belonging. They want to be able to tell their individual stories without feeling rejected, marginalized, and labeled as a negative force in the society in which they were raised. Nicole, who has lived in the United States since she was three years old, sums up the feelings of most respondents by saying, "The American Dream … isn't that everybody's goal?" Sara is a twenty-two-year-old political science major living in Oregon since she was seven. Her comments about what a DREAM Act and citizenship would mean to her are worth quoting at length:

> My goal is to finally become a citizen from here so I can help with all the rights. I do everything for this country but I feel like I don't get anything back, so maybe by then I can start. Maybe I can vote, you know be part of all the things that citizens are involved in.... My goal is to, I always wanted to work ... for a non-profit organization that's gonna help my community. That helped me so much through this whole process. I think I wouldn't have to live within the shadows anymore. I can be able to ... just one day my goal is to tell people because people right now don't know that I'm illegal. They think I'm legal because I go to school, have a job. We have an apartment, we have a car, so people think that I'm legal because there's nothing that I'm doing that shows that I'm illegal. So one day I just want to be able to talk about like, "yeah, I did all that without papers—it was hard but I did it." I think if the DREAM Act passed and I was able to become legal I think I would be able to talk to more people about it and show them that like, tell them more of who I am. 'Cause right now I feel like I have to limit myself. I have to live under the shadows for a little bit, limit myself. But after that happened, I wouldn't have to limit myself anymore ... I could talk about my life experiences and maybe change peoples' actions or thoughts or perceptions based on experience and my history 'cause they'll be able to understand that, we're not bad people, we're not here to steal your job, we're just regular people. The only difference is that we don't have nine numbers, that's it. And so personally that's going to help me grow like that.

Many, like Sara, see multiple potential benefits from passage of a federal DREAM Act, for herself as an individual and also for American society. They believe that the passage of this kind of legislation could reframe the debate at the national level while simultaneously empowering individuals in their everyday lives.

IN THE FINAL ANALYSIS

At the beginning of this chapter we noted that the American Dream is about the opportunity for upward social mobility through hard work. The DREAMers we spoke to have a deeper understanding of this concept. James Truslow Adams, an American historian and Pulitzer-winning writer, describes this more nuanced characterization as follows:

> The American Dream is that dream of a land in which life should be better and richer and fuller for everyone, with opportunity for each according to ability or achievement. It is a difficult dream for the European upper classes to interpret

adequately, and too many of us ourselves have grown weary and mistrustful of it. It is not a dream of motor cars and high wages merely, but a dream of social order in which each man and each woman shall be able to attain to the fullest stature of which they are innately capable, and be recognized by others for what they are, regardless of the fortuitous circumstances of birth or position.[37]

The young people we interviewed aspire to be fully incorporated into US society—economically, socially, and politically. However, their end goals extend beyond economic success and political voice—they include the idea of being recognized and treated as a part of the whole. While these DREAMers are somewhat pleased by the short-term opportunities deferred action can provide, most believe it is too little.

The bottom line is that only some of the problems faced by the DREAMers can be solved by DACA. DREAMers will continue to live in limbo even if they avail themselves of the protections afforded by DACA. Deferred action provides only a temporary respite from deportation and fails to provide any permanent status or solution for the particular DREAMers who qualify. Living in limbo means that DREAMers' lives are on hold. Educational, career, and social and political development possibilities are stunted. Because they are unable, given the current state of immigration laws in this country, to fully pursue their dreams, the growth and vitality of US society is also stunted.

Chapter 5

Political Activism and Ethnic Identity

Before, I was, you know—I didn't exist. I didn't have a number. So you're, you're a shadow, you know? But now, I'm gonna exist. You know, there's gonna be a record of me. I'm gonna have, like, an identification. I'm gonna have a number. So I am gonna feel, you know, the consequences of this immigration policy.

—Hugo, age twenty-three, from California,
responding to the deferred action program

Mauricio, a sociology major at UCLA, came to the United States with his parents when he was just a few months old. Like many of the DREAMers we spoke to for this book, he learned of his status as a high school senior, when he found he couldn't obtain a driver's license or fill out college financial aid forms. At first, he struggled with this new information. In his own words,

I was so uncomfortable with my immigration status, I was really ashamed, I didn't get an ID, my *matricula*, until my second year [of college] because I was just, like, I don't want to force a Mexican identity ... I was very resistant ... and then I turned 18 and I wanted to go out and I was like, "I guess I need an ID with my age on it, too," so, I forced myself to get one, and that was the first thing, I think, I was like, for a while, I kinda like questioned it, what the resistance was, like me having been, like, ashamed of my Mexican identity or was it because I was just resisting my status and the fact that I had never lived there before, and so I was trying to be critical of that feeling, like I had to question, like, do I have a sense of shame for who I am.

For the next few years, Mauricio tried to determine his identity and how he fit into American society, taking relevant classes at UCLA and becoming involved in a Latin American group on campus. "As I questioned my own, or tried to retain my own, culture ... like, what is this Americanization, I'm undocumented, I'm not allowed to be part of this society but I'm still holding true to these values and socializing myself into this society." In due course, Mauricio became heavily involved in student activities on behalf of the DREAM Act, and he now identifies strongly as Latino.

Theories of political socialization would lead us to believe that undocumented youth living through the political drama that is our current immigration reform debate would become interested in politics, mobilize to take action, and develop stronger feelings of panethnic identity. For many of our respondents, including Mauricio, this accurately describes their experiences as DREAMers. In contrast, others were led to turn inward, focusing on staying out of trouble and attending school, living in fear of being discovered and possibly deported. In this chapter, we take advantage of the open-ended format of the interviews to flesh out the interactions between DREAMer status, political attitudes and behavior, and ethnic identity, and to compare those richer understandings of these relationships to what we would expect to see given previous scholarship. Overall, we find that while some extant research is confirmed, other findings are perhaps more surprising, reflecting both the diversity of the DREAMer community and the complexity of these topics.

As noted by Gimpel, Lay, and Schuknecht, people do not become politically socialized in a vacuum; they are influenced by local social and political circumstances.[1] DREAMers share some contexts, but vary in others. All came to the United States as infants or children and without appropriate documents—most of those we interviewed came on tourist visas that they subsequently overstayed rather than via some stealthy made-for-Hollywood border crossing—and thus are influenced by their status. Some have experienced deportation or detainment because of their status, while others have eluded such traumas. Some live in the heavily Latino and heavily immigrant neighborhoods of southern Texas and California, while others are from the Pacific Northwest, communities with not only far fewer Latino immigrants but also very different political cultures. According to data from the Pew Hispanic Center, of the 11.2 million undocumented immigrants in the United States in 2010, 2.55 million resided in California and 1.65 million in Texas (6.8 percent and 6.7 percent of each state's total population, respectively), compared to only 230,000 in Washington state and 160,000 in Oregon (3.4 and 4.3 percent of those state populations, respectively).[2] Thus, just in terms of the size and density of the undocumented immigrant population, individuals in Texas and California experience a very different context. In addition, the states differ in terms of their broader ethnoracial diversity. According to the 2010 US Census, 37.6 percent of individuals living in California and Texas are Latino, as compared to only 11.7 percent of individuals living in Oregon and 11.2 percent of individuals living in Washington.

These contexts also affect their politicization and political behavior. As Rodney Hero notes, "mixtures or cleavages of various minority and/or racial/ethnic groups within a state—the types and levels of social *diversity* or complexity—are critical in understanding the politics and policy in the states" (emphasis in original).[3] Latinos in the heavily Latino states of California and Texas experience day-to-day life very differently than do Latinos living in the Pacific Northwest; this inevitably will affect their feelings of belonging, political empowerment, and Latino identity, regardless of their immigration status.

These four states also vary in terms of their political culture. Daniel Elazar defined three major types of political culture: individualistic, moralistic, and traditionalistic.[4] While often criticized, his typology has generally held up over time, and there is empirical evidence of deeply ingrained political values that differ substantially across regions of the United States.[5] Relevant here are the labels for the four states in which we conducted interviews. California and Washington are considered moralistic and individualistic, Texas is classified as traditionalistic and individualistic, and Oregon is moralistic. According to Elazar, these cultures are associated with different norms regarding individual political participation. Moralists consider participation for the sake of the common good to be the duty of all citizens, individualists endorse participation that aims to improve one's personal position, and traditionalists reserve participation for those considered to be elites. Applying this typology to the four states in which we conducted interviews, we would expect the least participation among respondents in Texas, and more participation elsewhere.

The interviews we conducted in Texas took place in the southern tip of the state, in the Rio Grande Valley. The context of this geographic location differs in that it is included in the US Border Patrol's system of internal checkpoints, as described in Chapter 4. This means that undocumented immigrants in the area face the constant threat of detection and deportation, even if they do not attempt to cross the border into Mexico. The Rio Grande Valley Sector of the Border Patrol is headquartered in Edinburg, the same city that hosts the University of Texas–Pan American, which many of our respondents from Texas have attended in the past or currently attend. The sector includes two interior checkpoints, one on each of the major highways leading north from the area (US Highway 77 and US Highway 281).

What this means for undocumented residents of the Rio Grande Valley, including our respondents, is that they cannot easily travel within the state. Data from the US Department of Homeland Security (DHS) confirm that undocumented immigrants in the Rio Grande Valley are more likely than undocumented immigrants in California, Oregon, or Washington to be apprehended.[6] For example, in 2011, 59,243 individuals were apprehended in the Rio Grande Valley Sector, compared to only 640 in Los Angeles and 668 in Seattle, Washington; so few apprehensions are made from Oregon that it is not listed in the US DHS reports. In sum, while all undocumented immigrants fear deportation to some extent, the US Border Patrol has a much stronger presence in Deep South Texas than in the other locations in which we conducted interviews, generating much stronger everyday fears, as was discussed in Chapter 4. This everyday fear is reflected in their levels of political engagement and participation.

During the interviews, we asked participants, "Were you involved in any of the immigration marches of 2006 or in any other action related to immigration policy?" Among respondents from Texas, almost all answered with a simple "no." A few gave more detailed answers that also support the idea of Texas as a traditionalistic state that discourages mass political behavior, particularly among those not considered legitimate, documented citizens. Santino, age twenty, noted, "I couldn't go because I might get arrested or, you know—I couldn't risk that." Julia, age twenty-three, said, "A lot of times I wanted to go but I was afraid to go." Only one Texas respondent, Fiorella, reported having taken part in one of the marches many years ago as a student. Fiorella, now twenty-five years old, came to the United States at age fourteen, and knew immediately of her status because she was asked for her Social Security number when she went to register for high school. That status later prevented her from officially graduating, although she otherwise had completed the requirements to do so. Despite her status and the traditionalist culture of Texas she went to a march in favor of immigration reform, but she lied about it when confronted by the teacher:

> A: We wanted to march … about immigration, [about] students becoming legal … we did it, like, from here to march, everybody skip [school]. We didn't go to school because we went to that.
> Q: You didn't go to school because you went to the march.
> A: Yes, anyway we found out that we had a test that day, for the same reason.
> Q: Oh, so they gave you guys a test that day so that you wouldn't go to the march.
> A: Yes, but we still went.
> Q: How were your teachers when you came back? Were they upset?
> A: No, they were asking where we went. And we're like, oh, well I was sick that day and everybody was like, "we went to the march!" And I wouldn't say I went to the march. But we just, a bunch of us went and liars some … I was one of the liars. Because I can't say I went because they were saying, like, you're not supposed to go … because, we're students, we're supposed to stay home.

Students in other states were more likely to respond to this question with a story about their activism, but less so in Washington and Oregon than in California, where the density and absolute numbers of Latinos and immigrants facilitated participation.

A majority (sixteen out of twenty-five) of our Washington state respondents said that they had participated in some immigration-related political activity, albeit usually just a march or two. Valentina, age nineteen, participated in a march in Seattle in 2012 with some fellow students, but found herself unable to gather enough local interest to participate further. "We were trying to do this awareness thing at school but we really couldn't make it 'cause there weren't enough people. Our school is really small so it's really hard to get stuff started." Alejandra, age twenty, came to the United States at age four and is a senior at the University of Washington, majoring in sociology and education. Unlike most Washington DREAMers, her activism is extensive:

> A: Yeah, I've been involved and helped organize for some of those things and—not really help organize, but I've gone in and brought in people to rallies and marches and all that good stuff, so, yeah.
>
> Q: Are there any other activities that you've done related to immigration policies that are not marches, but, like, other, like workshops, or?
>
> A: Yeah, I'm a co-founder of the Washington DREAM Act Coalition and like even now we're doing work to help students apply for the Deferred Action Plan. I am an intern this year for Sea Mar's LEAP program [the Latina/o Educational Achievement Project, a program of Sea Mar's Community Health Centers], which is all about HB 1079 students and helping to create policy changes. I mean, not just HB 1079s it's just education in general and then I interned at OneAmerica two summers ago, which is all about immigrants' rights, so I've always been very into immigration policy and doing whatever I can to make sure that good things are voted for. [Note: HB 1079 is the Washington state version of the DREAM Act.]

In general, however, Washington respondent activism was fairly minimal, and more likely to have occurred in 2006–2008 than more recently. Illustrative of this set of DREAMers is the story shared by Alessandra, an eighteen-year-old political science major at Whitworth University who came to the United States at age six. She plans to eventually become an immigration lawyer. Alessandra remembers going with her dad and younger brother to the 2006 march, when she was only twelve years old:

> I was still young then, but, I just felt really inspired, I guess it could be, like "little kid inspired," because I just saw a lot of people, just, you know, yelling and chanting and like being a community and I've never seen that type of atmosphere up until then. So, I guess it was really, really interesting and I guess subconsciously that's what, you know, inspired me to do what I'm doing right now.

The same proportion of our Oregon respondents, sixteen of twenty-five, also participated in at least one sort of political action related to immigration reform, usually marches but also actions at their schools to raise awareness or fight for in-state tuition rights for Oregon-based DREAMers. Overall, our Oregon respondents were slightly more likely to be politically active than our Washington respondents, but still significantly less so than our California respondents.

The stories of two participants who now live in Oregon but previously lived in California help illustrate how these shifts in geographic context affect participation. Benjamin, age nineteen, came to the United States at age seven and in 2012 was attending Portland Community College. But in 2006, Benjamin lived in San Bernardino, California. He remembers being an activist while living there:

> Yes, in 2006, out in California, it was a big deal. I lived in the San Bernardino, Inland Empire area, so a big, huge Hispanic population, and they had school walkouts. I participated in one of those. Also, during the boycott, my family participated in one of those where you didn't go out and eat or buy anything. And we've also been to a few marches over there—and here in Portland as well.

Mateo, age twenty-two, studies sociology at Portland Community College and Portland State University. He was also in California in 2006:

> A: They were doing the walkouts in 2006 in the high schools in California and they actually put us on lock-down for two and a half hours and after the lock-down, I want to say, actually during the lock-down a group of us decided to go walk outside of class and go banging on all the doors and try to get people to walk out and we had a group of like, 20, 30 students, and they caught us and they sent us to, like, security, and they were gonna suspend us, and then they were like, "whatever, just don't do it." And as soon as we came out, when they ended the lock-down, a huge group of students converged in the middle of the quad in our high school and everybody just started walking out.
>
> Q: Really, so it was a massive walkout?
>
> A: Yeah, massive walkout. I wanna say more than a thousand students walked out that day.

The interviewer then asked Mateo if he had participated in any more recent political actions, in Oregon. There, the environment is very different; instead of enjoying a supportive community that is ready to defy school authorities and walk out of class, even during a lock-down, he is working to raise awareness among his fellow college students that there are undocumented students on campus. In his own words,

> A: The group at PCC we call it, like, the Shadows Group, and it's coming out of the shadows, and it started last year when we started doing some protests at the college to start raising awareness of undocumented students on campus because I know that a lot of students, they're like, "Hey, there's illegal students out on campus but I know that none of them are in my class," and I know they would say that sometimes and like some of my friends would hear that and they're like, "well, I'm illegal," and, "oh, really, I never knew."
>
> Q: So they weren't aware.

A: Yeah, they're not, a lot of them weren't aware. So we did a bunch of stuff. We put signs on the grass that had stories, like, our stories, we put them on the grass, we had like 40 signs. We graffitied the bathrooms, I guess. We used the window markers, and they got mad at us for that. . . . We wore the purple shirts the first day that say, "Do I look undocumented?" We had 100 shirts and they ran out really fast. And, we had support, but we also had backlash against it. I know that one of my friends was intimidated by this person who threatened him for wearing the shirt.

In Texas, very few respondents were active; in Washington, a majority of our respondents were active, albeit at a fairly low level; and in Oregon we heard about slightly more intense levels of activism. In contrast, among our California respondents—perhaps due to the combination of the state's political culture and the density and size of the Latino (and undocumented) population—activism was widespread and extensive. Only one of our California respondents said that they had never participated in a march or other action; others who had participated in just one or a few marches seemed almost apologetic, as if they felt their involvement was below par. Most reported extensive activism, including not just marches but lobbying, mock graduations, and even hunger strikes.

For example, Esteban, age twenty-three, has participated in almost every sort of political behavior (aside from those reserved for citizens) that one might imagine: "Since 2006 I definitely participated in some of those marches but I became more involved in 2009. I was part of disobedience actions, marches, protests, direct actions, lobbying efforts, legislative visits—a bunch, I guess, the whole plate." Mauricio, quoted in the opening of this chapter, acknowledged the role of context in 2006. "In '06 I was still in high school and my parents didn't allow me to get out there and march, but I do remember organizing with the students in school to do our walkouts, just getting the word out within our school like, 'oh, this is what all the schools are going to be doing on this day, let's do it.'" Similarly, Santiago, age twenty-three, noted,

Yeah, I was in all of those [2006 marches]. I was involved in that . . . more of the fact that the people came out, you know, I wasn't, like, in hiding any more, like before, people weren't afraid as they were, like, back then, like when a cop will show up and everyone scatters like cockroaches kind of thing, you know, they all went out on a peaceful full force to show that there's a lot of us and you can't just say, like, "oh, we'll pass a bill to get rid of all you guys."

What is notable about Santiago's remarks is that he recognizes the importance of his local context. In a community (in Los Angeles) with a large undocumented population, he and other participants felt secure in marching through the streets, and did not feel the need to hide or run from authorities; this stands in contrast to respondents in Texas who live in a similarly situated community but with a different political context. In Oregon, however, respondents cited the danger of deportation as the precise reason they did not go to any marches. Daniela, age twenty-three, said, "No, I wasn't—for the same reason, that people were like, oh, you know, *allí te van a llevar* [there you will be taken]." Jorge, age twenty-one, commented, "I mean, you get a lot of Mexicans in one place and you're just scared of immigration popping up."

Geographic isolation from larger immigrant communities inhibited the participation of some would-be activists. Oregon resident Jimena, age twenty-two, has participated only via the Internet and telephone. "There's a couple [websites], like, DreamActivist.org and the DREAM Act page on Facebook, constantly puts people who are being detained and, to make phone calls to the Senators to help them to not be deported. I've been doing that for a while. Just, making people aware of the situation." Another Oregon resident, Zoe, age nineteen, noted that the marches were too far away and that she had no means of transportation to join them. Axel, age twenty-three, commented, "I'm from Spokane so there were no marches here in, like marches you guys have on the westside. However, I was involved with my church, we discussed there some of the immigration issues going on, but, marches like you guys do on the other side of the state, no."

Layered on top of these larger geographic differences in context and culture are the idiosyncratic contexts of each individual with respect to their families, their schools, and their local neighborhoods. In reviewing our conversations with the DREAMers we interviewed, it is clear that these varied contexts interacted with individual predispositions to generate a wide variety of political predispositions and behaviors. Thus our respondents' answers to questions about political interest and attitudes varied widely: some were uninterested in politics, apathetic about political parties and elections, and focused on their personal lives. Others were political science majors, vigorous public advocates for political change, and actively involved in conventional and unconventional political behavior, including protests, mock graduations, and hunger strikes.

Undocumented youth interviewed for this study were asked a series of questions about their levels of political interest, activity, trust, and ideology. Responses to the query about political interest were highly varied, with some respondents very political and clearly politicized by their immigration status and others alienated and uninterested, often reflecting feelings of detachment from the United States. Consistent with work by Carol Hardy-Fanta on how many politically active Latinas do not consider their actions to be political, many DREAMers who reported significant political involvement and leadership elsewhere in the interview responded that they were not interested in politics.[7] Responses to the queries about ideology confirmed existing research about the degree to which these terms are less well understood by the public than by political scientists, and also the confusion that results from the different uses of terms such as liberal and conservative in the United States and in sending countries.

The term political socialization was coined by sociologist Herbert H. Hyman in 1959, which he defined as an individual's "learning of social patterns corresponding to his societal positions as mediated through various agencies of society."[8]

Over time, the study of political socialization has matured and thickened, leading to development of subtheories of how attitudes are formed and their persistence over time. Of particular relevance to our study of DREAMers is the impressionable years model, which posits that individual attitudes are particularly susceptible in adolescence and early adulthood—precisely the period in the life cycle that most of our respondents became aware of their immigration status and were experiencing the context of the 2006 immigration marches and the DREAMer movement. In the impressionable years, generally understood as the period up to one's late twenties, individuals are experiencing politics as a "fresh encounter," making powerful first impressions.[9] They are becoming aware of the political world around them just as they are developing their sense of self and identity.[10]

Also relevant here is the idea of political cohorts: that individuals may reflect generational effects of particularly powerful shared historical experiences, such as the New Deal or the Vietnam War.[11] Our respondents all came to the United States within the past few decades as young people, and they are sharing the experiences of recent efforts to promote immigrant rights and immigration reform. As undocumented youth, they have been politically socialized in a context of heightened public interest in the issue and a shared community. In other words, they know they are not alone, that many other youth share their immigration status and associated challenges, and that the national political environment seems poised on the brink of dramatic reform. Thus, while many DREAMers have lived lives of fear and uncertainty, there is also a widely shared sense of hope and an underlying faith that they will soon have a chance to participate in the American Dream.

DREAMERS AND POLITICAL PARTIES

Latinos tend to affiliate with the Democratic Party, with the notable exception of Cuban-descent Latinos, who generally prefer the Republican Party. This aspect of Latino partisanship has persisted for some time.[12] Partisanship is stronger among citizens than noncitizens; among Latino immigrants, partisanship increases with time spent in the United States, as does preference (among non-Cubans) for the Democratic Party.[13] Cain, Kiewiet, and Uhlaner link increased preference for the Democratic Party to the more pro-immigrant reputation of the Democratic Party, and note that over time immigrants are more likely to have experienced discrimination and to identify as a member of a minority group.[14] Similarly, Wong notes that this hypothesized process is consistent with Philip Converse's political exposure model.[15] The consensus of previous research is that although Latino immigrants might not learn partisanship through intergenerational transmission, as do Anglos, they learn the preferred partisanship of their national-origin group (Democrat for Mexicans and Puerto Ricans, Republican for Cubans) over time.

We asked the DREAMers we spoke to how they felt about the political parties, and also about their analysis of the political motivations of President

Obama and 2012 Republican presidential candidate Mitt Romney. Both politicians made statements about immigration reform and the DREAM Act during the 2012 presidential election campaign. More indicated a preference for the Democratic Party than for the Republican Party, but for most this was a weak preference, tempered by their feelings of cynicism about politics in general and the motivations of individual politicians, including the president, in particular. Overall, respondents were quite ambivalent about the major political parties and mainstream politics, reporting low levels of trust in government and low levels of affinity toward the Democratic and Republican parties alike.

To a certain extent this seems to be due to very low levels of information about politics and political parties. For example, consider the following exchange with Joshua, a nineteen-year-old living in Oregon:

> Q: Which of the following political party labels best applies to you: Strong Republican, Republican, Strong Democrat, Democrat, Independent, or other?
> A: Oh my gosh, um, see, I'm like, I don't even know those labels, but I guess I would be a . . . Republican. Is that what Obama is?
> Q: No, he's a Democrat.
> A: Okay, a Democrat.

Paulina, a twenty-four-year-old living in Texas, came to the United States from Mexico at age four, and is now a PhD student in medical anthropology. She said she feels torn about paying attention to US politics, and is fairly dismissive of President Obama, calling his deferred deportation plan "just a tactic to get Latino votes." Paulina explained,

> I'm always just paying attention to, like, health care change and reform. But, I know there have been other times where I've totally not wanted to pay attention to anything that had to do with American politics. So it's, like, if this country rejects me and I'm not part of it, why should I care whether it has a good reform on this or that? And kinda gives you, like, I don't know, it makes you a little bitter towards it.

Similarly, Guadalupe, a twenty-three-year-old also living in Texas, noted,

> I kind of, like, wanna be informed with what is going on in the nation 'cause, like, I live here, you know, like it interests me in the curiosity of what's going on. And the reason that I'm not as much interested is, then again, like, I know I have no voice, you know?

In sum, our respondents were very much like most Americans, and most young people, in that they reported very low trust in government and very little interest in politics. While they were unfamiliar with basic facts about the US government, they were well informed about President Obama's deferred deportation plan and the DREAM Act, and many reported a link between their interest in those topics and their immigration status. While they were almost universally cynical about politics and uninterested in political parties or institutional politics, they were much more likely than the average young person in the United States to have taken part in direct actions, including protests, hunger strikes, or other civil disobedience, and also in direct lobbying on the issue of immigration reform. Rather than viewing politics as something related exclusively to mainstream political parties, institutions, and elections, their life experiences—and their inability to vote—has led them to develop a specific model of political attitudes and behaviors that sees such action as much more normal and acceptable. DREAMers have been politicized and mobilized by their status and the context of ongoing political debates over immigration policy.

Martina, a twenty-year-old living in Washington, came to the United States at age two. She believes that others view her as inferior because of her immigration status, and generally feels very insecure about her place in US society and distrustful of the US government. At the same time, Martina noted that she felt empowered by her participation in the 2006 immigration marches:

> I felt really strong. It was a good experience because I remember, like, everybody was wearing white that day and I felt, like, we were actually going to do something, and it was very motivating. It was very different and I am really glad I attended that. I remember there was like so much people that day and they were so much, like, advertising. There were buses everywhere and it was just good. I remember that day, I had a sandwich, and the speech, and there was just, like, it made me feel really proud of my culture 'cause I saw everybody with their flags and I, just, every different shapes and sizes of people and I realized that, like, something's gonna happen sooner or later. Like, I felt really strong that day.

In contrast, Carolina, an eighteen-year-old who also lives in Washington, was empowered by the marches at first, as an eighth grader, but less so over time:

> Two times I went to the marches in downtown Seattle that advocated for immigration.... I think the first time I went I was kind of empowered to see so many people that believed in the same cause, in the immigration cause, and that was kind of inspiring. And then, I think after a while I was like, "Is it really that effective and is my presence there a big deal, do I really want to miss school to go make a point?" So then after a while I stopped going.

Other DREAMers we spoke to also shared stories of how their immigration status had politicized them. Simon, a twenty-one-year-old living in California, came to the United States on a tourist visa at age ten. At age fifteen, he went to the local community college to register for a physics class, hoping to boost his chances

of getting into a good four-year private college after high school. When he realized that his lack of papers meant he would be charged $800 as an out-of-state
resident for just one class, he went home crying. Simon now prefers to focus on
his education, and is focused on his educational and career goals above all else.
Yet, at the same time, he noted that his immigration status has forced him to
pay attention to politics. In fact, he has been extremely active in the DREAM
Act movement, participating in marches in 2006 and 2010, and also taking part
in a fourteen-day hunger strike at California senator Dianne Feinstein's office to
influence her to vote the DREAM Act out of the Judiciary Committee.

A more extreme story of politicization comes from Juan Diego, a twenty-
four-year-old living in California. Juan Diego knew at a young age that he was
undocumented; he was deported at age six and he was brought back to the United
States three years later. He has strong memories of the incident and of being held
in the deportation facility, not allowed to visit the restroom. Juan Diego notes
that this feeling of not being welcome, of being perceived as different, has motivated him to be very interested in American politics. He stated in this regard,
"Mi motivacion es de que no nomas quiero superarme a mi mismo, pero tambien
a los demás" [My motivation is that not only do I want myself to overcome (or
succeed), but I want to help others to succeed also]. Yet, Juan Diego has no
interest in voting, and is extremely cynical about politicians and the political
parties, and declined to choose one with which he would identify. Instead, he
has harnessed his energies into organizing and participating in student walkouts,
protests, and marches.

Francisco, a twenty-three-year-old living in California, is a nationally known
undocumented student whose immigration status was made public while he was
serving as student body president of Fresno State University. We first shared his
story in Chapter 3, including how the public revelation of his immigration status
led to worldwide media attention. Francisco originally came to the United States
as a preschooler, but only learned he was undocumented and not a legal resident
as a senior in high school. Francisco only came to understand the full implications of his status when he started his college education and could not get access
to financial aid. At first, his status did not affect him greatly, but over time he
became more involved in student politics and was eventually elected student body
president, a position that normally comes with a stipend. A story in the campus
newspaper about his having declined the stipend led a reporter from the local city
newspaper, the *Fresno Bee*, to ask him if he was undocumented, and he answered
honestly. Worldwide media attention quickly followed, as well as an investigation
by the federal government for alleged voter registration fraud and online blogs
calling for his immediate deportation. Not surprisingly, Francisco is extremely
active in working for immigration reform, and attributes his interest in politics
to his undocumented status. In his own words:

> Well, the only way that I can get relief is through Congress, I guess, is through
> the political process. It is through the American government and I connected

that. When I found out that it was going to take an act of Congress for me to get my immigration status fixed here in this country, then I connected not only the government, the political process, but connected elections, candidates, issues, society, and then it branched out to party politics and how those things are determined in various communities. Then I started getting very good at understanding that, a lot, very well. So I connected myself and took it upon myself to not only get educated through media, through reading, but I decided to major in Political Science and that became my field.... I got involved in College Democrats on campus because they have influence on who gets nominated for that respective district area. So I knew if we were to influence the nomination process, the endorsements, the party platform, it'd make immigration, the DREAM Act, higher education, one of the key tenets of that. That's one of the reasons why I got involved that way.

Other respondents echoed Francisco's comments. Esteban originally went to college to major in aerospace engineering. Faced with the reality of his undocumented status, he changed to political science and became politically active in his community, participating in marches, protests, lobbying, and civil disobedience actions. He recognizes that he is motivated by self-interest: "I would think that if I would have been documented I would have continued pursuing my aerospace engineer major. I don't think I would have been involved. So I think the fact that I'm undocumented, that led me to be politically involved." Salvador put it more succinctly: "My life has become political." Elizabeth commented, "You just have to be on top of your game, know what's going on, what laws are affecting you." Jose, now twenty-five years old, came to Los Angeles from Guadalajara at age thirteen. He knew from the start that he was undocumented, and has always felt that he does not belong here in the United States. He shared the story of how he became involved in the DREAM Act movement despite the uncertainty about his future:

We don't know what is gonna happen. You know, we don't have that—we're living in the moment, we're living day-by-day. You know, we may get deported next year, we may get deported in five years. So how can you make a plan or how can you plan your life in the next ten years if you don't know where you are going to be.... I did interviews on TV and I said, like, oh I'm Jose and I'm an undocumented student. And that was very empowering and that was very liberating. And, for me, because, you know I grew up with zero documentation. And I grew up with the fear of being deported. When I, when I started saying it, like, yes, I'm undocumented, you know, it feels great.

These politicized and politically active DREAMers call to mind the words of Henry David Thoreau, written in his 1849 essay *Civil Disobedience*. Thoreau is writing about the need to resist the US government due to its continued support of slavery and the initiation of the Mexican-American War, but his words are easily applicable to other instances where members of a civil society believe the laws to be unjust:

> Unjust laws exist: shall we be content to obey them, or shall we endeavor to amend them, and obey them until we have succeeded, or shall we transgress them at once? ... If the injustice is part of the necessary friction of the machine of government, let it go, let it go ... but if it is of such a nature that it requires you to be the agent of injustice to another, then, I say, break the law. *Let your life be a counter-friction to stop the machine.* [emphasis added][16]

In contrast to the engaged DREAMers, there were also many who were not involved, and not interested in taking personal action. Instead of being inspired by the uncertainty of their status, they were detached. Waiting for the DREAM Act, or to see if they would qualify for deferred deportation status, they viewed their lives fatalistically as being in limbo. As Renata put it, "it's like living on the shelf." Living in fear—of being pulled over by the police, of being deported—meant their lives were truncated. Julia came to the United States from Mexico at age four and has always known her immigration status. From the beginning, her parents warned her to stay out of trouble and avoid deportation. Today, Julia says she feels like she lives in a virtual cage. She has not attended any immigration marches or direct actions, despite wanting to participate, out of fear.

ETHNIC IDENTITY

A robust scholarly debate focuses on the power of ethnic identity, and particularly on panethnic identity, as well as on the various predictors of and paths toward strong feelings of panethnic and/or "American" identity. The multiple paths to assimilation documented by Portes and Rumbaut and Alba and Nee have been used by a variety of scholars to investigate identity politics—the adoption of pan-ethnic or nonethnic identifiers by immigrants and their descendants.[17] Identity matters in part because it reflects the degree and manner in which immigrants are assimilating, but also because it has behavioral consequences, influencing partisanship, vote choice, and political behavior more generally.[18] Panethnic Latino identity can also be the foundation of coethnic and bi-/multiracial coalition building and inspire political participation.[19]

Yet, most immigrants do not arrive in the United States with self-identities that match the ethnoracial categories most prevalent in this country, and native-born Americans have sometimes struggled to fit newcomers within the existing categories.[20] Instead, as time in the United States increases, Latino immigrants are less likely to self-identify as a member of a national-origin group (e.g., as Mexican or Salvadoran) and more likely to identify as "just American," as a member of a panethnic group (e.g., Latino or Hispanic), or as both American and as Hispanic/Latino.[21] There is some evidence that the shift to an "American" identity as opposed to a panethnic or ethnic identity is related to experiences of discrimination or exclusion; other research links shifts in identity to differences in phenotype and skin tone, which vary widely among Latinos.[22] Using 2006 Latino National Survey (LNS) data, Jones-Correa and Leal find that Latino immigrant identity shifts from "Latino" to "American" as time in the United States increases, but that transnational ties, the racial/ethnic identity of friends and coworkers, and desire to return to one's home country are even stronger predictors of identity.[23] Jones-Correa and Leal also note that research has yet to determine "exactly what respondents mean" when they use panethnic identifiers such as "American" or "Latino."

A shared collective experience should lead to stronger feelings of panethnic identity such as Latino or Hispanic.[24] Jones-Correa and Leal find that Latinos who have a panethnic identity are more likely to be politically active—signing petitions, attending meetings, and displaying public support for a candidate; Masuoka finds that involvement in Latino politics and perceptions of discrimination are strong predictors of adoption of a panethnic identity.[25] This led us to expect that our respondents who had been more involved in the immigration marches of 2006 or the DREAMers movement would be more likely to prefer a panethnic identity, as would those who perceived high levels of discrimination in the United States.

We asked our respondents about their ethnic and panethnic identity, including whether they preferred the term American, Mexican American, Latino/Hispanic, or Mexican, among other choices. Their open-ended responses to that question, as well as a follow-up question about the strength of their panethnic Latino identity, provide powerful insight into how these terms are understood by young DREAMers, helping unpack those terms as suggested in existing work. Overall, we found that DREAMers identified both as Mexican, often verbally noting how this reflected the reality of their immigration status, but also as Americans or Latinos, reflecting their upbringing and psychological attachment to the United States. John García notes that Mexican immigrants who become US citizens are asserting a new psychological affiliation with the host country—immigrants with a strong American identity were more likely to naturalize or plan to naturalize, while those who considered themselves foreigners or strangers in the country were less likely to do so.[26] This pattern, however, is interrupted by current US policies regarding DREAMers; even if they strongly consider themselves to be Americans they are unable to naturalize; and the causal process is reversed when they learn of their status and they begin to consider themselves more as either Mexicans or outsiders. An illustrative example comes from Adrian, a twenty-four-year-old who came to the United States at age three and did not learn of his undocumented status until he was seventeen when he tried to get a driver's license and secure a work permit. This experience has led him to reconsider the American identity that he had adopted during those years. Adrian noted,

I used to consider myself American, but in these last couple of years I realized that one has to be realistic about who they are and where they're from, so at this point and for the last couple of years I consider myself either Mexican or Latino, but more Mexican than anything.

These conflicted feelings of identity and belonging are also common to the undocumented youth we spoke to who were a bit older when they came to the United States. Guadalupe, now twenty-three, came to the United States at age ten and was always aware of her status. She commented,

> I grew up here the second part of my life, and, like, I feel something, sometimes, that I kind of belong here. Not that I'm from here, because I'm never gonna deny that I'm Mexican. But, I don't know what it is now to live there, like, I don't know, the cultures, like a lot of culture from there, because of the fact that I've grown up here, that I've met people from here, that I've gotten used to the culture from here, like the way people speak, you know. So I kind of feel that kind of, like, acceptance in a way, and I don't feel like I don't belong.

Luna, an eighteen-year-old living in Washington, came to the United States at age eleven, on a tourist visa, but didn't realize she was an undocumented immigrant until she was in high school. Since then, she says, she has frequently considered going back to her home country of Mexico. She noted in this regard, "But, it's going back to a place that I don't know. I don't remember that place.... Over here—I don't like to feel unwanted, you know, so there is an, always an option to go back." Asked about her ethnic identity, Luna responded, "Chicano, Mexican-American—even though I should be Mexican, but I don't feel 100% Mexican."

The DREAMers' comments about identity echo the voices of feminist Chicana theorists Gloria Anzaldúa and Emma Pérez. Anzaldúa writes that Chicanos "straddle the borderlands"—they are neither Anglos nor Mexicans.[27] For undocumented youth, this straddling across borders is even more acute, and more legal—they do not just feel that they are straddling the border because they are Latinos in the United States. They are not Anglos, but they do not feel fully Mexican given the years spent here; their identity as undocumented immigrants means that they have physically crossed a border that they are not legally authorized to have crossed. Pérez argues that Mexican immigrants never fully assimilate into US culture, but instead always retain a degree of Mexican culture.[28] For DREAMers, there is a legal barrier to full assimilation that forces a full stop by, at the latest, the latter years of high school, as young people hoping to attend college or get a driver's license find themselves, often for the first time, faced with the reality of their immigration status. However much they may consider themselves to be Americans, or Mexican Americans, their identity is solidly defined by US politics and society as other, as foreigner, as Mexican. Some DREAMers embrace this otherness, working to improve their Spanish language abilities or to learn more about Mexican culture and politics. Others work to "prove" their American-ness, to adopt US culture and the English language even more forcefully. These choices and conflicting identity pressures are shared by legal immigrants, but for undocumented youth the choices are often more limited.

These straddled identities are revealed in comments from the DREAMers we interviewed. Simon, age twenty-one, has lived in the United States almost continuously since age eight. Simon noted that if the DREAM Act passes, "I see myself, like, I finally belong to the U.S., to the U.S. society in terms of paperwork and status. Like, I feel like I belong right now, but I am limited. So, I feel like I won't be limited anymore, with that, with the federal DREAM Act.... I'll be able to work and function as a regular citizen." Later, he noted, "Sometimes I feel Chicano, but then I change my mind ... I'm not American." Josefina's response to the query about ethnic identity illustrates the conflicting attachments of many DREAMers. Josefina, now twenty-one years old, came to the United States when she was only one year old, and did not learn of her status until she was a senior in high school. Her comments about identity are revealing:

A: I think I'm Mexican.... I mean, I don't know, I'm like, because I'm not, like you know, how my parents are here, I guess, people are considered to be Mexican-American either because they're born here and their parents are Mexican, or if your parents were born here and you ... I don't know, because I do feel myself as American, but then I do love being Mexican.

Q: Yeah.

A: Because I was born here and I kind of, I kind of feel this is my home.

Q: Born here?

A: [laughing] I'm not, I mean, not born here, but you know, like ... I feel like I was born here, that's why ... I think I would say Mexican-American/Chicano.

Other DREAMers we spoke to gave similar answers, reflecting internal struggles over their identity and sense of belonging to the United States. Raquel, age twenty-four, came to the United States at age eight. She commented, "I guess, Mexican ... I mean, I guess ... it's 'cause, like, I feel like, if I was to go to Mexico I feel like, I don't even belong there ... 'cause I was raised, like, American ... so, but I, I'm not, I'm not Chicano 'cause I'm *Mexican* Mexican. So I guess Mexican." Samuel, age nineteen, came to the United States at age five. He acknowledged the disconnect between his official nationality and his perception of his identity:

Mexican ... well, like, I know I'm Mexican definitely but ... I know I'm Mexican, but I definitely see myself as a little whitewash ... Mexican-American as well. I mean, I have, only my roots tie me to Mexico, I haven't really visited, I don't really know much, so ...

Diego, now twenty-four years old and living in Texas, remembers crossing the river into the United States with his family when he was nine years old. Despite always knowing his immigration status, he identifies as Mexican American: "I consider myself Mexican American. I was born in Mexico, but I have been able to pick up the culture and learn a different language and I consider myself a Mexican American even though I'm not legal." Similarly, Constanza, age twenty-three, who also crossed over at age nine, commented, "I'm Mexican, but even though I don't have a legal status I still consider myself a Mexican-American."

The DREAMers we interviewed said that others with whom they had shared their status shared this perception of them as Americans. Many noted that when they revealed their status to friends or other individuals, they expressed surprise, commenting on their excellent English skills or other outward signs of belonging. For example, Linda, age twenty-seven, described a conversation with her employer, a woman for whom she was working as a nanny, that was precipitated by Linda's declining the woman's offer to take extra time off on Election Day to go vote. After explaining that she wouldn't need it because she couldn't vote due to her undocumented status, the employer responded, "but you went to college and you're a grad student and your English is fine and, you know, you're so American." Linda came to the United States at age two and learned of her undocumented status and its consequences in high school, as did many of our respondents, when she found herself unable to participate in study abroad programs or get a driver's license. Linda self-identifies as Mexican and, although she hopes to eventually become a US citizen, she plans to leave the United States. Her undocumented status means her only work experience has been as a nanny, although she has earned a master's degree, and she believes that she will be better able to take advantage of her education in other countries.

Other youth we interviewed made clear that they recognize the complexity of their identities and how they intersect with their immigration statuses. Alejandra, age twenty, came to the United States when she was four years old. She identifies as Mexican with a strong Latina identity. In her own words:

> It's interesting 'cause like I identify myself a lot like, like I'm Latina here in the United States but not really as a Mexican per se 'cause I mean, like, I have the cultural background for the Mexican culture but, like, I know nothing about their politics, like, I know nothing about the country, I don't even know what states are in that country to be honest. I'm more American than I am Mexican, but I'm still proud to say that I'm a Latina and I advocate for Latino friends and their movements, um ... so, Mexican I would say not very much, but as a Latina in the United States I would, I classify myself very highly with that.

Santino, a twenty-year-old living in Texas, came to the United States at age eleven. Many of the DREAMers we interviewed came to the United States *como la gente*, with tourist visas, and then stayed. In contrast, Santino crossed with a *coyote* (trafficker), and was always aware of his undocumented status. He worked hard to leave his past behind and, as he put it, "learn everything an American had to do, learn my history, learn, you know, my culture, you know, I started getting acculturated with the American culture, you know, pretty much leaving everything that I was behind." He focused on learning English and says he can no longer have a full conversation in Spanish. Santino notes,

> From what I was to now, like, I'm not that person anymore, like, I'm an American. I feel like I'm an American and that I have every right that an American has, but just because I wasn't born in this country, like, you know, I don't deserve that ... like all these years I've been trying to be like an American, as much as I could be.

As a senior in college, Santino realized that his lack of a Social Security number meant his college options were severely limited, despite his efforts to fit in and his being voted "most likely to succeed" at his high school. He learned that Texas state law allowed him to attend the University of Texas–Pan American without documents; he obtained scholarships, and again worked to acculturate by joining leadership programs and a fraternity. "From then on, like, coming into college it felt like, that I wasn't an illegal again anymore." But facing graduation, with no DREAM Act in sight, he is again coming to the realization that his options are severely limited. "What am I gonna do with my life? I can't get a job anywhere. And if I do get a job, my degree is not gonna be paid what it's worth. So then I start realizing again that, wait, I'm an illegal." Yet, asked how he identifies, Santino quickly and unequivocally answers, "American."

Jorge, age twenty-one, came to the United States at age five but has always known his immigration status. Asked his preferred identity, he quickly responded, "Mexican," but added, "and Mexican-American too, 'cause, I mean, I was raised here." Bianca, age twenty-five, came to the United States at age eleven, thinking it was merely a vacation to visit her father, as had been the case on an earlier trip. But this time she stayed in the United States, and six years later, at age seventeen, she realized the implications of her undocumented status. Bianca gave her ethnic identity as "Mexican and Chicana, but not Mexican-American. So it's just Mexican 'cause I was born and raised there and then Chicana because of my ethnologies.... I would say Chicana for sure and Mexican, but not American." Sara, now twenty-two years old, came to the United States at age nine. "Before I would say Mexican, but I grew up so much of my life here that I don't know.... I would say Hispanic."

Another exchange that provides insight into how the identity question is a complex one for DREAMers comes from Francisco, who came to the United States at age three but believed until the end of high school that he was a legal resident.

> A: I'm going to say Latino/Hispanic, and I know this has been always been asked a question of me is like, do you consider yourself as an ... you say you're an American, you feel you're an American. But I don't feel it yet. I'm pretty American, I'm pretty Americanized, pretty well.
>
> Q: But you're not necessarily Mexican ...

A: 'Cause I don't know much of the culture. I can, I look Mexican, I came from Mexico, I speak Spanish somewhat ... it's gone down a little bit. But since the fact that I don't really, want to, I don't tend to categorize myself, I don't say I'm Latino, 'cause, well, hey, I'm very ... inclusive of everybody, like, I don't see a difference between people from Cuba and El Salvador, even though there is.

As these interviews make clear, the sense of belonging and not belonging is at the forefront of the identities of DREAMers. Some came to the United States as infants, others as adolescents, and all have eventually learned of their immigration status. Thus they find themselves torn between the American identities that they have developed during their childhoods and the reality of their outsider identities, their lack of "nine digits" that mark one as a full member of US society. For some, this has led them to embrace their Mexican or other Latino national-origin identity, while others remain solidly self-identified as American, members of the only country they truly know. As has been noted elsewhere and by many of our respondents, undocumented status means the inability to travel.[29] Thus, documented immigrants and native-born US citizens of Latino descent are able to travel to Mexico and other sending countries, to keep in touch with their extended families and the culture of their heritage. Undocumented immigrants, in contrast, cannot travel without fear of being discovered and unable to return, and thus are less likely to be familiar with their home countries or to feel that they belong anywhere else. For them, the irony of their "true" Mexican or other nationality is sharply at odds with their lived reality.

CONCLUSION

President Obama's program of deferred deportation, and the prospect on the horizon of true immigration reform that would allow DREAMers to permanently regularize their status, shapes the political and daily realities of undocumented youth, including the ones we interviewed for this book. Listening to their stories, we were struck by the degree to which they have constantly and continually been forced to think about the way in which they fit into US society. Young Latinos who were born in the United States or who enjoy permanent resident status face racism and are often mistaken for undocumented immigrants. As Villanueva notes, even professional Latinos whose families have lived in the United States for generations are haunted by a perpetual "outsider" or "illegal alien" image.[30] Latinos (and Asians and Arabs) are often "racially categorized as foreign-born outsiders, regardless of actual citizenship status."[31] Those here in the United States with documents, or who are citizens, can push back against this external labeling. Because their legal identity does not conform to outsider stereotypes, their sense of belonging is more resilient. For some, this leads to a racialized identity with notable attitudinal and behavioral consequences.[32] What is relevant here is that their sense of identity cannot be as sharply influenced by the prejudices and perceptions of others because of their known realities. In contrast, undocumented youth have a more tenuous reality with which to push back against assigned identities as outsiders. They may have lived for decades in the United States, and may have only learned of their immigration status as older teenagers, but their lack of documents is a reality that conforms to society's "othering" of their identities, making it more difficult for them to determine how and where they truly fit in.

Some of our respondents always knew about their undocumented status. Adriana remembers crossing the river into the United States at age eight, and recalling that she knew something about it was wrong. Now twenty-three years old, she has lived for years in fear, limiting her interactions with society, and declining to become involved in activities at school or to participate in immigration marches or other protest actions aimed at pushing for political reform. Others, like Francisco and Hugo, learned of their status much later in life and have no memory of coming to the United States; they, like other DREAMers we interviewed with similar stories, were much more likely to reject their official status of not belonging, and to be heavily involved in extracurricular and community activities.

Anzaldúa and Pérez talk of Latinos as *trapped in the borderlands*, as belonging neither here nor there. This is the reality of many of the DREAMers we talked to. They are legally not Americans, lacking proper documentation that would allow them to pursue their educational and career goals, or even just to live without fear and travel farther than the local supermarket. But they are also not truly Mexicans (or members of other national-origin groups) because they came to the United States as young children and have been unable to visit, and in many cases because they were raised believing that they legally belonged here. Some are fighting back, pushing for the DREAM Act and hoping to eventually realize their goals. Others are considering leaving the United States, taking their skills and educations abroad. All are exploring their identities. All are looking to belong.

Chapter 6

Conclusion

Dreaming of Justice

Luna came to the United States on a tourist visa when she was eleven years old, in the company of her parents and sister. Now an eighteen-year-old high school senior, she only learned of her immigration status two years ago and has found the new knowledge incredibly unsettling. She states,

> It's just the feeling of feeling unwanted. Like, even though you have not done anything bad, because I don't feel I've ever done anything bad, I'm still, like— not getting punished, but, like, restricted. I haven't been able to know how to drive because of being afraid of being stopped by a policeman and just being asked questions. Sometimes I get invited to participate in traveling programs. I am not allowed to leave the country so I have to say no as much as I want to leave, you know, to travel the world, because that's one of my biggest dreams. Also, financial aid; I really want to go to college, really bad, and I've been preparing myself this whole high school experience and I feel I cannot get financial aid, you know, I'm working harder than a lot of other people and I do qualify for it. Those types of things they do affect me, my daily life. You don't have options, you cannot travel, you cannot work, you know, you cannot do a lot of stuff because of that.

Her fear of calling a policeman extends to many other aspects of Luna's life, even including fear of calling 911 when she needs help, which might lead to deportation. She doesn't work because she didn't want to use a false Social Security number. Despite the challenge of finding adequate funding, she does plan to attend college next year. "I want to go to the University of Washington and then I want to apply for as many scholarships as possible to be able to pay. That's, like, the main plan but as a 1079 student[1] you have to have a backup plan because your future is not secure, ever. So you always have to think of plan B and plan C." She looks forward to a future where she will feel more like a full member of society.

> It's not like I don't feel normal right now, but I do feel like I have some special things—I don't feel like I have full rights. And it will make me feel a little bit more free [if the DREAM Act passes] and be able to do what I want to do.... More freedom—make my own decisions based on what I want, not really worrying about a future that much, with fear of where am I gonna end up if I take this decision.

Deferred deportation means Luna can work and save money, "in case something happens"—she is still unsure if she will be able to go to college or even stay in the United States. "Nothing is for sure for us, you know ... things change all the time."

We began this book by asking the important and timely question, what does the denial of citizenship and full participation to American-raised youth teach us about our political values and about the racialization of Latinos? The undocumented students we interviewed have lived the majority of their lives in political, legal, and economic limbo. Among other things, this has in many cases meant having a parent deported, or living in constant fear of deportation. We found that this has been a significant fear in our respondents' lives even though we failed to ask a specific question about deportations in our interview questionnaire. Perhaps this is not surprising considering President Obama's deportation record resulting in 5,000 children who have been placed in foster care in recent years.

There are many life experiences our sample of respondents has faced that are in clear contradiction to the widespread liberty and justice frame of the right to "life, liberty, and the pursuit of happiness" so familiar to most Americans.[2] Instead they have been racialized as lawbreakers who need to be removed from the country, even those who are university student-body presidents who have lived in the United States for most of their lives. Similar to blacks in the Jim Crow South, Latinos, especially immigrants, are criminalized in this country. For example, one of the authors for this study attended a university forum about the hunger strike of over seven hundred people detained at the Northwest Detention Center in Tacoma. During the question and answer period a student from the audience asked the presenter, "Why shouldn't they be deported? What they have done is like breaking into your house." Equating the act of migrating to the United States to work, and in many cases to be reunited with one's family, to the act of a burglar breaking into one's home to steal or cause someone harm is a clear example of the anti-Latino subframe of the white racial frame, not to mention a total lack of compassion or empathy to the inhumane conditions that the people engaging in the hunger strike were protesting.[3] Yet, the view of immigrants as criminals as represented by this student's remarks is quite common.

Golash-Boza argues, immigrants are not criminals; rather, our immigration laws are failing us all, particularly immigrants and their families, which include US citizens who are being separated from their parents. She states, "What renders some migrants 'illegal' is *the lack of legislation* that enables undocumented migrants to obtain proper documentation" (emphasis added).[4] Examining immigration policies—including the rise of deportations among immigrants mostly from Latin America—from a human rights perspective, Golash-Boza argues for the importance of viewing immigrants as human beings, of understanding that immigrants to the United States come from countries with a history of political and economic ties to the United States, and that racism is very much at the heart of the United States' immigration and deportation policies.[5] However, these punitive immigration policies will be very difficult to change until more people care about the lives of immigrants and their children, and until immigrants are not criminalized and racialized. In the meantime, the denial of full participation to undocumented youth raised in the United States has taken a heavy toll on the DREAMers we interviewed for this research.

Throughout this book we have shared the stories of undocumented Latino youth examining their pre- and post-DACA experiences. Many of the DREAMers in this study have been torn between optimism, completing college and even graduate degrees in pursuit of their dreams, and pessimism, wondering if their undocumented status would mean they might never have the opportunity to fulfill those dreams due to the inability to work in their chosen career after graduation. DACA allowed some DREAMers to obtain two-year renewable work permits, but how much did DACA really allow our study participants to pursue their goals and to live a life of liberty and justice? We asked our study participants how they thought DACA would change their lives, and specifically what opportunities they believed would be open to them that were previously closed. We wanted to understand the impact of DACA on our sample of DREAMers' lives in political, material, and symbolic ways. We also wanted to know what it meant to spend the majority of their lives undocumented, specifically asking our study participants how they pursued the American Dream as undocumented Latino youth.

What did we find? Not surprisingly, the Latino youth we interviewed have had far fewer options for a promising future than their American citizen siblings, friends, and peers who were raised and socialized in the United States along with them. President Barack Obama's DACA policy does not provide a path to citizenship for these youth, and they continue to live in legal limbo, but it has provided our study participants some measure of legal protection that they did not have before. They are protected from deportation and can legally work in the United States, at least in the short term. However, deferred action was not the answer our sample of DREAMers has been waiting for their entire adult lives. Far from it. As many of them noted, President Obama's announcement occurred within the context of the 2012 presidential election; as a number of our interview respondents observed, they felt as though they were "pawns in a political game." Many commented that DACA is not what they were hoping for with statements such as, "This is not the DREAM Act. This is not legalization. This is crumbs, crumbs of what we have been asking for." Not only is DACA not the DREAM Act, which would result in an eventual path to citizenship for the DREAMers, but the Obama administration ruled in late August 2012 that even those allowed to stay in the United States would still *not* be considered "legally present," thus excluding them from coverage under federal health care programs and keeping them in a precarious state in between documented and undocumented resident.

Despite this precarious status for DREAMers, the DACA program has proved enormously popular. By January 2014, more than 521,000 deferrals had been approved by Citizenship and Immigration Services, which handles 2,000 applications a day.[6] Yet, many are left out: not all undocumented youth are eligible, and not all of those eligible are willing to apply.[7] According to a 2013 study from the Pew Hispanic Center, there are hundreds of thousands of undocumented youth living in the United States who are not eligible for deferred action.[8] This includes approximately 770,000 youth who are not yet eligible because they are younger than sixteen, as well as about 320,000 who are not eligible because they did not complete high school. Another 2.4 million youth arrived in the United States after age fifteen or have lived here fewer than five years; these youth are also ineligible for DACA.[9] DACA is clearly not the answer for all the undocumented Latino youth. While DACA comes as a great relief to half a million undocumented youth, it clearly falls short of a real immigration policy solution. And there is little possibility that Congress will deliver such a solution any time soon. In late January 2014, House Republican leaders released a blueprint for immigration reform; after a fierce backlash from Tea Party conservatives, House Speaker John Boehner backed away from the plan, instead claiming that the GOP would not support immigration reform until Obama was no longer president, as he could not be trusted to implement it fairly and impartially.[10]

We wanted to more fully understand the ways in which growing up as undocumented Latino youth impacted DREAMers' lives. Specifically, we asked our sample of DREAMers how old they were when they came to the United States. We asked as well what their families were like. We wanted to know if they live in families with mixed legal status. We asked how decisions about their future were affected by their undocumented status. We asked how they believed their lives would change post-DACA, and how DACA would affect their long-term goals, where they saw themselves in five and ten years. Responding to this last question, Juan, one of the DREAMers we interviewed, said, "[In] ten years, I see myself with a good education, a stable life, and pretty much that's it. A stable life. I don't ask for nothing, just to have a stable life where I'm somebody, where I'm counted as a person." In the previous chapters of this book we have explored that sense of longing, of belonging. We have explored, through the eyes of 101 young Latinos, what it means to pursue the American Dream for those who are undocumented, who just want to be "counted as a person," but who deserve so much more.

Understanding the experiences of undocumented Latino youth is important for a number of reasons. First, as highlighted in Chapter 1, their experiences help to counter the widespread stereotypes about Latinos in the United States. A number of our respondents told stories about how others reacted to their revealing their status, often with disbelief, because they did not work in the fields, spoke unaccented English, and did so well in school. Particularly for our respondents in the less-heavily Latino states of the Pacific Northwest, the friends, teachers, and coworkers to whom they came out often had never before met (to their knowledge) an undocumented immigrant, and "knew" only what they had been led to believe about undocumented immigrants from the mass media or unfriendly politicians.

Second, their experiences of living in the shadows have significant implications for the health of American democracy. It is clearly important that we explore ways to incorporate DREAMers into society if we wish to have a healthy democracy, and that we take immediate action to do so. As a nation, it is hard to maintain our liberty and justice frame while undocumented immigrants are systematically oppressed. What are needed are sound, rational policy solutions in line with the economic and political realities that have created the large numbers of undocumented people in this country. Members of our increasingly diverse nation will be hard-pressed to maintain faith, belief, and trust in the ability of American society to meet the needs of *all* of its citizens and residents as long as we have an entire group of people who were raised in the United States but remain stuck between legal borders in the position of second-class resident status, or worse, are uprooted and deported to a country they do not know, as Golash-Boza highlights in countless examples in her study.[11] The ongoing exclusion of DREAMers is perpetuating an American apartheid and this sad state of affairs will negatively affect our democracy. As law professor and longtime immigrant rights advocate Bill Ong Hing states in his book *Deporting Our Souls,*

> The age of hysteria over immigration in which we live leads to tragic policies that challenge us as a moral society. Policies that are unnecessarily harsh—that show a dehumanizing side of our character—are senseless. They bring shame to us as a civil society.[12]

Furthermore, a healthy democracy, according to Harvard professor Michael Sandel, requires we share in common life experiences. Sandel contends,

> Democracy does not require perfect equality, but it does require that citizens share in a common life. What matters is that people of different backgrounds and social positions encounter one another, and bump up against one another, in the course of everyday life. For this is how we learn to negotiate and abide our differences, and how we come to care for the common good.[13]

Currently, immigrants are being legally prevented from sharing in many aspects of this "common life" Sandel talks about. A large number of our sample of

DREAMers work at fast food restaurants, as nannies, or not at all; only a fraction work in the careers for which they have trained. Some were high school valedictorians and presidents, some are college graduates, and some have even earned postgraduate degrees—yet they lack the nine digits that would allow them to fully use their talents in the workplace and to participate in our democratic institutions. Some have dreams of joining the air force, or working as medical researchers on a potential new cure for diabetes; most, however, work at low-skilled service jobs, behind the scenes and in the shadows. The comprehensive immigration reform bill considered by Congress in 2013 would have allowed these young DREAMers to reach for the American Dream, to become doctors and scientists, air force pilots and police officers, artists and lawyers. More importantly, for the health of the nation, it would have allowed them to one day vote, to participate in civic engagement efforts in their communities. As our political leaders continue to battle over how best to reform our broken immigration system—either through passage of a comprehensive immigration reform bill, or with further executive actions such as DACA—it should be informed by the reality that the continual exclusion of immigrants and DREAMers comes at a great cost to us as a democratic nation. Political justice demands an end to the legal exclusion of DREAMers from the benefits of citizenship.

Similarly to other historical periods such as during the era of Jim Crow in the American South, our core values of liberty and justice are called into question when examining the treatment of immigrants and especially of those raised in the United States.[14] For example, Massey states,

> Although the current system of temporary worker migration could certainly benefit from improvements to protect workers from exploitation, the most serious task remaining for immigration reformers is the legalization of the 11 million persons who are currently unauthorized, especially the 3 million or more persons who entered as minors and grew up in the United States. The lack of legal status constitutes an insurmountable barrier to social and economic mobility, not only for the undocumented immigrants themselves, but for their citizen family members. *Not since the days of slavery have so many residents in the United States lacked the most basic social, economic, and human rights.* [emphasis added][15]

As Joe Feagin points out, our liberty and justice frame emerged out of slavery with metaphors of bondage used by the framers of the US Constitution as they developed their arguments for independence from England.[16] Yet, the liberty and justice frame continues to be taught to our children in direct contradiction to the racial oppression of immigrants among us. As Golash-Boza notes, because immigration enforcement is no longer a matter of border security but also what she calls "internal security," this has created a situation whereby immigration becomes an issue throughout all US communities, not just at the border.[17]

Finally, we would point out that as the largest ethnic and racial group in the country, Latinos as a group matter greatly. They comprise the demographic history and future of the United States, but are underrepresented in politics and in high-status occupations. They represent 16.9 percent of the population as of 2012 US Census estimates but only 3 to 4 percent of engineers, doctors, lawyers, pharmacists, and even elementary and high school teachers. They are not represented in significant numbers in our governing institutions either. Fewer than 5 percent of members of Congress are Latino, and Latinos represent only 3.3 percent of all elected officials nationwide. Latinos have made great strides in this area in the last fifteen years, increasing their numbers from 3,743 elected officials in 1996 to 5,850 in 2011, a 53 percent increase, but they are still grossly underrepresented.[18] The largest ethnic and racial minority group is greatly underrepresented in our government institutions and among our professions. What does this poor representation portend for the future of our country? Clearly, our institutions of government and our professions are failing to keep up with the changing demographics of American society. The United States is an increasingly multicultural society, and this diversity should be reflected in all spheres of influence and power in American society. Yet, continued dominance of the white racial frame, perpetuated in part by our broken immigration system, means this underrepresentation will also continue. Allowing undocumented Latino immigrants to regularize their status and pursue citizenship will send a message to all Americans that Latinos are an important and valid part of US society, generating increasing opportunities for Latinos to pursue elected office and higher-status occupations. And it will bring us closer to fulfilling our political values of "liberty and justice for all" that many of them grew up reciting in the Pledge of Allegiance.

As we documented in previous chapters, Latinos have a long history with the United States. As reviewed in Chapter 2, many scholars have demonstrated that the United States has been promoting a contradictory set of public policies with Mexico that has both encouraged and discouraged migration. This has created what Hing describes as an "interdependence between regions."[19] Latinos have had a long-standing relationship with the United States that is multidimensional and complex. As Hing states, "Beyond the economic situation in Mexico, a socioeconomic phenomenon is at play. The phenomenon is the long, historical travel patterns between Mexico and the United States, coupled with the interdependency of the two regions."[20] Any examination of immigration policy that does not take this interdependence into account will be not only ahistorical, but also most likely flawed. In other words, moving forward on immigration reform in a just, compassionate, and humane manner requires admitting that our own policies have contributed to the creation of a 5-million-person-strong underground community of undocumented Latino youth. Passage of a DREAM Act by the US Congress would, in part, mean taking responsibility for those young lives that have been put in legal limbo not through any fault of their own but because of US policies and politics.

SUMMARY OF OVERALL FINDINGS

The DREAMers we talked to face extraordinary challenges, including family separation, poverty, fear, discrimination, as well as more subtle everyday limitations on their economic, political, educational, and social experiences. For example, for the majority of their lives they could not legally work, even if they have graduated from college. Even with DACA, they cannot participate in civic and political activities without fear of retribution, as Francisco learned the hard way when he served (unpaid) as student body president at California State University, Fresno. Even with DACA, they cannot attend elite universities where they have been accepted because they do not qualify for federal financial aid. For the majority of their lives they could not travel with their friends or family for fear of deportation. In fact, many stated they spent a great deal of their lives with great fear and anxiety whenever they had to leave their house, for fear of deportation. They have even had to worry about dating someone for fear they will be perceived as using them for their *papeles*, or even worse, being threatened with deportation if the relationship ended badly. Throughout their lives they have been constantly reminded that they are outsiders who are unwanted by many American institutions and people, as Luna described in the opening vignette to this chapter. DREAMers are often burdened with the kind of difficulties and uncertainty that led Luna to comment, "Nothing is for sure for us, you know ... things change all the time." Nevertheless, despite the struggles they have faced, many of the young people we talked to remain courageous and hopeful that one day Congress will approve the DREAM Act or comprehensive immigration reform and they will finally, truly, belong to American society. Others have given up believing that the precarious situation in which they live will ever change. They have come to accept the fact that notions such as the American Dream do not apply to them, regardless of how hard they work. Some of these undocumented Latino youth have become so deeply disillusioned with the political system and with American society they have decided to leave the United States.

In Chapter 2, we reviewed the long history of political discussion and (in)action that preceded President Obama's decision in the summer of 2012 to take unilateral executive action and announce the Deferred Action for Childhood Arrivals (DACA) program. We began with a review of the sources of the DREAMers, starting with the economic and cultural hegemony of the United States over most of its southern neighbors. The massive unmet demand for unskilled labor in numerous sectors of the US economy, the loss of jobs in Mexico since 1994, and the low cap on legal work visas have combined to create a flow of undocumented workers to the United States. Increased border enforcement has forced the replacement of the old pattern of circular migration with one of permanent residency; not surprisingly, workers then are often joined by their families, including young children—DREAMers. Raised in the United States, these youth then graduate from high school without documents and without a Social Security number, but feeling very much like Americans. Many states have taken action to encourage these youth to continue their educations, offering them in-state college tuition, while other states, in contrast, have passed legislation to bar undocumented students from paying in-state tuition (or to ban them from state colleges and universities altogether). We reviewed the history of federal DREAM Acts, starting with the first introduced bill in April 2001 by Chicago Democrat Luis Gutiérrez, through the nearly successful passage of the Comprehensive Immigration Reform Act of 2006 (which included the DREAM Act provisions), and concluding with final efforts of the 112th Congress, in the summer of 2012. With the presidential election approaching, Democrats hoped to pass a DREAM Act to help ensure Obama's reelection, while Republicans were similarly committed to blocking the president from having a victory on the issue on which to campaign. It was this political environment in which the president chose to act.

In Chapter 2 we also reviewed various projections of the cost of various versions of the DREAM Act from the nonpartisan Congressional Budget Office (CBO) as well as nongovernmental organizations and research centers. The CBO estimated an overall reduction in the federal budget deficit from 2010 to 2020, but increased deficits starting in 2021. The Center for American Progress, a progressive think tank, estimated that the DREAM Act would generate millions of new jobs and would add $329 billion to the US economy by 2030. Even larger estimates of economic benefits were generated by a 2010 study from the North American Integration and Development Center at the University of California, Los Angeles. We also reviewed economic projections from groups opposed to the DREAM Act, such as the Center for Immigration Studies.

In Chapter 3 we described the demographic makeup and family background information of our sample of DREAMers. Most of them arrived in the United States at a very young age—typically under seven years old. The majority of them (70 percent) grew up in households where family members had mixed legal statuses. In other words, some of the members of their immediate family were undocumented and some of them, usually younger siblings, were US citizens. This has had a profound effect on their day-to-day lives, ranging from sharing in the fear of the potential (and in some cases, real) separation from their families due to deportations, to watching siblings travel out of state, perhaps to study at an elite university, while the DREAMer was attending a local community college. Our respondents discussed family members who were US citizens who likewise had their options limited because others used their documents for work and travel that were desperately needed to support their struggling families.

All of our DREAMers made decisions about their futures based on their undocumented status, from declining acceptance to elite universities to being resigned to taking life "one day at a time." They also made daily decisions based on their status. The reality for DREAMers is that living undocumented in the United States means that one's circumstances can change at any moment. If your mom or dad is late coming home from work, you might wonder if they are just stuck in traffic, or if they have been detained and taken to a detention center. You have to choose between risking driving the car (without a license) to get to class on time, or taking the two-hour bus ride and risking annoying your professor (again) because you're late (again). Some common themes that emerged from their experiences of living life without legal authorization included persistent fear, resentment, and a deep sense of vulnerability. The DREAMers we spoke to shared examples of both positive and negative treatment received once people knew they were undocumented. We can all remember squabbles with our childhood friends, but how many Americans can relate to the story of a girl whose friend's parents threatened to call and have them deported if the girls didn't stop fighting? Teenage romance is a veritable rollercoaster of emotions and insecurity, but how often does a messy breakup mean also worrying that the person you once trusted with the secret of your undocumented status might call the authorities and report you? Being undocumented in the United States makes even these relatively common and usually benign coming-of-age experiences all the more dangerous and stressful for the DREAMers among us.

In Chapter 4 we focused on our DREAMers' reactions to President Obama's DACA policy. A clear pattern emerged that the DREAMers we interviewed knew about deferred action, even though the policy change had been announced just weeks prior to our conversations. While most identified ways in which their own lives would be positively impacted by deferred action, they raised serious questions about the motivations behind the president's actions. They expressed feelings of disappointment, cynicism, and anger, as well as uncertainty, thankfulness, and hope as they talked about their reactions to DACA. Despite the clear preference for more encompassing comprehensive immigration reform measures, most respondents thought that President Obama did the right thing in moving ahead with an executive order rather than waiting for legislative solutions from Congress. Interviews with our DREAMers revealed a clear trend: they want to see the passage of a federal DREAM Act. A number of interviewees discussed this need and plan to continue organizing to this policy end.

Also in Chapter 4 we shared the widespread desire of DREAMers to have the opportunity to pursue the American Dream and to be fully incorporated into the fabric of the United States. Our DREAMers aspire to be fully incorporated into US society—economically, socially, and politically. They dream of being acknowledged as part of the society in which they grew to adulthood. The short-term opportunities provided by the deferred action program follow over two decades of organizing, but resolve only some of the problems faced by DREAMers, and they continue to live in limbo. Deferred action, by definition, is temporary and fails to provide any permanent status or solution for DREAMers who qualify. Living in limbo means continued limits on educational, career, and social and political development possibilities. Because undocumented youth are unable, given the current state of immigration laws in this country, to fully pursue their dreams, the growth and vitality of US society are also impacted.

As we described in Chapter 5, the political socialization and ethnic identities of the youth we interviewed varied widely. Some became politicized activists—undocumented and unafraid—while others turned inward, focusing on staying in school and out of trouble, reflecting the diversity of their personal situations but also the political contexts of the four different states in which they reside. Our study participants were quite ambivalent about the major political parties and mainstream politics in general, reporting low levels of trust in government and low levels of affinity toward either the Democratic or Republican parties. Yet, while our sample of DREAMers was very much like most Americans, and most young people, in that they reported very low trust in government and very little interest in politics, they were very well-informed about President Obama's deferred deportation plan and the DREAM Act, and many reported a link between their interest in those topics and their immigration status. While they were almost universally cynical about politics and uninterested in political parties or institutional politics, they were much more likely than the average young person in the United States to have taken part in direct actions, including protests, hunger strikes, or other civil disobedience, and also to have taken part in direct lobbying on the issue of immigration reform. Rather than viewing politics as something related exclusively to mainstream political parties, institutions, and elections, their life experiences—and their inability to vote—have led them to develop a specific model of political attitudes and behaviors that sees such action as conventional and effective. DREAMers have been politicized and mobilized by their status and the context of ongoing political debates over immigration policy. Waiting for the DREAM Act, or to see if they would qualify for deferred deportation status, many saw their lives as being in limbo. As Renata put it, "it's like living on the shelf."

In Chapter 5 we also reviewed our DREAMers' answers to queries about their ethnic and panethnic identity. Overall, we found that they identified as Mexican, often noting how this reflected the reality of their immigration status, but also as Americans or Latinos, reflecting their upbringing and psychological attachment to the United States. For DREAMers, there is a legal barrier to full assimilation that forces a full stop by, at the latest, the latter years of high school, as young people hoping to attend college or secure a driver's license find themselves, often for the first time, faced with the reality of their immigration status. However much they may consider themselves to be Americans, or Mexican Americans, their identity is solidly defined by US politics and American society as other, as foreigner, as Mexican. Some DREAMers embrace this otherness, working to improve their Spanish language abilities or to learn more about Mexican culture and politics. Others work to "prove" their American-ness, to adopt US culture and the English language even more forcefully. They find themselves torn between the American identities that they have developed during their childhoods and the reality of their outsider identities, their lack of nine digits that mark one as a full member of US society. For some, this has led them to embrace their Mexican or other Latino national-origin identity, while others remain solidly self-identified as American, members of the only country they truly know.

IMPLICATIONS

The Process of "De-Americanization"²¹ and One-Way Assimilation

When one looks at American society through the eyes of the DREAMers, one learns that there are still great injustices perpetuated in twenty-first-century America toward people of color and immigrants. Despite widespread notions that we are a postracial society, the stories shared by our sample of DREAMers clearly demonstrate a strong anti-Latino frame and underscore the fact that the United States is not as tolerant, welcoming, or inclusive of immigrants as many would like to believe. For example, recall from Chapter 3 the story shared by Damian. He remembers being told by a financial aid counselor at UCLA, "Don't waste your time. Go get a job and get, get your ass to work. You won't be able to go to college, you won't be able to pay tuition at a, at a university. Don't waste your time." This revealing account underscores the pervasive anti-Latino frame discussed in Chapter 1. Latinos are racialized to be laborers, not professionals. In this example, a young Latino male was racialized by a financial aid counselor despite his obvious academic promise, having been accepted by four schools in the prestigious UC system. Examples of this sort, of reinforcement of the white racial frame, are a constant in American society, one encouraged and enhanced by the othering of undocumented immigrants.

Despite the rhetoric espoused by President Obama that the United States of America represents "the story of ambition and adaptation, hard work and education, assimilation and upward mobility,"²² the interview data we gathered in this study indicate that as a country we cannot get beyond the racist exclusion of immigrants and in this case, not even the children of immigrants who personally had nothing to do with the decision to emigrate. Despite the legal theory embraced in *Plyler* that we should not punish children for the decisions of their parents, DREAMers are punished time and again by US society for their undocumented status. This resistance to the political and social incorporation of people of color has a deep foundation in the United States. We almost destroyed ourselves as a nation during the Civil War over the efforts of the Confederate States to keep African Americans enslaved. Throughout our nation's history, the incorporation of people who are not Anglo-Saxon Protestants into the privilege of American citizenship has been met with resistance. Currently, this resistance extends even to children who have been raised in America, many of whom came here as infants or small children. As Reverend Dennis H. Holtschneider states in the Foreword to *Living Illegal*,

> Throughout history, society has confronted a fear of incorporating the stranger. The United States justified slavery and Jim Crow by claiming those of African descent were less than human. Women were portrayed as too simple-minded and emotionally unstable to vote.... Today, entire classes of unauthorized

immigrants have been demonized by unfair portrayals of immigrants' perceived negative effects on the United States' economy, crime rate, and social order. The benefits of their influence are rarely brought to light, let alone discussed. Rarely do we hear stories about the contributions unauthorized immigrants make to small businesses, churches, or once-failing neighborhoods.[23]

The current racialization of Latino immigration and Latino immigrants is highlighted by being defined out of the American community and by the oppressive circumstances the DREAMers have had to live under as outsiders in this country. Our findings underscore Ron Schmidt's conclusion that the racialization of undocumented immigrants plays a significant role in immigration policy debates. "[I]n turn, this phenomenon plays an important role in the maintenance of racial hierarchy in the United States, thereby undermining the country's ongoing project toward becoming an ethno-racial democracy."[24]

This racialization of unauthorized immigrants also creates what Bill Ong Hing calls "de-Americanization": racially profiling groups out of the notion of what is an American. It has resulted in defining DREAMers as "not *real* Americans, not part of us" (emphasis in original).[25] Hing argues that this process has the insidious ability to perpetuate itself in multiple generations. Michelson's work on immigrants' adapting to the racialized identity of their coethnics underscores Hing's argument. As Latino immigrants spend more time in the United States, they become more aware of discrimination and racism against Latinos, of hostility toward their culture on the part of the host society. Those who come to view the US government as racist, to believe that government officials mistreat Latinos and immigrants, tend to acculturate "not into mainstream America society, but into a racialized Latino community."[26] According to Hing, the process of de-Americanization is not only generationally reproduced, but in addition it goes beyond classic xenophobia. He states in this regard,

> De-Americanization is not simply xenophobia because more than fear of foreigners is at work. This is a brand of nativism cloaked in a Eurocentric sense of America that combines hate and racial profiling.[27]

Hing's concept of de-Americanization is applicable to the lived experiences of immigrants and to the stories we heard time and again among our sample of DREAMers. For example, recall Jorge's quote from Chapter 3 that "[B]eing an illegal immigrant shapes who you are, so ... when you're growing up, like what you become and who you, how you act and whatnot." Ninety-eight percent of our sample of DREAMers told us that being undocumented affected their decisions about what to do with their lives after high school. Many of our sample of DREAMers expressed the notion that they were perceived as "undeserving" of social programs such as the following example from Romina's comments from Chapter 3: "[I]t kind of brings me down. Like I was in migrant services in high school. Well, some students would always say that we had it easy because they would give us everything." Ironically, even though because of her status Romina is not eligible for many scholarships and programs, she understands the all too common perception among others that she is undeserving of scholarships and programs, and that some people even believe that Latinos and other ethnic and racial minorities receive *more* scholarships than do white Americans. This is just one example of the de-Americanization that Hing describes.

Yet the reality is that the United States is an ethnoracial society; however, we are very far from having an ethnoracial democracy. If we truly want to become an ethnoracial democracy then we must go forward with immigration policy that moves beyond our history of xenophobia and the de-Americanization of people of color. We must engage in a paradigm shift in regard to how we treat immigrants among us, especially the undocumented youth who have been with us for the majority of their young lives. Because of the white racial frame, all Latinos encounter discrimination, whether they are undocumented immigrants or citizens, students or professionals. As a nation, we must become aware of and challenge the continuing notions of the white racial frame. One strategy for doing this can be found in a study written by Adam Simon and Frank Gilliam, which argues that while it is important to begin with a moral argument, it is also important to be strategic and know when to switch one's tactics when handling anti-immigrant attacks focused on the rule of law.[28] In a survey experiment of 8,000 registered voters, Simon and Gilliam found that switching from a moral argument to a pragmatist argument is much more effective at convincing voters of the importance of comprehensive immigration reform than is the commonly held notion of sticking to one's message. However, the key is beginning with a moral argument such as is found in the liberty and justice frame with ideas such as fairness, justice, tolerance, and respect.[29]

Strategies for confronting the white racial frame are important because those portraying America as a postracial society are wrong. As Feagin states, "this new colorblind rhetoric has just papered over what are still blatantly racist views of Americans of color that have continued in most whites' framing of this society."[30] This awareness of racism in the United States is the first challenge that must be overcome before immigration policy can turn away from its punitive direction. Despite their efforts to belong, DREAMers are de-Americanized, to the detriment of all Americans.

Assimilation has too often been seen as a one-way street, as noted in Chapter 1. In their recent study *Latinos Facing Racism*, Feagin and Cobas document the historical and contemporary racialization of Latinos in the United States. They argue that popular narratives of Latinos as either threatening to destroy Western civilization or as the latest example of an immigrant group ready to shed its home culture and assimilate into mainstream society are both wrong. Rather, Latinos continue to be racialized and the "melting pot" does not include and never has included them. In fact, assimilation has too often meant immigrants have been forced to give up their culture and fully adopt an American culture. This comes at a great cost to immigrants and their families, who despite assimilation will face racialization and discrimination based upon phenotype.[31] Newcomers are encouraged to adapt to American society by learning English and internalizing our customs and mores. DREAMers have done all of this and more—and it is still not enough. The notion of one-way assimilation must give way to one that recognizes the value of a variety of cultures and mores, that values equally all members of the increasingly diverse American population.

The Importance of Civic, Economic, and Legal
Integration of Undocumented Youth

Fully and legally incorporating undocumented Latino youth in a manner that addresses the alienation and resentment their experiences of growing up in the shadows have fostered will greatly strengthen our country. As illustrated by the impressive accomplishments of our 101 respondents, this group is made up of clearly capable and enterprising young people who long to make full use of their talents and ambition. For the most part, they know no other home and they are here to stay. But instead of working in their chosen or preferred professions, where they can contribute more to society, they are often trapped in low-status and menial jobs. Instead of voting and taking part in other mainstream and conventional forms of political behavior, many have taken to the streets, demonstrating and marching for immigration reform. In our increasingly diverse society, we must at least explore the possibility that our political, civic, and professional circles will be affected by the United States' demographic changes—positively through effective inclusion, or negatively through continued exclusion. If we wish to sustain a healthy society, maintain faith in our government and in our society, then it is critically important that we systematically explore ways to incorporate DREAMers into the American polity. As Hing argues,

> [T]he integration of newcomers into civic life is critical, from the perspectives of both the receiving communities and the newcomers themselves. The early integration and civic involvement of newcomers should be a high priority because that involvement is a key to better social, economic, and cultural integration of the newcomer and his or her family.... In short, the integration of newcomers is good for local communities and good for the nation.[32]

As a nation we pride ourselves on the liberty and justice frame ideals written in the Declaration of Independence: "We hold these truths to be self-evident, that all men are created equal, that they are endowed by their Creator with certain unalienable Rights, that among these are Life, Liberty and the pursuit of Happiness." However, the ideals of this founding principle have not extended to our young immigrant youth. As noted throughout this book, the political and social inclusion of people of color in the United States has never been achieved. We have a legacy of legalized segregation and racism from which we are still suffering residual impacts, ranging from enduring institutional and individual racism, persistent segregation, and a lack of proportional representation in our higher-status professions and among elected officials. We have come a long way. "We the people" now includes more of us than ever before. Yet, as illustrated by the stories shared by the DREAMers we interviewed, we still have a long way to go. The United States is a nation of immigrants, and we must treat our young immigrants—our DREAMers—in a way that reflects the values of this great nation.

Until we see immigrants as contributors rather than as a cost to the United States the punitive focus of the immigration debate will not change. As reviewed in Chapter 2, passage of a federal DREAM Act would likely be of enormous economic benefit to the US economy. Many studies demonstrate that the millions of undocumented immigrants who are working in the United States are providing valuable services and generating wealth across the economy, from small businesses to large corporations. Allowing DREAMers and other undocumented immigrants in the United States to be fully incorporated and come out of the shadows is thus not only the right thing to do politically and morally, it is the right thing to do for the sake of the US economy.

Building an Ethnoracial Democracy Begins
with Humane Immigration Reform

Humane immigration reform must begin by changing the way we view immigrants. Former Florida governor Jeb Bush recently challenged the widespread negative view that undocumented immigrants are criminals. In an interview with Fox News he stated,

> The way I look at this is someone who comes to our country *because they couldn't come legally*, they come to our country because their families—the dad who loved their children—was worried that their children didn't have food on the table. And they wanted to make sure their family was intact, and they crossed the border because they had no other means to work to be able to provide for their family.... [T]here should be a price paid, but it shouldn't rile people up that people are actually coming to this country to provide for their families. [emphasis added][33]

By viewing undocumented immigrants in this light rather than as criminals we can begin the work of politically and socially incorporating them and their American-raised children. The principles of the Founding Fathers challenge us to move away from the current, punitive treatment of these lifelong US residents. Rather than penalizing immigrants through our immigration policies, which have largely focused on border enforcement and deportations, we need immigration policies that truly embrace "your tired, your poor/your huddled masses yearning to breathe free."[34] The work of building a true ethnoracial democracy requires that we create just, fair, and inclusive immigration policies. Americans have an opportunity to turn away from our xenophobic history and our current anti-immigrant stance to be a nation that is welcoming and accepting of newcomers and people of diverse cultural, racial, and ethnic backgrounds—beginning with undocumented youth.

Listening to the stories of our sample of DREAMers, we learned about the lives of hardworking, good kids who have grown up in the United States seeking to achieve the American Dream like everyone else. Some always knew they were undocumented, but they did not quite understand what it meant; others first learned as teenagers. Just as they were attempting, like other teenagers around them, to assert their independence—to go away to college, to get a first job, to learn to drive—they found themselves stopped in their tracks by a system that does not recognize their long-term identities or their lack of agency in becoming undocumented. Imagine that. Imagine yourself back in high school, those heady days of summer romance and adventure, and suddenly finding that although all of your friends were doing these marvelous, grown-up activities, you could not. *No Social Security number. No legal recourse. No voice.* After recovering from the initial shock, you would want people to understand your story, to treat you with dignity and respect, and to welcome you legally into the American polity. You would want our government to pass legislation that would fix this situation, for us and for the millions of youth who only want the chance to pursue the American Dream. In short, you would want a responsive, just, and humane immigration policy. You would want to be treated fairly. You would want to be seen as a human being.

We must have the wisdom and the tenacity to continually seek ways to improve our government, our professional institutions, and our commitments to one another by extending the promise of America's most cherished principles to immigrants and especially to the DREAMers. As Luis Fraga states, "Public policy is the primary way in which Americans have always demonstrated their commitment to each other."[35] If we make a commitment to DREAMers through humane immigration policy, our entire society will be enriched by not only the economic and cultural benefits that they will bestow upon American society, but also because we will stop undermining our democratic values through the continual exclusion of undocumented Latino youth who have so much to contribute to society. In the process we will be one step closer to achieving an ethnoracial democracy for the first time in our nation's history.

However, at present the US Congress seems to prefer a course of action divorced from reason; their choice has been one that erodes our societal values of justice, freedom, equality, and democracy, and has created a permanent underclass for these lifelong residents of this country, the DREAMers. It is a policy approach that serves to reinforce the United States' racial hierarchy.[36] This hierarchy (and the white racial frame) is being perpetuated by the current refusal by Congress to move forward on immigration reform. As we went to press, Republicans in the House of Representatives were again blocking progress on the issue. In late January 2014, House GOP leaders released a list of principles on immigration reform meant to move the issue forward. Backlash from within the party was swift and fierce:

[T]he Tea Party Patriots group set in motion 900,000 automatic phone calls in 90 Republican House districts, connecting tens of thousands of voters to their members of Congress. The hashtag #NoAmnesty blazed across Twitter. About the same time, FreedomWorks, another anti-tax, limited-government group, was pulling in signatures on its "fire the speaker" petition against the House speaker, John A. Boehner.[37]

Boehner quickly reversed course, pledging to not move forward on immigration reform during the Obama administration because, he said, the president could not be trusted to enforce any such law fairly and impartially. The flawed comprehensive bill that had been so tortuously put together by the US Senate's Gang of Eight, promising to move forward only on select pieces of the bill (such as border fencing and farmworker visas), seemed dead. The *New York Times* editorialized on August 3, 2013, about the importance of forcing House Republicans to fix the broken system: "[A]s Congress dawdles, deportations are continuing at a record pace—thousands of lives and families torn apart every month, hundreds of thousands every year." President Obama does not have the constitutional authority to end deportations on his own, but he seems increasingly willing to use executive action—as he did with the deferred action program—to do something.[38] And still, Congress dawdles. The *New York Times* again editorialized on April 5, 2014, about options President Obama should and can act on in light of Congress's failure to pass comprehensive immigration reform, including ending deportations among people who would qualify for legalization under SB 744, extending deferred action to the parents of DREAMers, ending Secure Communities programs that create terror in immigrant communities, and ending "the deportation machinery."[39] They state, "It's hard to know when he will finally stir himself to do something big and consequential."[40] As this book went to press, speaker John Boehner urged his Republican House colleagues to move forward on immigration reform, but observers noted that progress was unlikely during a midterm election year and thus that little was to be expected from Congress before 2015.

In the meantime, the DREAMers continue to live in legal limbo while hoping that one day they will have justice.

Appendix

Undocumented Youth Interview Questionnaire

Before beginning interview: Did you read the consent form that I gave to you and agree to participate in this interview? [ ] Y [ ] N

Do you understand that your participation in this project is voluntary, and that you may discontinue participation at any time? [ ] Y [ ] N

SECTION A: AGE & EDUCATIONAL BACKGROUND

A1.   What is your age? _____
Note to Interviewer: If under 18, stop interview.

A2.   *Interviewer record gender:* [ ] Male   [ ] Female

A3.   Do you have a high school diploma?   [ ] Y [ ] N

A4.   If yes, are you currently enrolled in college/
university? [ ] Y [ ] N

A5.   Where do you go to school when you are enrolled? *Interviewer: record school name* _____

If you are a college graduate, what college/university did you attend and what was your major? *Interviewer: record alma mater and major college/university:*

_____

Major area of study: _____

A6.   What level of education was attained by your parents?
      Mother: _____
      Father: _____

SECTION B: IMMIGRANT BACKGROUND & EXPERIENCES

B1.   Place of birth (state and country)

      _____

B2.   Are you a US Citizen, permanent resident, or other?
      US Citizen _____
      Permanent resident _____
      Other _____

B3.   Where were your parents born? (city, state if US; country if not US)
      Mother: _____
      Father: _____

B4.   How old were you when you came to the United States?
      _____

B5.   How did you find out about your immigration status? *Probe*—How old
      were you?

      _____

      _____

      _____

B6.   What is your family like—are the other members of your immediate
      family of the same immigration status as you, or is it a mix?
      [   ] Same Status   [   ] Mix
      Probe—Does this family member's immigration status affect your daily life? If
      so, in what ways does it affect you?

      _____

      _____

      _____

B7.   Do any friends or teachers/staff at school know about your
      status?   [   ] Y   [   ] N

B8.   Have you had to "come out" to some people? If so, what was that like?
      Did this change how they perceived you?

      _____

      _____

      _____

B9.   Have you been "outed" without your permission? If so, what were the
particular circumstances? Did you suffer any negative consequences as a
result? If so, give an example or examples.

_____

_____

_____

B10. Have you found that those who know about your status treat you
differently than those who don't know? If so, in what ways does their
treatment of you differ?

_____

_____

_____

B11. Have you made decisions about where to go to school after high school
and what to do after graduation that are related to your immigration
status? If so, please explain.

_____

_____

_____

SECTION C: DREAM ACT & PRES. OBAMA'S IMMIGRATION DECLARATION

C1.   Are you familiar with President Obama's Executive Order directing the
Department of Homeland Security to end the deportation of school-
aged undocumented youth?   [   ] Y   [   ] N

If so, in what ways do think your immediate circumstances will change?

_____

_____

_____

C2.   This action taken by the President was rather controversial.
How would you describe your own opinion of this
action?   [   ] Favorable   [   ] Unfavorable

Please explain: _____

_____

_____

Probe—Do you believe your future circumstances will be different because of
this change in immigration policy?   [   ] Y   [   ] N

If so, how do you think your future circumstances will be different?

_____

_____

C3.   Do you think it would have been better for President Obama to continue to wait for a permanent immigration reform law passed by Congress rather than to take this executive action?   [   ] Y   [   ] N

C4.   With the 2012 presidential elections approaching, Republican Presidential Candidate Governor Mitt Romney has refused to say whether he would revoke President Obama's Executive Order on deportation. How do you feel about this decision on Gov. Romney's part?   [   ] Approve   [   ] Disapprove   [   ] No Opinion

C5.   Do you plan on getting a renewable 2-year work permit, given this announcement?   [   ] Y   [   ] N
If no, please explain why not: _____
_____
_____

C6.   If you are a current student, will this policy decision change the way you engage socially with other students and in campus life?
        [   ] Yes, I will be more engaged
        [   ] No, I will not change in my level of engagement with other students and campus life
        [   ] Not applicable; not currently a student

C7.   If you work, will this policy decision change the way you engage socially with your co-workers?
        [   ] Yes, I will be more engaged socially at work
        [   ] No, I will not change in my level of engagement with others where I work
        [   ] Not applicable; not currently working

C8.   Where do you see yourself in five years? In ten years?
        Five years: _____
_____
        Ten years: _____
_____

C9.   Are you familiar with the DREAM Act?   [   ] Y   [   ] N
If so, how would passage of the DREAM Act likely affect your educational, occupational, and personal decisions in each of the following four areas?
        A. At school:
        _____
        B. After graduation:
        _____

C. With work/career choices:

_____

D. Personally with respect to marriage, family formation, etc.:

_____

SECTION D: POLITICAL VALUES AND PERSONAL IDENTITY

D1.   How much attention do you pay to politics in the US?
[   ] Very Little   [   ] Some   [   ] A Good Deal   [   ] A Great Deal

D2.   How interested would you say you are in American politics?
[   ] Not Interested   [   ] Somewhat Interested   [   ] Quite Interested

D3.   Are you interested in working on political
       campaigns?   [   ] Y   [   ] N
If not interested, why not?

_____

_____

D4.   Would you like to be able to vote one day?   [   ] Y   [   ] N

D5.   As a student, to what extent did you participate in student organizations,
       clubs, or other campus-based extra-curricular activities?
       [   ] Not at all   [   ] Some   [   ] A Good Deal
       [   ] A Great Deal

D6.   To what extent do you trust each of the following to generally "do the
       right thing" for the public?
       I.   The federal government:
            [   ] Little Trust   [   ] Some Trust   [   ] Much Trust
       II. Your state government:
            [   ] Little Trust   [   ] Some Trust   [   ] Much Trust
       III. Your local government:
            [   ] Little Trust   [   ] Some Trust   [   ] Much Trust

D7.   Were you involved in any of the immigration marches of 2006, or in
       any other action related to immigration policy? If yes, please explain.

_____

_____

_____

D8. Which of the following political party labels best applies to you? (check only one)
[ ] Strong Republican   [ ] Strong Democrat   [ ] Independent
[ ] Republican   [ ] Democrat   [ ] Other

D9. Thinking about your views concerning *economic issues* (such as taxes, government spending), where would you place yourself on the scale below: (check only one)
[ ] Very Conservative   [ ] Somewhat Conservative
[ ] Moderate   [ ] Somewhat Liberal   [ ] Very Liberal

D10. Thinking about your views concerning *social issues* (such as women's rights, gay rights), where would you place yourself on the scale below: (check only one)
[ ] Very Conservative   [ ] Somewhat Conservative
[ ] Moderate   [ ] Somewhat Liberal   [ ] Very Liberal

D11. When asked to describe your ethnic identity, which term would you be most likely to use?
[ ] American   [ ] South American
[ ] Mexican American/Chicano   [ ] Central American
[ ] Puerto Rican   [ ] Dominican
[ ] Cuban   [ ] Latino/Hispanic _____
[ ] Mexican

D12. How would you rate your sense of Latino identity?
[ ] Very strong   [ ] Strong
[ ] Moderate   [ ] Weak   [ ] Very weak

Thank you. Could you recommend one or two people with similar immigration status to yours that I could talk with next?

Notes

CHAPTER 1

* All the names in this book are pseudonyms.

1. The criteria include (1) brought to the United States before sixteen years of age and have remained in the United States for five years, (2) are under age thirty, (3) have no criminal record, (4) have a high school diploma (or equivalent) or have served in the military. See Janet Napolitano, *Exercising Prosecutorial Discretion with Respect to Individuals Who Came to the United States as Children* (Washington, DC: Government Printing Office, 2012).

2. Barack Obama, "Remarks by the President on Immigration," Rose Garden, June 15, 2012, www.whitehouse.gov/the-press-office/2012/06/15/remarks-president-immigration (retrieved February 20, 2013).

3. "What Obama's Immigration Move Means for Undocumented Youth, Politics," *PBS NewsHour*, June 15, 2012, www.pbs.org/newshour/bb/politics/jan-june12/dreamact_06-15 .html.

4. See Aristide Zolberg, *A Nation by Design: Immigration Policy in the Fashioning of America* (Cambridge, MA: Harvard University Press, 2006).

5. For example, see Rogers M. Smith, *Civic Ideals: Conflicting Visions of Citizenship in U.S. History* (New Haven, CT: Yale University Press, 1997); and Mae M. Ngai and Jon Gjerde, *Major Problems in American Immigration History*, 2nd ed. (Boston: Wadsworth/ Cengage Learning, 2011).

6. See Ronald Schmidt Sr., "Racialization and the Unauthorized Immigration Debate," paper presented at the annual meeting of the American Political Science Association, 2013.

7. Marshall Ganz, "Why Stories Matter," *Sojourners*, March 2009, http://sojo.net /magazine/2009/03/why-stories-matter (retrieved August 21, 2013).

8. Ibid.

9. Ibid.

10. Smith, *Civic Ideals*, "Introduction."

11. Ibid., 1.

12. Ngai and Gjerde, *Major Problems*; Ronald Takaki, *A Different Mirror: A History of Multicultural America* (Boston: Back Bay Books, 1993); Lisa García Bedolla, *Fluid Borders: Latino Power, Identity, and Politics in Los Angeles* (Berkeley: University of California Press, 2005).

13. Ngai and Gjerde, *Major Problems*.

14. Leo R. Chavez, *Shadowed Lives: Undocumented Immigrants in American Society* (Independence, KY: Cengage Learning, 1997), 186–187.

15. Leo Chavez, *The Latino Threat: Constructing Immigrants, Citizens, and the Nation* (Stanford, CA: Stanford University Press, 2008).

16. Sandra Lilley, "Poll: 1 Out of 3 Americans Inaccurately Think Most Hispanics Are Undocumented," NBC Latino, September 12, 2012, http://nbclatino.com/2012/09/12/poll -1-out-of-3-americans-think-most-hispanics-are-undocumented/.

17. Isabel Sawhill and John E. Morton, "Economic Mobility: Is the American Dream Alive and Well?," Economic Mobility Project Report (Washington, DC: Pew Charitable Trusts, 2007).

18. Barack Obama, *The Audacity of Hope: Thoughts on Reclaiming the American Dream* (New York: Knopf, 2008), 260.

19. Ron Haskins, "Economic Mobility of Immigrants in the United States," Economic Mobility Project Report (Washington, DC: Pew Charitable Trusts, 2009), 1.

20. See ibid.; Camille Guerin-Gonzales, *Mexican Workers and American Dreams: Immigration, Repatriation, and California Farm Labor, 1900–1939* (New Brunswick, NJ: Rutgers University Press, 1994); Sheryll Cashin, *The Failures of Integration: How Race and Class Are Undermining the American Dream* (New York: Perseus, 2004).

21. Joe R. Feagin, *The White Racial Frame: Centuries of Racial Framing and Counter-Framing* (New York: Routledge, 2010).

22. Richard Alba, "Mexican Americans and the American Dream," *Perspectives on Politics* 4, no. 2 (2006): 289.

23. Peralta Eyder, "National Council of La Raza Dubs Obama 'Deporter-in-Chief,'" interview with Janet Murguía, National Public Radio, March 4, 2014, www.npr.org /blogs/thetwo-way/2014/03/04/285907255/national-council-of-la-raza-dubs-obama -deporter-in-chief.

24. Please see Nancy LeTourneau's blog, "Some History and Facts for Those Claiming That President Obama Is "Deporter-in-Chief," at http://immasmartypants.blogspot .com/2014/03/some-history-and-facts-for-those.html (retrieved March 14, 2014).

25. We are indebted to Joe Feagin for assistance with these issues.

26. Ginger Thompson and Sarah Cohen, "More Deportations Follow Minor Crimes, Records Show," *New York Times*, April 6, 2014, www.nytimes.com/2014/04/07/us/more -deportations-follow-minor-crimes-data-shows.html?_r=0 (retrieved April 24, 2014).

27. David Nakamura, "With an Immigration Deal Possible, Advocates Mount New Push to End Deportations," *Washington Post*, February 3, 2014, www.washingtonpost.com /politics/with-an-immigration-deal-possible-advocates-mount-new-push-to-end-deportations /2014/02/03/ee6feaa8-8ce7-11e3-98ab-fe5228217bd1_story.html (retrieved March 11, 2014).

28. We are indebted here to discussions of these issues with Joe Feagin.

29. Detention Watch Network, "The Influence of the Private Prison Industry in the Immigration Detention Business," May 2011, www.detentionwatchnetwork.org/sites /detentionwatchnetwork.org/files/PrivatePrisonPDF-FINAL%205-11-11.pdf (retrieved March 11, 2014).

30. Feagin, *White Racial Frame*, 37.

31. Editorial Board, "Yes, He Can, on Immigration," *New York Times*, April 5, 2014, www.nytimes.com/2014/04/06/opinion/sunday/yes-he-can-on-immigration.html (retrieved April 24, 2014).

32. Michael A. Olivas, *No Undocumented Child Left Behind: Plyler v. Doe and the Education of Undocumented Schoolchildren* (New York: New York University Press, 2012).

33. Ibid., 8.

34. Ibid.

35. Ibid., 36.

36. Ibid., 74.

37. Ibid., 61.

38. Marie Friedmann Marquardt, Timothy J. Steigenga, Philip J. Williams, and Manuel A. Vásquez, *Living "Illegal": The Human Face of Unauthorized Immigration* (New York: The New Press, 2013).

39. Douglas Massey, Jorge Durand, and Nolan J. Malone, *Beyond Smoke and Mirrors: Mexican Immigration in an Era of Economic Integration* (New York: Russell Sage Foundation, 2002).

40. Mark Hugo Lopez and Ana Gonzalez-Barrera, "If They Could, How Many Unauthorized Immigrants Would Become U.S. Citizens?" (Washington, DC: Pew Research Center, June 2013), www.pewresearch.org/fact-tank/2013/06/27/if-they-could-how-many-unauthorized-immigrants-would-become-u-s-citizens/.

41. Roberto G. Gonzales and Leo R. Chavez, "'Awakening to a Nightmare': Abjectivity and Illegality in the Lives of Undocumented 1.5-Generation Latino Immigrants in the United States," *Current Anthropology* 53, no. 3 (June 2012): 255–281.

42. Ibid., 262.

43. Ibid., 265.

44. Ibid., 267.

45. Veronica Terriquez and Caitlin Patler, "Aspiring Americans: Undocumented Youth Leaders in California," Policy Brief, California Young Adult Study, Center for the Study of Immigrant Integration, University of Southern California, June 2012.

46. Joe R. Feagin and José A. Cobas, *Latinos Facing Racism: Discrimination, Resistance, and Endurance* (Boulder, CO: Paradigm Publishers, 2013), 31.

47. Ibid.

48. Ibid., 13.

49. Ibid., 15.

50. Ashley Parker, "G.O.P. Congressman's Remarks Undermine Party's Immigration Efforts," *New York Times*, July 24, 2013, http://thecaucus.blogs.nytimes.com/2013/07/23/g-o-p-congressman-undermines-partys-immigration-efforts/?_r=0 (retrieved July 30, 2013).

51. See Jessica Lavariega Monforti, "Immigration: Trends, Demographics, and Patterns of Political Incorporation," in *Perspectives on Race, Ethnicity, and Religion: Identity Politics in America*, ed. Valerie Martinez-Ebers and Manochehr Dorraj, 52–72 (New York: Oxford University Press, 2009).

52. Feagin, *White Racial Frame*, 163–165.

53. Ibid., 164–165.

54. Ibid.

55. Ronald Schmidt Sr., "Racialization and the Unauthorized Immigration Debate," paper presented at the annual meeting of the American Political Science Association, Chicago, August 31, 2013.

56. Luis R. Fraga et al., *Latino Lives in America: Making It Home* (Philadelphia: Temple University Press, 2010); José A. Cobas, Jorge Duany, and Joe R. Feagin, eds., *How the United States Racializes Latinos: White Hegemony and Its Consequences* (Boulder, CO: Paradigm Publishers, 2009); Vicki L. Ruíz, *From Out of the Shadows: Mexican Women in Twentieth-Century America* (New York: Oxford University Press, 2008); Maria Chávez, *Everyday Injustice: Latino Professionals and Racism* (Lanham, MD: Rowman and Littlefield, 2011).

57. Quote from one of our research assistants, who is also an undocumented college student who arrived in the United States at the age of seven.

58. See Min Zhou, "Segmented Assimilation: Issues, Controversies, and Recent Research on the New Second Generation," *International Migration Review* 31, no. 4, Special Issue: Immigrant Adaptation and Native-Born Responses in the Making of Americans (Winter 1997): 975–1008.

59. Feagin and Cobas, *Latinos Facing Racism*.

60. Ibid.

61. Ibid., 6.

62. Ronald Schmidt Sr., *Language Policy and Identity Politics in the United States* (Philadelphia: Temple University Press, 2000), 109.

63. For example, see Chávez, *Everyday Injustice*; Fraga et al., *Latino Lives in America*; Kevin R. Johnson, *How Did You Get to Be a Mexican? A White/Brown Man's Search for Identity* (Philadelphia: Temple University Press, 1999); Bill Ong Hing, *Defining America through Immigration Policy* (Philadelphia: Temple University Press, 2004); or Eduardo Bonilla-Silva, *Racism without Racists: Color-Blind Racism and Racial Inequality in Contemporary America* (New York: Rowman and Littlefield, 2010).

64. Feagin and Cobas, *Latinos Facing Racism,* 14.

65. Joe R. Feagin and José A. Cobas, "Latinos/as and the White Racial Frame: The Procrustean Bed of Assimilation," *Sociological Inquiry* 78, no. 1 (2008): 45.

66. This is a quote from an email conversation about how current college students have been socialized to believe we live in a "post-racial" society. Oftentimes they are seeped in the white racial frame, so they have a difficult time with data that demonstrate we have racial inequality in the United States. This email exchange took place on September 19, 2013.

67. Bill Ong Hing, *To Be an American: Cultural Pluralism and the Rhetoric of Assimilation* (New York: New York University Press, 1997), 3.

68. Feagin, *White Racial Frame,* 14.

69. Ibid.

70. See ibid., chapter 2.

71. Ngai and Gjerde, *Major Problems.*

72. Ibid., 387.

73. Ibid., 387–388.

74. Christine Marie Sierra, Teresa Carrillo, Louis DeSipio, and Michael Jones-Correa, "Latino Immigration and Citizenship," *PS: Political Science and Politics* 33, no. 3 (September 2000): 535. Also see Lavariega Monforti, "Immigration," 52–72.

75. Sierra et al., "Latino Immigration and Citizenship," 535.

76. Lisa García Bedolla, *Latino Politics* (Cambridge, UK: Polity, 2009). The histories of Puerto Rican, Cuban, and Central and South American immigrant groups are also provided in this book.

77. Ibid.

78. Ricardo Romo, "Responses to Mexican Immigration, 1910–1930," *Aztlán* 6 (1975): 173–194.

79. See Francisco E. Balderrama and Raymond Rodriguez, *Decade of Betrayal: Mexican Repatriation in the 1930s* (Albuquerque: University of New Mexico Press, 2006).

80. Kitty Calavita, *Inside the State: The Bracero Program, Immigration, and the I.N.S.* (New York: Routledge, 1992).

81. This is an argument made in a public presentation by Pulitzer Prize–winning author Junot Diaz at the University of Puget Sound, Tacoma, Washington, September 17, 2013.

82. Ronald Schmidt Sr., Yvette M. Alex-Assensoh, Andrew L. Aoki, and Rodney E. Hero, *Newcomers, Outsiders, and Insiders: Immigrants and American Racial Politics in the Early Twenty-First Century* (Ann Arbor: University of Michigan Press, 2010), 67.

83. Sierra et al., "Latino Immigration and Citizenship," 535.

84. Massey, Durand, and Malone, *Beyond Smoke and Mirrors,* 3.

85. Ronald Schmidt Sr., "Racialization and the Unauthorized Immigration Debate," paper presented at the Western Political Science Association, Portland, March 23, 2012.

86. Ibid., 12–13.

87. Ibid., 13.

88. Ibid., 14.

89. See www.azleg.gov/legtext/49leg/2r/bills/sb1070s.pdf for details.

90. See http://legiscan.com/AL/text/HB56/id/321074 for details.

91. Schmidt, "Racialization and the Unauthorized Immigration Debate" (2012), 26.

92. Chávez, *Everyday Injustice.*

93. Maria Chávez, "Targeting Latino Children Is Not the Answer," Racism Review, May 10, 2011, www.racismreview.com/blog/2011/05/10/targeting-latino-children-is-not-the-answer/.

94. For the full transcript of President Obama's speech, see www.nytimes.com/2013/01/30/us/politics/full-transcript-of-president-obamas-remarks-on-immigration-reform.html?pagewanted=all&pagewanted=print (retrieved March 5, 2013).

95. David Nakamura, "Obama to Refocus Attention on Immigration, Gun Control," *Washington Post*, March 1, 2013, www.washingtonpost.com/politics/obama-to-refocus-attention-on-immigration-gun-control/2013/03/01/64fbe2d0-81ef-11e2-a350-49866afab584_story.html (retrieved March 3, 2013).

96. See transcripts at www.nytimes.com/2013/01/30/us/politics/full-transcript-of-president-obamas-remarks-on-immigration-reform.html?pagewanted=all&pagewanted=print (retrieved March 5, 2013).

97. Ibid.

98. Ibid.

99. Special thanks to Landyn Rookard for assistance with the summary of Senate Bill 744.

100. Fernanda Santos, "Border Security Rule Costs Bill Support," *New York Times*, June 26, 2013, www.nytimes.com/2013/06/27/us/politics/border-security-rule-costs-bill-support.html?_r=0 (retrieved August 3, 2013).

101. David Damore, "Message Not Received: House Republicans and Immigration Reform," Latino Decisions, July 25, 2013, www.latinodecisions.com/blog/2013/07/25/message-not-received-house-republicans-and-immigration-reform/ (retrieved August 3, 2013).

102. Ibid.

103. David Damore, "How Latino Voters May Decide Control of the U.S. House of Representatives," Latino Decisions, July 9, 2013, www.latinodecisions.com/blog/2013/07/09/how-latino-voters-may-decide-control-of-the-u-s-house-of-representatives/ (retrieved August 3, 2013).

104. Lamar Smith, "Immigration Enforcement Key to Success," *USA Today*, March 4, 2013, www.usatoday.com/story/opinion/2013/03/04/lamar-smith-on-immigration-enforcement/1960287/ (retrieved March 5, 2013).

105. Ibid.

106. Ashley Parker and Jonathan Martin, "Senate, 68 to 32, Passes Overhaul for Immigration," *New York Times*, June 27, 2013, www.nytimes.com/2013/06/28/us/politics/immigration-bill-clears-final-hurdle-to-senate-approval.html?pagewanted=all (retrieved August 3, 2013).

107. Editorial Board, "Yes, He Can."

108. Ibid.

109. Ibid.

110. Obama, *Audacity of Hope*, 260.

CHAPTER 2

1. Jim Rutenberg and Jeff Zeleny, "Perry and Romney Come Out Swinging at Each Other in G.O.P. Debate," *New York Times*, September 22, 2011, www.nytimes.com/2011/09/23/us/politics/perry-and-romney-come-out-swinging-at-each-other-in-gop-debate.html?ref=politics.

2. Hernan Ramirez and Pierrette Hondagneu-Sotelo, "Mexican Immigrant Gardeners: Entrepreneurs or Exploited Workers?," *Social Problems* 56, no. 1 (February 2009): 70–88.

3. Jeffrey S. Passel, "The Size and Characteristics of the Unauthorized Migrant Population in the U.S.," Research Report (Washington, DC: Pew Hispanic Center, March 2006), http://pewhispanic.org /files/reports/61.pdf.

4. David Coates, *Answering Back: Liberal Responses to Conservative Arguments* (New York: Continuum International Publishing Group, 2009).

5. Philip L. Martin, *Trade and Migration: NAFTA and Agriculture* (Washington, DC: Institute for International Economics, 1993).

6. Coates, *Answering Back.*

7. Daniel J. Tichenor, *Dividing Lines: The Politics of Immigration Control in America* (Princeton, NJ: Princeton University Press, 2002).

8. Jason Juffras, "IRCA and the Enforcement Mission of the Immigration and Naturalization Service," in *The Paper Curtain: Employer Sanctions' Implementation, Impact, and Reform,* ed. Michael Fix, 31–63 (Lanham, MD: University Press of America, 1991).

9. B. Lindsay Lowell and Zhongren Jing, "Unauthorized Workers and Immigration Reform: What Can We Ascertain from Employers?," *International Migration Review* 28, no. 107 (1994): 427–448.

10. Dan DeVivo and Valeria Fernández, "Crossing Arizona: Rooting Out the Problem," in *Getting Immigration Right: What Every American Needs to Know,* ed. David Coates and Peter Siavelis (Dulles, VA: Potomac Books, 2009), 131.

11. David Coates and Peter Siavelis, eds., *Getting Immigration Right: What Every American Needs to Know* (Dulles, VA: Potomac Books, 2009).

12. Quoted in David A. Martin, "Eight Myths about Immigration Enforcement," *Journal of Legislation and Public Policy* 10, no. 3 (2007): 525–533.

13. *Plyler v. Doe* 457 U.S. 202 (1982).

14. Jeffrey M. Jones, "Slim Majority of Americans Would Vote for DREAM Act Law," Gallup, December 10, 2010, www.gallup.com/poll/145136/Slim-Majority-Americans-Vote-DREAM-Act-Law.aspx.

15. "Immigration Law—Education—California Extends Instate Tuition Benefits to Undocumented Aliens. Act Relating to Public Postsecondary Education, Ch. 814, 2001 Cal. Adv. Legis. Serv. 5122 (Deering) (Codified at CAL. Educ. Code § 68130.5 (Deering Supp. 2002))," *Harvard Law Review* 115, no. 5 (March 1, 2002): 1548–1554.

16. Gray Davis, Letter to Members of the California Assembly, "Veto Message of AB 1197," September 29, 2000, www.leginfo.ca.gov/pub/99-00/bill/asm/ab_1151-1200/ab_1197_vt _20000929.html (retrieved January 4, 2013).

17. "Immigration Law," 1554.

18. Wendy Erisman and Shannon Looney, *Opening the Door to the American Dream: Increasing Higher Education Access and Success for Immigrants* (Washington, DC: Institute for Higher Education Policy, 2007).

19. Stella M. Flores, "The First State Dream Act: In-State Resident Tuition and Immigration in Texas," *Educational Evaluation and Policy and Analysis* 32, no. 4 (December 2010): 435–455.

20. Ibid.; Stella Flores and Jorge Chapa, "Latino Immigrant Access to Higher Education in a Bipolar Context of Reception," *Journal of Hispanic Higher Education* 8, no. 1 (2009): 90–109; Neeraj Kaushal, "In-State Tuition for the Undocumented: Education Effects on Mexican Young Adults," *Journal of Policy Analysis and Management* 27, no. 4 (2008): 771–792.

21. Yudhijit Bhattacharjee, "Law Leads to Degrees but Not Jobs in Texas," *Science* 308, no. 5727 (June 2005): 1397.

22. Mike Cason, "HB56 Two Years Later: Settlement Takes Bite Out of Alabama's Immigration Law," November 3, 2013, http://blog.al.com/wire/2013/11/hb56_two_years _later_constitut.html (retrieved February 20, 2014).

23. The Epidavros Project, "The Senators' Bargain: Last Best Chance," *Twelve Stories: How Democracy Works Now*, www.howdemocracyworksnow.com/story/last-best-chance (retrieved January 5, 2013).

24. Dave Montgomery, "Senate to Vote on Whether to Take Up Limited Immigration Bill," *McClatchy*, October 23, 2007, www.mcclatchydc.com/2007/10/23/20766/senate-to -vote-on-whether-to-take.html#storylink=cpy (retrieved January 5, 2013).

25. Dick Durbin, "DREAM Act as an Amendment to the Defense Authorization Bill," Dick Durbin, US Senator for Illinois, Assistant Majority Leader, July 13, 2007, http:// durbin.senate.gov/public/index.cfm/statementscommentary?ID=eb72e30c-a50f-4e92-b2f5 -4e3643703a9e (retrieved January 5, 2013).

26. Patrick J. Leahy, "Development, Relief, and Education for Alien Minors Act of 2007," *Congressional Record* 153, 160 (October 22, 2007): S13203.

27. Harry Reid, "Development, Relief, and Education for Alien Minors Act of 2007," *Congressional Record* 153, 162 (October 24, 2007): S13301.

28. Mitch McConnell, "Development, Relief, and Education for Alien Minors Act of 2007," *Congressional Record* 153, 162 (October 24, 2007): S13304.

29. Kay Bailey Hutchison, "Development, Relief, and Education for Alien Minors Act of 2007," *Congressional Record* 153, 162 (October 24, 2007): S13304.

30. Dick Durbin, "Development, Relief, and Education for Alien Minors Act of 2007," *Congressional Record* 153, 162 (October 24, 2007): S13305.

31. Luis Miranda, "Get the Facts on the DREAM Act," The White House, December 1, 2010, www.whitehouse.gov/blog/2010/12/01/get-facts-dream-act.

32. "Reid, McCain Spar over Immigration Add-On in Defense Bill," FoxNews.com, September 16, 2010, www.foxnews.com/politics/2010/09/16/reid-mccain-spar-immigration -add-defense/ (retrieved January 6, 2013).

33. Suzanne Gamboa, "DREAM Act Dies with Rejection of Defense Bill," Boston.com, September 21, 2010, www.boston.com/news/nation/articles/2010/09/21/dream_act_dies _with_rejection_of_defense_bill/ (retrieved January 6, 2013).

34. Ibid.

35. "Development, Relief, and Education for Alien Minors Act of 2010," *Congressional Record* 156, 161 (December 8, 2010): H8223.

36. Chet Edwards, "Development, Relief, and Education for Alien Minors Act of 2010," *Congressional Record* 156, 161 (December 8, 2010): H8230.

37. Rush Holt, "Development, Relief, and Education for Alien Minors Act of 2010," *Congressional Record* 156, 161 (December 8, 2010): H8242.

38. John Conyers, "Development, Relief, and Education for Alien Minors Act of 2010," *Congressional Record* 156, 161 (December 8, 2010): H8226.

39. Lamar Smith, "Development, Relief, and Education for Alien Minors Act of 2010," *Congressional Record* 156, 161 (December 8, 2010): H8226.

40. Ibid., H8237.

41. Tom Graves, "Development, Relief, and Education for Alien Minors Act of 2010," *Congressional Record* 156, 161 (December 8, 2010): H8230.

42. Elton Gallegly, "Development, Relief, and Education for Alien Minors Act of 2010," *Congressional Record* 156, 161 (December 8, 2010): H8239.

43. Steve King, "Development, Relief, and Education for Alien Minors Act of 2010," *Congressional Record* 156, 161 (December 8, 2010): H8228.

44. Robert Menendez, "Development, Relief, and Education for Alien Minors Act of 2010," *Congressional Record* 156, 162 (December 9, 2010): S8664.

45. Jeff Sessions, "Development, Relief, and Education for Alien Minors Act of 2010," *Congressional Record* 156, 162 (December 9, 2010): S8665.

46. David Vitter, "Development, Relief, and Education for Alien Minors Act of 2010," *Congressional Record* 156, 162 (December 9, 2010): S8228.

47. "Obama Mocks Border Enforcement: 'They'll Need a Moat with Alligators,'" Real Clear Politics, May 10, 2011, www.realclearpolitics.com/video/2011/05/10/obama_mocks _border_enforcement_theyll_need _a_moat_with_alligators.html (retrieved January 7, 2013).

48. Stephen Dinan, "Obama Says Border Is Secure Enough to Begin Legalization," *Washington Times*, May 10, 2011, www.washingtontimes.com/news/2011/may/10/obama-says -border-secure-enough-begin-legalization (retrieved January 17, 2013).

49. Dick Durbin, "A Bill to Authorize the Cancellation of Removal and Adjustment of Status of Certain Alien Students Who Are Long-Term United States Residents and Who Entered the United States as Children and for Other Purposes," *Congressional Record* 157, 64 (May 11, 2011): S2886.

50. Dick Durban, Senate Judiciary Committee, Subcommittee on Immigration, Refugees, and Border Security, "Hearing on 'The Dream Act,'" June 28, 2011.

51. Margaret D. Stock, Senate Judiciary Committee, Subcommittee on Immigration, Refugees, and Border Security, "Hearing on 'The Dream Act,'" June 28, 2011.

52. Steven A. Camarota, Senate Judiciary Committee, Subcommittee on Immigration, Refugees, and Border Security, "Hearing on 'The Dream Act,'" June 28, 2011.

53. John Cornyn, Senate Judiciary Committee, Subcommittee on Immigration, Refugees, and Border Security, "Hearing on 'The Dream Act,'" June 28, 2011.

54. Congressional Budget Office, *S. 3992, Development, Relief, and Education for Alien Minors Act of 2010*, Cost Estimate (December 2, 2010): 2.

55. Ibid.

56. Juan Carlos Guzmán and Raúl C. Jara, *The Economic Benefits of Passing the DREAM Act* (Washington, DC: Center for American Progress, October 2012).

57. Raul Hinojosa Ojeda and Paule Cruz Takash, *No DREAMers Left Behind: The Economic Potential of DREAM Act Beneficiaries* (Los Angeles: North American Integration and Development Center, University of California, Los Angeles, October 2010), 3.

58. Ibid., iv.

59. Steven A. Camarota, "Estimating the Impact of the DREAM Act," memorandum (Washington, DC: Center for Immigration Studies, December 2010).

CHAPTER 3

1. Amy Gutmann and Dennis Thompson, *The Spirit of Compromise: Why Governing Demands It and Campaigning Undermines It* (Princeton, NJ: Princeton University Press, 2012).

2. Leisy J. Abrego and Roberto G. Gonzales, "Blocked Paths, Uncertain Futures: The Postsecondary Education and Labor Market Prospects of Undocumented Latino Youth," *Journal of Education for Students Placed at Risk* 15, no. 1–2 (2010): 144–157.

3. Ibid., 145.

4. Valerie Strauss, "Hispanic High School Graduates Pass Whites in College Enrollment Rate," *Washington Post*, May 11, 2013, www.washingtonpost.com/blogs/answer -sheet/wp/2013/05/11/hispanic-high-school-graduates-pass-whites-in-college-enrollment -rate/?print=1 (retrieved July 1, 2013).

5. Richard Fry and Paul Taylor, "Hispanic High School Graduates Pass Whites in Rate of College Enrollment," Pew Hispanic Center, May 9, 2013, www.pewhispanic.org/2013/05/09 /hispanic-high-school-graduates-pass-whites-in-rate-of-college-enrollment/ (retrieved July 1, 2013).

6. William G. Bowen and Derek Bok, *The Shape of the River: Long-Term Consequences of Considering Race in College and University Admissions* (Princeton, NJ: Princeton University Press, 1998).

7. www.raceforward.org/research/reports/shattered-families?arc=1.

8. The comments in this section were originally published by Maria Chávez at www.racismreview.com/blog/2010/07/23/children-march-against-anti-immigrant-federal-action/.

9. See www.migrationpolicy.org/.

10. Maria Chávez, *Everyday Injustice: Latino Professionals and Racism* (Lanham, MD: Rowman and Littlefield, 2011).

11. Ibid.

12. Cybelle Fox, *Three Worlds of Relief: Immigration and the American Welfare State from the Progressive Era to the New Deal* (Princeton, NJ: Princeton University Press, 2012).

13. Maria L. Chávez, Brian Wampler, Ross E. Burkhart, "Left Out: Trust and Social Capital among Migrant Seasonal Farmworkers," *Social Science Quarterly* 87, no. 5 (December 2006): 1012–1029.

14. Annette Bernhardt, Michael W. Spiller, and Diana Polson, "All Work and No Pay: Violations of Employment and Labor Laws in Chicago, Los Angeles and New York City," *Social Forces* 91, no. 3 (2013): 725–746.

15. As reported in *On the Media*, September 30, 2013, "My Detainment Story, or: How I Learned to Stop Feeling Safe in My Own Country and Hate Border Agents," www.onthemedia.org/story/my-detainment-story-or-how-i-learned-stop-feeling-safe-my-own-country-and-hate-border-patrol/.

16. Chávez, *Everyday Injustice*.

17. Sonya Sotomayor, *My Beloved World* (New York: Knopf, 2013).

18. Joe Feagin, *The White Racial Frame: Centuries of Racial Framing and Counter-Framing* (New York: Routledge, 2010).

19. Aristide R. Zolberg, *A Nation by Design: Immigration Policy in the Fashioning of America* (Cambridge: Harvard University Press, 2006).

20. Lisa García Bedolla, *Fluid Borders: Latino Power, Identity, and Politics in Los Angeles* (Berkeley: University of California Press, 2005), 5.

CHAPTER 4

1. Rogers M. Smith, *Civic Ideals: Conflicting Visions of Citizenship in U.S. History* (New Haven, CT: Yale University Press, 1997).

2. Aristide R. Zolberg, *A Nation by Design: Immigration Policy in the Fashioning of America* (Cambridge, MA: Harvard University Press, 2006).

3. Douglas S. Massey, "America's Immigration Policy Fiasco: Learning from Past Mistakes," 2013, www.mitpressjournals.org/doi/pdf/10.1162/DAED_a_00215 (retrieved July 17, 2013).

4. Jennifer L. Hochschild, *Facing Up to the American Dream* (Princeton, NJ: Princeton University Press, 1996).

5. David Leal, "Latinos, Public Opinion, and Immigration Reform," in *Immigration Reform: A System for the 21st Century*, Latin America Initiative Research Project Working Paper, James Baker Institute for Public Policy, Rice University, 2013, www.bakerinstitute.org/publications/LAI-pub-LealLatinosImmigrationReform-040213.pdf.

6. See www.publicagenda.org/files/Immigration.pdf.

7. Kevin Johnson, *The "Huddled Masses" Myth: Immigration and Civil Rights* (Philadelphia: Temple University Press, 2004).

8. See ibid.; Zolberg, *A Nation by Design*; and Massey, "America's Immigration Policy Fiasco." Also see Jessica Lavariega Monforti, "Immigration: Trends, Demographics, and Patterns of Political Incorporation," in *Perspectives on Race, Ethnicity, and Religion: Identity Politics in America*, ed. Valerie Martinez-Ebers and Manochehr Dorraj, 52–72 (New York: Oxford University Press, 2009).

9. Roger Daniels, *Guarding the Golden Door: American Immigration Policy and Immigrants since 1882* (New York: Hill and Wang, 2004); Lisa García Bedolla, *Latino Politics* (Cambridge, UK: Polity, 2009).

10. See Zolberg, *A Nation by Design*.

11. Doris Meissner, Donald M. Kerwin, Muzaffar Chishti, and Claire Bergoni, *Immigration Enforcement in the United States: The Rise of a Formidable Machinery* (Washington, DC: Migration Policy Institute, 2013).

12. Ralph Guzmán, "The Political Socialization of the Mexican American People," PhD diss., University of California, Los Angeles, 1970; F. Chris Garcia, *Political Socialization of Chicano Children: A Comparative Study with Anglos in California Schools* (New York: Praeger, 1973); Rodolfo O. de la Garza, Louis DeSipio, F. Chris Garcia, John García, and Angelo Falcón, *Latino Voices: Mexican, Puerto Rican, and Cuban Perspectives on American Politics* (Boulder, CO: Westview, 1992); Robert D. Putnam, principal investigator, "The Social Capital Community Benchmark Survey," Saguaro Seminar (Cambridge: Harvard University, John F. Kennedy School of Government, 2001), www.ropercenter.uconn.edu/data_access/data/datasets/social_capital_community_survey.html#.Ty64hF34QVA.

13. Melissa R. Michelson, "Political Trust among Chicago Latinos," *Journal of Urban Affairs* 23 (2001): 323–334.

14. Melissa R. Michelson, "The Corrosive Effect of Acculturation: How Mexican-Americans Lose Political Trust," *Social Science Quarterly* 84, no. 4 (2003): 918–933; Melissa R. Michelson, "All Roads Lead to Rust: How Acculturation Erodes Latino Immigrant Trust in Government," *Aztlán: A Journal of Chicano Studies* 32, no. 2 (Fall 2007): 21–46.

15. Jessica Lavariega Monforti and Melissa R. Michelson, "Multiple Paths to Cynicism: Social Networks, Identity, and Linked Fate among Latinos," in *En Ciencia Política: The Search for Latino Identity and Racial Consciousness*, ed. Tony Affigne, Evelyn Hu-DeHart, and Marion Orr, 92–112 (New York: New York University Press, 2014).

16. GAO cites *United States v. Martinez-Fuerte*, 428 U.S. 543, 545 (1976).

17. Luis R. Fraga, John A. Garcia, Rodney E. Hero, Michael Jones-Correa, Valerie Martinez-Ebers, and Gary M. Segura, *Latino Lives in America: Making It Home* (Philadelphia: Temple University Press, 2010).

18. Samuel Huntington, "The Hispanic Challenge," *Foreign Policy*, March/April 2004, www.public.asu.edu/~nornradd/documents/HispanicChallenge.pdf.

19. See Fraga et al., *Latino Lives in America*.

20. Leo Chavez, *The Latino Threat* (Stanford, CA: Stanford University Press, 2013), 182.

21. Paul Burka, "Immigration, Border Security, and the Rio Grande Valley," *TexasMonthly* Burkablog, June 17, 2013, www.texasmonthly.com/burka-blog/immigration-border-security-and-rio-grande-valley.

22. "New Poll: After SB1070 Decision Obama Widens Lead over Romney among Latinos," Latino Decisions, July 18, 2012, www.latinodecisions.com/blog/2012/07/18/after-sb1070-decision-obama-widens-lead-over-romney/.

23. Neil King Jr., "Obama Gains among Latinos," *Wall Street Journal*, June 27, 2012, http://online.wsj.com/article/SB10001424052702303561504577492642990259950.html.

24. Elise Foley, "Deportation Hits Another Record under Obama Administration," *Huffington Post*, December 21, 2012, www.huffingtonpost.com/2012/12/21/immigration-deportation_n_2348090.html#slide=1089995.

25. A. Finifter, "Dimensions of Political Alienation," *American Political Science Review* 64, no. 2 (June 1970): 389–410.

26. A. Hancock, *The Politics of Disgust and the Public Identity of the "Welfare Queen"* (New York: New York University Press, 2004).

27. T. Catalano, "Anti-Immigrant Ideology in U.S. Crime Reports: Effects on the Education of Latino Children," *Journal of Latinos and Education* 12, no. 4 (2013): 254–270.

28. E. E. Schattschneider, *The Semi-Sovereign People* (New York: Holt, 1960).

29. Dylan Byers, "Univision's Jorge Ramos Grills Obama," Politico, September 20, 2012, www.politico.com/blogs/media/2012/09/univisions-ramos-grills-obama-on-immigration-136194.html.

30. There are many books that provide an in-depth analysis of Latino politics in California. For one that focuses on more contemporary developments, see Juan Gómez-Quiñones, *Chicano Politics: Reality and Promise 1940–1990*, The Calvin P. Horn Lectures in Western History and Culture (Albuquerque: University of New Mexico Press, 1990).

31. Matt Barreto, Sylvia Manzano, Ricardo Ramírez, and Kathy Rim, "Solidaridad and Politics by Other Means: Latino Participation in the 2006 Immigration Protest Rallies," *Urban Affairs Review* 44, no. 5 (2009): 736–764.

32. David Montejano, *Anglos and Mexicans in the Making of Texas, 1836–1986* (Austin: University of Texas Press, 1987).

33. Ibid., 32.

34. Benjamin Heber Johnson, *Revolution in Texas: How a Forgotten Rebellion and Its Bloody Suppression Turned Mexicans into Americans* (New Haven: Yale University Press, 2003).

35. Roque Planas, "Deportation: More Than 200,000 Parents Removed Who Say They Have a U.S. Citizen Child since 2010," *Huffington Post*, December 17, 2012, www.huffingtonpost.com/2012/12/17/deportation-more-than-200000-parents-removed-citizen-child_n_2316692.html.

36. See Hochschild, *Facing Up to the American Dream*.

37. James Truslow Adams, *The Epic of America* (Safety Harbor, FL: Simon Publications, 2001).

CHAPTER 5

1. James G. Gimpel, J. Celeste Lay, and Jason E. Schuknecht, *Cultivating Democracy: Civic Environments and Political Socialization in America* (Washington, DC: Brookings Institution Press, 2003).

2. Jeffrey S. Passel and D'Vera Cohn, "Unauthorized Immigrant Population: National and State Trends, 2010" (Washington, DC: Pew Hispanic Center, 2011).

3. Rodney E. Hero, *Faces of Inequality: Social Diversity in American Politics* (New York: Oxford University Press, 1998), 6.

4. Daniel J. Elazar, *American Federalism: A View from the States* (New York: Harper and Row, 1984).

5. Rodney E. Hero and Caroline J. Tolbert, "A Racial/Ethnic Diversity Interpretation of Politics and Policy in the States of the U.S.," *American Journal of Political Science* 40 (1996): 851–871; Joel Lieske, "Regional Subcultures of the United States," *Journal of Politics* 55 (1993): 86–113.

6. US Department of Homeland Security, *Yearbook of Immigration Statistics: 2011* (Washington, DC: USDHS, Office of Immigration Statistics, 2012).

7. Carol Hardy-Fanta, *Latina Politics, Latino Politics: Gender, Culture, and Political Participation in Boston* (Philadelphia: Temple University Press, 1993).

8. Herbert H. Hyman, *Political Socialization: A Study in the Psychology of Political Behavior* (Berkeley: University of California Press, 1959), 54.

9. Karl Mannheim, *Essays on the Sociology of Knowledge* (London: Routledge and Kegan Paul, 1952).

10. Erik H. Erikson, *Identity, Youth, and Crisis* (New York: W. W. Norton, 1968).

11. David O. Sears and Sheri Levi, "Childhood and Adult Political Development," in *Oxford Handbook of Political Psychology*, ed. David O. Sears, Leonie Huddy, and Robert Jervis, 60–109 (New York: Oxford University Press, 2003).

12. Rodolfo O. de la Garza, Louis DeSipio, F. Chris Garcia, John García, and Angelo Falcón, *Latino Voices: Mexican, Puerto Rican, and Cuban Perspectives on American Politics* (Boulder, CO: Westview Press, 1992); Luis R. Fraga, Ali A. Valenzuela, and Danielle Harlan, "Patterns of Latino Partisanship: Foundations and the Prospects for Change," paper presented at the annual meeting of the Western Political Science Association, 2009.

13. Bruce E. Cain, D. Roderick Kiewiet, and Carole J. Uhlaner, "The Acquisition of Partisanship by Latinos and Asian Americans," *American Journal of Political Science* 35, no. 2 (May 1991): 390–422; Carole Jean Uhlaner and F. Chris Garcia, *Foundations of Latino Party Identification: Learning, Ethnicity, and Demographic Factors among Mexicans, Puerto Ricans, Cubans, and Anglos in the United States* (Irvine, CA: Center for the Study of Democracy Research Monograph Series, 1998); Janelle S. Wong, "The Effects of Age and Political Exposure on the Development of Party Identification among Asian American and Latino Immigrants in the United States," *Political Behavior* 22, no. 4 (December 2000): 341–371; Zoltan Hajnal and Taeku Lee, "Out of Line: Immigration and Party Identification among Latinos and Asian Americans," in *Transforming Politics, Transforming America: The Political and Civic Incorporation of Immigrants in the United States*, ed. Taeku Lee, S. Karthick Ramakrishnan, and Ricardo Ramírez (Charlottesville: University of Virginia Press, 2006); R. Michael Alvarez and Lisa García Bedolla, "The Foundations of Latino Voter Partisanship: Evidence from the 2000 Election," *Journal of Politics* 65, no. 1 (2003): 31–49.

14. Cain, Kiewiet, and Uhlaner, "The Acquisition of Partisanship."

15. Wong, "The Effects of Age and Political Exposure."

16. Henry David Thoreau, *Civil Disobedience* (1849), in *Walden and Civil Disobedience*, ed. Paul Lauter (Boston and New York: Houghton Mifflin, 2000), 17–23.

17. Alejandro Portes and Rubén G. Rumbaut, "The Second Generation and the Children of Immigrants Longitudinal Study," *Ethnic and Racial Studies* 28, no. 6 (2005): 983–999; Richard D. Alba and Victor G. Nee, *Remaking the American Mainstream: Assimilation and Contemporary Immigration* (Cambridge, MA: Harvard University Press, 2003).

18. Raymond E. Wolfinger and Steven J. Rosenstone, *Who Votes?* (New Haven, CT: Yale University Press, 1980); Yen Le Espiritu, *Asian American Panethnicity: Bridging Institutions and Identities* (Philadelphia: Temple University Press, 1992); Michael S. Lewis-Beck, Helmut Norpoth, William G. Jacoby, Herbert F. Weisberg, *The American Voter Revisited* (Ann Arbor: University of Michigan Press, 2008).

19. Lisa García Bedolla, *Fluid Borders: Latino Power, Identity, and Politics in Los Angeles* (Berkeley: University of California Press, 2005); John A. García, "Pan Ethnicity: Politically Relevant for Latino/a Political Engagement?," in *Black and Latino/a Politics: Issues in Political Development in the United States*, ed. William Nelson Jr. and Jessica Lavariega Monforti (Miami, FL: Barnhardt and Ashe, 2006).

20. John Higham, *Send These to Me: Immigrants in Urban America* (Baltimore, MD: Johns Hopkins University Press, 1984); Alejandro Portes and Rubén G. Rumbaut, *Immigrant America: A Portrait* (Berkeley: University of California Press, 2006).

21. Tanya Golash-Boza, "Dropping the Hyphen? Becoming Latino(a)-American through Racialized Assimilation," *Social Forces* 85, no. 1 (September 2006): 27–55; Jack Citrin, Amy

Lerman, Michael Murakami, and Kathryn Pearson, "Testing Huntington: Is Hispanic Immigration a Threat to American Identity?," *Perspectives on Politics* 5, no. 1 (2007): 31–48.

22. Felix M. Padilla, *Latino Ethnic Consciousness: The Case of Mexican Americans and Puerto Ricans in Chicago* (Notre Dame, IN: University of Notre Dame Press, 1985); Rogers M. Smith, *Civic Ideals: Conflicting Visions of Citizenship in U.S. History* (New Haven, CT: Yale University Press, 1997); Lisa García Bedolla, Jessica L. Lavariega Monforti, and Adrian Pantoja, "A Second Look: Is There a Latina/o Gender Gap?," *Journal of Women, Politics and Policy* 28, no. 3–4 (2007): 147–171; Golash-Boza, "Dropping the Hyphen?"; Jessica Lavariega Monforti, "Rhetoric or Meaningful Identifiers? Latina/os and Panethnicity?," *Latino/a Research Review* 6, no. 1–2 (2006): 7–32.

23. Michael Jones-Correa and David L. Leal, "Becoming 'Hispanic': Secondary Panethnic Identification among Latin American–Origin Populations in the United States," *Hispanic Journal of Behavioral Sciences* 18, no. 2 (1996): 214–254.

24. José Calderón, "'Hispanic' and 'Latino': The Viability of Categories for Panethnic Unity," *Latin American Perspectives* 19, no. 4 (1992): 37–44.

25. Jones-Correa and Leal, "Becoming 'Hispanic'"; Natalie Masuoka, "Together They Become One: Examining the Predictors of Panethnic Group Consciousness among Asian Americans and Latinos," *Social Science Quarterly* 87, no. 5 (2006): 993–1011.

26. John A. García, "Political Integration of Mexican Immigrants: Explorations into the Naturalization Process," *International Migration Review* 15, no. 4 (1981): 608–625.

27. Gloria Anzaldúa, *Borderlands/La Frontera: The New Mestiza* (San Francisco: Spinsters/Aunt Lute Book Company, 1987).

28. Emma Pérez, *The Decolonial Imaginary: Writing Chicanas into History* (Bloomington: Indiana University Press, 1999).

29. Douglas S. Massey and Fernando Riosmena, "Undocumented Migration from Latin America in an Era of Rising US Enforcement," *The Annals of the American Academy of Political and Social Science* 630, no. 1 (2010): 294–321.

30. Margaret A. Villanueva, "Racialization and the US Latina Experience: Economic Implications," *Feminist Economics* 8, no. 2 (2002): 147.

31. Angelo N. Ancheta, *Race, Rights, and the Asian American Experience* (New Brunswick, NJ: Rutgers University Press, 1998), 64.

32. Melissa R. Michelson, "All Roads Lead to Rust: How Acculturation Erodes Latino Immigrant Trust in Government," *Aztlán: A Journal of Chicano Studies* 32, no. 2 (Fall 2007): 21–46; Melissa R. Michelson, "The Corrosive Effect of Acculturation: How Mexican-Americans Lose Political Trust," *Social Science Quarterly* 84, no. 4 (December 2003): 918–933.

CHAPTER 6

1. This is a law approved in 2003 by the Washington state legislature allowing undocumented students to be considered Washington state residents for the purposes of higher education.

2. Joe Feagin, *The White Racial Frame: Centuries of Racial Framing and Counter-Framing* (New York: Routledge, 2010).

3. This lack of empathy is what Joe Feagin refers to as alexithymia. For example, see ibid., chapter 8; and Joe Feagin and José Cobas, *Latinos Facing Racism: Discrimination, Resistance, and Endurance* (Boulder, CO: Paradigm Publishers, 2013).

4. Tanya Golash-Boza, *Immigration Nation: Raids, Detentions and Deportations in Post-9/11 America* (Boulder, CO: Paradigm Publishers, 2011), 33.

5. Ibid.

6. Julia Preston, "Program Benefiting Some Immigrants Extends Wait for Others," *New York Times*, February 9, 2014, A20.

7. Mark Hugo Lopez and Ana Gonzalez-Barrera, "If They Could, How Many Unauthorized Immigrants Would Become U.S. Citizens?" (Washington, DC: Pew Hispanic Center, June 27, 2013), www.pewresearch.org/fact-tank/2013/06/27/if-they-could-how-many-unauthorized-immigrants-would-become-u-s-citizens/ (retrieved June 27, 2013).

8. Jeffrey S. Passel and Mark Hugo Lopez, "Up to 1.7 Million Unauthorized Immigrant Youth May Benefit from New Deportation Rules" (Washington, DC: Pew Hispanic Center, August 14, 2012), www.pewhispanic.org/2012/08/14/up-to-1-7-million-unauthorized-immigrant-youth-may-benefit-from-new-deportation-rules/ (retrieved June 27, 2013).

9. Ibid.

10. Jonathan Weisman, "Boehner Doubts Immigration Bill Will Pass in 2014," *New York Times*, February 7, 2014, A1.

11. Golash-Boza, *Immigration Nation*, see chapter 3.

12. Bill Ong Hing, *Deporting Our Souls: Values, Morality, and Immigration Policy* (New York: Cambridge University Press, 2006), 7.

13. Michael J. Sandel, *What Money Can't Buy: The Moral Limits of Markets* (New York: Farrar, Straus and Giroux, 2012), 203.

14. We are indebted here to discussions of these issues with Joe Feagin.

15. Douglas S. Massey, "America's Immigration Policy Fiasco: Learning from Past Mistakes," 2013, www.mitpressjournals.org/doi/pdf/10.1162/DAED_a_00215, 13.

16. Feagin, *White Racial Frame*, see chapter 2.

17. Golash-Boza, *Immigration Nation*.

18. Vanessa Cárdenas and Sophia Kerby, *The State of Latinos in the United States* (Washington, DC: Center for American Progress, 2012), www.americanprogress.org/wp-content/uploads/issues/2012/08/pdf/stateoflatinos.pdf.

19. Hing, *Deporting Our Souls*, 4.

20. Ibid.

21. The concept of "de-Americanization" is found in ibid.

22. Barack Obama, *The Audacity of Hope: Thoughts on Reclaiming the American Dream* (New York: Knopf, 2008), 260.

23. Dennis H. Holtschneider, "Foreword," in *Living Illegal: The Human Face of Unauthorized Immigration*, ed. Marie Freidmann Marquardt, Timothy J. Steigenga, Philip J. Williams, and Manuel A. Vasquez (New York: The New Press, 2013), x.

24. Ronald Schmidt Sr., "Racialization and the Unauthorized Immigration Debate," paper presented at the annual meeting of the American Political Science Association, Chicago, August 31, 2013.

25. Hing, *Deporting Our Souls*, 163.

26. Melissa R. Michelson, "All Roads Lead to Rust: How Acculturation Erodes Latino Immigrant Trust in Government," *Aztlán: A Journal of Chicano Studies* 32, no. 2 (Fall 2007): 40.

27. Hing, *Deporting Our Souls*, 163.

28. Adam Simon and Frank Gilliam, "Don't Stay on Message: What 8,000 Respondents Say about Using Strategic Framing to Move the Public Discourse on Immigration," FrameWorks Institute, 2013, http://frameworksinstitute.org/assets/files/Immigration/dont_stay_on_message_values_11_2013.pdf?utm_source=Immigration+03%2F11%2F14+Email&utm_campaign=Framing+Immigration+03%2F11&utm_medium=email (retrieved March 13, 2014).

29. We are indebted here to discussions of these issues with Joe Feagin.

30. Feagin, *White Racial Frame*, 97.

31. There are many examples of scholarship in this area. For just one example of current racism faced by people of color see Eduardo Bonilla-Silva, *Racism without Racists: Color-Blind Racism and Racial Inequality in Contemporary America* (New York: Rowman and Littlefield, 2010).

32. Hing, *Deporting Our Souls*, 166.

33. Ed O'Keefe, "Jeb Bush: Many Illegal Immigrants Come out of an 'Act of Love,'" *Washington Post*, April 6, 2014, www.washingtonpost.com/blogs/post-politics/wp/2014/04/06 /jeb-bush-many-illegal-immigrants-come-out-of-an-act-of-love/.

34. These words come from the poem "The New Colossus" by Emma Lazarus that is mounted on the pedestal of the Statue of Liberty.

35. Luis Fraga, "Racial and Ethnic Politics in a Multicultural Society," Charles E. Gilbert lecture presented at Swarthmore College, Swarthmore, PA, November 16, 2000, 5.

36. Schmidt, "Racialization and the Unauthorized Immigration Debate," 28.

37. Jonathan Weisman and Ashley Parker, "Boehner Is Hit from the Right on Overhaul for Immigration," *New York Times*, February 8, 2014, A1, www.nytimes.com/2014/02/08 /us/politics/boehner-is-hit-from-the-right-on-immigration.html.

38. Rebecca Shabad, "Obama Says He's Open to Taking Executive Action on Immigration," *The Hill*, January 31, 2014, http://thehill.com/blogs/blog-briefing-room /news/197137-obama-says-hes-open-to-executive-action-on-immigration.

39. Editorial Board, "Yes, He Can, on Immigration," *New York Times*, April 5, 2014, www.nytimes.com/2014/04/06/opinion/sunday/yes-he-can-on-immigration.html (retrieved April 24, 2014).

40. Ibid.

Bibliography

www.azleg.gov/legtext/49leg/2r/bills/sb1070s.pdf.

http://legiscan.com/AL/text/HB56/id/321074.

www.migrationpolicy.org.

www.raceforward.org/research/reports/shattered-families?arc=1.

Abrego, Leisy J., and Roberto G. Gonzales. "Blocked Paths, Uncertain Futures: The Postsecondary Education and Labor Market Prospects of Undocumented Latino Youth." *Journal of Education for Students Placed at Risk* 15, no. 1–2 (2010): 144–157.

Acuña, Rodolfo. *Occupied America: A History of Chicanos.* New York: HarperCollins Publishers, 1988.

Adams, David Wallace. *Education for Extinction: American Indians and the Boarding School Experience, 1875–1928.* Lawrence: University Press of Kansas, 1995.

Adams, James Truslow. *The Epic of America.* Safety Harbor, FL: Simon Publications, 2001.

Alba, Richard. "Mexican Americans and the American Dream." *Perspectives on Politics* 4, no. 2 (2006): 289–296.

Alba, Richard D., and Victor G. Nee. *Remaking the American Mainstream: Assimilation and Contemporary Immigration.* Cambridge, MA: Harvard University Press, 2003.

Alvarez, R. Michael, and Lisa García Bedolla. "The Foundations of Latino Voter Partisanship: Evidence from the 2000 Election." *Journal of Politics* 65, no. 1 (2003): 31–49.

Ancheta, Angelo N. *Race, Rights, and the Asian American Experience.* New Brunswick, NJ: Rutgers University Press, 1998.

Anzaldúa, Gloria. *Borderlands/La Frontera: The New Mestiza.* San Francisco: Spinsters/Aunt Lute Book Company, 1987.

Associated Press. "McCain, Graham, Flake Met with House Hardliners to Promote Immigration Plan." *Washington Post,* March 1, 2013. www.washingtonpost.com/politics/congress/senate-aide-mccain-graham-flake-met-with-house-hardliners-to-promote-immigration-plan/2013/03/01/8612120e-8295-11e2-a671-0307392de8de_story.html.

Balderrama, Francisco E., and Raymond Rodriguez. *Decade of Betrayal: Mexican Repatriation in the 1930s.* Albuquerque: University of New Mexico Press, 2006.

Barreto, Matt, Sylvia Manzano, Ricardo Ramírez, and Kathy Rim. "Solidaridad and Politics by Other Means: Latino Participation in the 2006 Immigration Protest Rallies." *Urban Affairs Review* 44, no. 5 (2009): 736–764.

Bernhardt, Annette, Michael W. Spiller, and Diana Polson. "All Work and No Pay: Violations of Employment and Labor Laws in Chicago, Los Angeles and New York City." *Social Forces* 91, no. 3 (2013): 725–746.

Bhattacharjee, Yudhijit. "Law Leads to Degrees but Not Jobs in Texas." *Science* 308, no. 5727 (June 2005): 1397.

Bonilla-Silva, Eduardo. *Racism without Racists: Color-Blind Racism and Racial Inequality in Contemporary America*. New York: Rowman and Littlefield, 2010.

Bowen, William G., and Derek Curtis Bok. *The Shape of the River: Long-Term Consequences of Considering Race in College and University Admissions*. Princeton, NJ: Princeton University Press, 1998.

Burka, Paul. "Immigration, Border Security, and the Rio Grande Valley." *TexasMonthly* Burkablog, June 17, 2013. www.texasmonthly.com/burka-blog/immigration -border-security-and-rio-grande-valley.

Byers, Dylan. "Univision's Jorge Ramos Grills Obama." Politico, September 20, 2012. www.politico.com/blogs/media/2012/09/univisions-ramos-grills-obama-on -immigration-136194.html.

Cain, Bruce E., D. Roderick Kiewiet, and Carole J. Uhlaner. "The Acquisition of Partisanship by Latinos and Asian Americans." *American Journal of Political Science* 35, no. 2 (May 1991): 390–422.

Calavita, Kitty. *Inside the State: The Bracero Program, Immigration, and the I.N.S.* New York: Routledge, 1992.

Calderón, José. "'Hispanic' and 'Latino': The Viability of Categories for Panethnic Unity." *Latin American Perspectives* 19, no. 4 (October 1, 1992): 37–44.

Camarota, Steven A. "Estimating the Impact of the DREAM Act." Memorandum. Washington, DC: Center for Immigration Studies, December 2010. www.cis.org /dream-act-cost.

Cárdenas, Vanessa, and Sophia Kerby. *The State of Latinos in the United States*. Washington, DC: Center for American Progress, 2012. www.americanprogress.org /wp-content/uploads/issues/2012/08/pdf/stateoflatinos.pdf.

Cashin, Sheryll. *The Failures of Integration: How Race and Class Are Undermining the American Dream*. New York: Perseus, 2004.

Cason, Mike. "HB56 Two Years Later: Settlement Takes Bite Out of Alabama's Immigration Law." November 3, 2013. http://blog.al.com/wire/2013/11/hb56_two_years _later_constitut.html.

Catalano, T. "Anti-Immigration Ideology in U.S. Crime Reports: Effects on the Education of Latino Children." *Journal of Latinos and Education* 12, no. 4 (2013): 254–270.

Chavez, Leo R. *Shadowed Lives: Undocumented Immigrants in American Society*. Independence, KY: Cengage Learning, 1997.

———. *The Latino Threat*. Stanford, CA: Stanford University Press, 2013.

———. *The Latino Threat: Constructing Immigrants, Citizens, and the Nation*. Stanford, CA: Stanford University Press, 2008.

Chávez, Maria. *Everyday Injustice: Latino Professionals and Racism*. Lanham, MD: Rowman and Littlefield, 2011.

———. "Targeting Latino Children Is Not the Answer." Racism Review, May 10, 2011. www.racismreview.com/blog/2011/05/10/targeting-latino-children-is-not-the -answer/.

Chávez, Maria L., Brian Wampler, and Ross E. Burkhart. "Left Out: Trust and Social Capital among Migrant Seasonal Farmworkers." *Social Science Quarterly* 87, no. 5 (2006): 1012–1029.

Citrin, Jack, Amy Lerman, Michael Murakami, and Kathryn Pearson. "Testing Huntington: Is Hispanic Immigration a Threat to American Identity?" *Perspectives on Politics* 5, no. 1 (2007): 31–48.

Coates, David. *Answering Back: Liberal Responses to Conservative Arguments*. New York: Continuum International Publishing Group, 2009.

Coates, David, and Peter Siavelis, eds. *Getting Immigration Right: What Every American Needs to Know*. Dulles, VA: Potomac Books, 2009.

Cobas, José A., Jorge Duany, and Joe R. Feagin, eds. *How the United States Racializes Latinos: White Hegemony and Its Consequences*. Boulder, CO: Paradigm Publishers, 2009.

Congressional Budget Office. *S. 3992, Development, Relief, and Education for Alien Minors Act of 2010*. Cost Estimate. December 2, 2010.

Damore, David. "How Latino Voters May Decide Control of the U.S. House of Representatives." Latino Decisions, July 9, 2013. www.latinodecisions.com/blog/2013/07/09 /how-latino-voters-may-decide-control-of-the-u-s-house-of-representatives/.

———. "Message Not Received: House Republicans and Immigration Reform." Latino Decisions, July 25, 2013. www.latinodecisions.com/blog/2013/07/25 /message-not-received-house-republicans-and-immigration-reform/.

Daniels, Roger. *Guarding the Golden Door: American Immigration Policy and Immigrants since 1882*. New York: Hill and Wang, 2004.

Davis, Gray. Letter to Members of the California Assembly. "Veto Message of AB 1197." September 29, 2000. www.leginfo.ca.gov/pub/99-00/bill/asm/ab_1151-1200/ab _1197_vt_20000929.html.

de la Garza, Rodolfo O., Louis DeSipio, F. Chris Garcia, John García, and Angelo Falcón. *Latino Voices: Mexican, Puerto Rican, and Cuban Perspectives on American Politics*. Boulder, CO: Westview Press, 1992.

del Castillo, Richard Griswold. *The Treaty of Guadalupe Hidalgo: A Legacy of Conflict*. Norman: University of Oklahoma Press, 1992.

Detention Watch Network. "The Influence of the Private Prison Industry in the Immigration Detention Business." May 2011. www.detentionwatchnetwork.org/sites /detentionwatchnetwork.org/files/PrivatePrisonPDF-FINAL%205-11-11.pdf.

"Development, Relief, and Education for Alien Minors Act of 2010." *Congressional Record* 156, no. 161 (December 8, 2010): H8223.

DeVivo, Dan, and Valeria Fernández. "Crossing Arizona: Rooting Out the Problem." In *Getting Immigration Right: What Every American Needs to Know*, edited by David Coates and Peter Siavelis, 115–132. Dulles, VA: Potomac Books, 2009.

Dinan, Stephen. "Obama Says Border Is Secure Enough to Begin Legalization." *Washington Times*, May 10, 2011. www.washingtontimes.com/news/2011/may/10/obama-says -border-secure-enough-begin-legalization/.

Doherty, Brendan J., and Melissa Cully Anderson. "Message Tailoring in Spanish: Courting Latino Voters in the 2000 Presidential Advertising Campaign." In *Lights, Camera, Campaign!: Media, Politics, and Political Advertising*, edited by David A. Schultz, 121–148. New York: Peter Lang Publishers, 2004.

Durbin, Dick. "DREAM Act as an Amendment to the Defense Authorization Bill." Dick Durbin, US Senator for Illinois, Assistant Majority Leader, July 13, 2007. http://durbin.senate.gov/public/index.cfm/statementscommentary?ID=eb72e30c -a50f-4e92-b2f5-4e3643703a9e.

———. "A Bill to Authorize the Cancellation of Removal and Adjustment of Status of Certain Alien Students Who Are Long-Term United States Residents and Who Entered the United States as Children and for Other Purposes." *Congressional Record* 157, 64 (May 11, 2011): S2886.

Editorial Board. "Yes, He Can, on Immigration." *New York Times*, April 5, 2014. www .nytimes.com/2014/04/06/opinion/sunday/yes-he-can-on-immigration.html.

Elazar, Daniel J. *American Federalism: A View from the States.* New York: Harper and Row, 1984.

The Epidavros Project. "The Senators' Bargain: Last Best Chance." *Twelve Stories: How Democracy Works Now.* www.howdemocracyworksnow.com/story/last-best-chance.

Erikson, Erik H. *Identity, Youth, and Crisis.* New York: W. W. Norton, 1968.

Erisman, Wendy, and Shannon Looney. *Opening the Door to the American Dream: Increasing Higher Education Access and Success for Immigrants.* Washington, DC: Institute for Higher Education Policy, 2007.

Espiritu, Yen Le. *Asian American Panethnicity: Bridging Institutions and Identities.* Philadelphia: Temple University Press, 1992.

Eyder, Peralta. "National Council of La Raza Dubs Obama 'Deporter-in-Chief.'" Interview with Janet Murguía. National Public Radio, March 4, 2014. www.npr.org /blogs/thetwo-way/2014/03/04/285907255/national-council-of-la-raza-dubs -obama-deporter-in-chief.

Feagin, Joe R. *The White Racial Frame: Centuries of Racial Framing and Counter-Framing.* New York: Routledge, 2010.

Feagin, Joe R., and José A. Cobas. "Latinos/as and the White Racial Frame: The Procrustean Bed of Assimilation." *Sociological Inquiry* 78, no. 1 (2008): 39–53.

———. *Latinos Facing Racism: Discrimination, Resistance, and Endurance.* Boulder, CO: Paradigm Publishers, 2013.

Finifter, A. "Dimensions of Political Alienation." *American Political Science Review* 64, no. 2 (June 1970): 389–410.

Flores, Stella M. "The First State Dream Act: In-State Resident Tuition and Immigration in Texas." *Educational Evaluation and Policy and Analysis* 32, no. 4 (December 2010): 435–455.

Flores, Stella, and Jorge Chapa. "Latino Immigrant Access to Higher Education in a Bipolar Context of Reception." *Journal of Hispanic Higher Education* 8, no. 1 (2009): 90–109.

Foley, Elise. "Deportation Hits Another Record under Obama Administration." *Huffington Post*, December 21, 2012. www.huffingtonpost.com/2012/12/21/immigration -deportation_n_2348090.html#slide=1089995.

Fox, Cybelle. *Three Worlds of Relief: Immigration and the American Welfare State from the Progressive Era to the New Deal.* Princeton, NJ: Princeton University Press, 2012.

Fraga, Luis. "Racial and Ethnic Politics in a Multicultural Society." Charles E. Gilbert lecture presented at Swarthmore College, Swarthmore, PA, November 16, 2000.

Fraga, Luis Ricardo, John A. García, Rodney Hero, Michael Jones-Correa, Valerie Martinez-Ebers, and Gary M. Segura. *Latino Lives in America: Making It Home.* Philadelphia: Temple University Press, 2010.

Fraga, Luis R., Ali A. Valenzuela, and Danielle Harlan. "Patterns of Latino Partisanship: Foundations and the Prospects for Change." Paper presented at the annual meeting of the Western Political Science Association, 2009.

Fry, Richard, and Paul Taylor. "Hispanic High School Graduates Pass Whites in Rate of College Enrollment." Washington, DC: Pew Hispanic Center, May 9, 2013. www.pewhispanic.org/2013/05/09/hispanic-high-school-graduates-pass-whites-in-rate-of-college-enrollment/.

"Full Transcript of President Obama's Remarks on Immigration Reform." *New York Times*, January 29, 2013. www.nytimes.com/2013/01/30/us/politics/full-transcript-of-president-obamas-remarks-on-immigration-reform.html.

Gamboa, Suzanne. "DREAM Act Dies with Rejection of Defense Bill." Boston.com, September 21, 2010. www.boston.com/news/nation/articles/2010/09/21/dream_act_dies_with_rejection_of_defense_bill/.

Ganz, Marshall. "Why Stories Matter." *Sojourners*. http://sojo.net/magazine/2009/03/why-stories-matter.

Garcia, F. Chris. *Political Socialization of Chicano Children: A Comparative Study with Anglos in California Schools*. New York: Praeger, 1973.

García, John A. "Pan Ethnicity: Politically Relevant for Latino/a Political Engagement?" In *Black and Latino/a Politics: Issues in Political Development in the United States*, edited by William Nelson Jr. and Jessica Lavariega Monforti. Miami, FL: Barnhardt and Ashe, 2006.

———. "Political Integration of Mexican Immigrants: Explorations into the Naturalization Process." *International Migration Review* 15, no. 4 (1981): 608–625.

García Bedolla, Lisa. *Fluid Borders: Latino Power, Identity, and Politics in Los Angeles*. Berkeley: University of California Press, 2005.

———. *Latino Politics*. Cambridge, UK: Polity, 2009.

García Bedolla, Lisa, Jessica L. Lavariega Monforti, and Adrian Pantoja. "A Second Look: Is There a Latina/o Gender Gap?" *Journal of Women, Politics and Policy* 28, no. 3–4 (2007): 147–171.

Gimpel, James G., J. Celeste Lay, and Jason E. Schuknecht. *Cultivating Democracy: Civic Environments and Political Socialization in America*. Washington, DC: Brookings Institution Press, 2003.

Golash-Boza, Tanya. *Immigration Nation: Raids, Detentions and Deportations in Post-9/11 America*. Boulder, CO: Paradigm Publishers, 2011.

———. "Dropping the Hyphen? Becoming Latino(a)-American through Racialized Assimilation." *Social Forces* 85, no. 1 (September 1, 2006): 27–55.

Gómez-Quiñones, Juan. *Chicano Politics: Reality and Promise 1940–1990*. The Calvin P. Horn Lectures in Western History and Culture. Albuquerque: University of New Mexico Press, 1990.

Gonzales, Roberto G., and Leo R. Chavez. "'Awakening to a Nightmare': Abjectivity and Illegality in the Lives of Undocumented 1.5-Generation Latino Immigrants in the United States." *Current Anthropology* 53, no. 3 (2012): 255–281.

Guerin-Gonzales, Camille. *Mexican Workers and American Dreams: Immigration, Repatriation, and California Farm Labor, 1900–1939*. New Brunswick, NJ: Rutgers University Press, 1994.

Gutiérrez, David. *Walls and Mirrors: Mexican Americans, Mexican Immigrants, and the Politics of Ethnicity*. Berkeley, CA: University of California Press, 1995.

Gutmann, Amy, and Dennis F. Thompson. *The Spirit of Compromise: Why Governing Demands It and Campaigning Undermines It.* Princeton: Princeton University Press, 2012.

Guzmán, Juan Carlos, and Raúl C. Jara. *The Economic Benefits of Passing the DREAM Act.* Washington, DC: Center for American Progress, October 2012.

Guzmán, Ralph. "The Political Socialization of the Mexican American People." PhD diss., University of California, Los Angeles, 1970.

Hajnal, Zoltan, and Taeku Lee. "Out of Line: Immigration and Party Identification among Latinos and Asian Americans." In *Transforming Politics, Transforming America: The Political and Civic Incorporation of Immigrants in the United States,* edited by Taeku Lee, S. Karthick Ramakrishnan, and Ricardo Ramírez. Charlottesville: University of Virginia Press, 2006.

Hancock, A. *The Politics of Disgust and the Public Identity of the "Welfare Queen."* New York: New York University Press, 2004.

Hardy-Fanta, Carol. *Latina Politics, Latino Politics: Gender, Culture, and Political Participation in Boston.* Philadelphia: Temple University Press, 1993.

Haskins, Ron. "Economic Mobility of Immigrants in the United States." Economic Mobility Project Report. Washington, DC: Pew Charitable Trusts, 2009.

Hero, Rodney E. *Faces of Inequality: Social Diversity in American Politics.* New York: Oxford University Press, 1998.

Hero, Rodney E., and Caroline J. Tolbert. "A Racial/Ethnic Diversity Interpretation of Politics and Policy in the States of the U.S." *American Journal of Political Science* 40 (1996): 851–871.

Higham, John. *Send These to Me: Immigrants in Urban America.* Baltimore, MD: Johns Hopkins University Press, 1984.

Hing, Bill Ong. *To Be an American: Cultural Pluralism and the Rhetoric of Assimilation.* New York: New York University Press, 1997.

———. *Defining America through Immigration Policy.* Philadelphia: Temple University Press, 2004.

———. *Deporting Our Souls: Values, Morality, and Immigration Policy.* New York: Cambridge University Press, 2006.

Hochschild, Jennifer L. *Facing Up to the American Dream.* Princeton, NJ: Princeton University Press, 1996.

Holtschneider, Dennis H. "Foreword." In *Living Illegal: The Human Face of Unauthorized Immigration,* edited by Marie Freidmann Marquardt, Timothy J. Steigenga, Philip J. Williams, and Manuel A. Vasquez. New York: The New Press, 2013.

Huntington, Samuel. "The Hispanic Challenge." *Foreign Policy,* March/April 2004. www.public.asu.edu/~nornradd/documents/HispanicChallenge.pdf.

Hyman, Herbert H. *Political Socialization: A Study in the Psychology of Political Behavior.* Berkeley: University of California Press, 1959.

"Immigration Law—Education—California Extends Instate Tuition Benefits to Undocumented Aliens. Act Relating to Public Postsecondary Education, Ch. 814, 2001 Cal. Adv. Legis. Serv. 5122 (Deering) (Codified at CAL. Educ. Code § 68130.5 (Deering Supp. 2002))." *Harvard Law Review* 115, no. 5 (March 1, 2002): 1548–1554.

Johnson, Benjamin Heber. *Revolution in Texas: How a Forgotten Rebellion and Its Bloody Suppression Turned Mexicans into Americans.* New Haven, CT: Yale University Press, 2003.

Johnson, Kevin R. *How Did You Get to Be a Mexican? A White/Brown Man's Search for Identity*. Philadelphia: Temple University Press, 1999.

————. *The "Huddled Masses" Myth: Immigration and Civil Rights*. Philadelphia: Temple University Press, 2004.

Jones, Jeffrey M. "Slim Majority of Americans Would Vote for DREAM Act Law." Gallup, December 10, 2010. www.gallup.com/poll/145136/Slim-Majority-Americans-Vote-DREAM-Act-Law.aspx.

Jones-Correa, Michael, and David L. Leal. "Becoming 'Hispanic': Secondary Panethnic Identification among Latin American–Origin Populations in the United States." *Hispanic Journal of Behavioral Sciences* 18, no. 2 (May 1, 1996): 214–254.

Juffras, Jason. "IRCA and the Enforcement Mission of the Immigration and Naturalization Service." In *The Paper Curtain: Employer Sanctions' Implementation, Impact, and Reform*, edited by Michael Fix, 31–63. Lanham, MD: University Press of America, 1991.

Kaushal, Neeraj. "In-State Tuition for the Undocumented: Education Effects on Mexican Young Adults." *Journal of Policy Analysis and Management* 27, no. 4 (2008): 771–792.

King, Neil, Jr. "Obama Gains among Latinos." *Wall Street Journal*, June 27, 2012. http://online.wsj.com/article/SB10001424052702303561504577492642990259950.html.

Lavariega Monforti, Jessica. "Immigration: Trends, Demographics, and Patterns of Political Incorporation." In *Perspectives on Race, Ethnicity, and Religion: Identity Politics in America*, edited by Valerie Martinez-Ebers and Manochehr Dorraj, 52–72. New York: Oxford University Press, 2009.

————. "Rhetoric or Meaningful Identfiers? Latina/os and Panethnicity?" *Latino/a Research Review* 6, no. 1–2 (2006): 7–32.

Lavariega Monforti, Jessica, and Melissa R. Michelson. "Multiple Paths to Cynicism: Social Networks, Identity, and Linked Fate among Latinos." In *En Ciencia Política: The Search for Latino Identity and Racial Consciousness*, edited by Tony Affigne, Evelyn Hu-DeHart, and Marion Orr, 92–112. New York: New York University Press, 2014.

Leal, David. "Latinos, Public Opinion, and Immigration Reform." In *Immigration Reform: A System for the 21st Century*. Latin America Initiative Research Project Working Paper, James Baker Institute for Public Policy, Rice University, 2013. www.bakerinstitute.org/publications/LAI-pub-LealLatinosImmigrationReform-040213.pdf.

LeTourneau, Nancy. "Some History and Facts for Those Claiming That President Obama Is "Deporter-in-Chief." http://immasmartypants.blogspot.com/2014/03/some-history-and-facts-for-those.html.

Lewis-Beck, Michael S., Helmut Norpoth, William G. Jacoby, and Herbert F. Weisberg. *The American Voter Revisited*. Ann Arbor: University of Michigan Press, 2008.

Lieske, Joel. "Regional Subcultures of the United States." *Journal of Politics* 55 (1993): 86–113.

Lilley, Sandra. "Poll: 1 Out of 3 Americans Inaccurately Think Most Hispanics Are Undocumented." NBC Latino, September 12, 2012. http://nbclatino.com/2012/09/12/poll-1-out-of-3-americans-think-most-hispanics-are-undocumented/.

Lopez, Mark Hugo, and Ana Gonzalez-Barrera. "If They Could, How Many Unauthorized Immigrants Would Become U.S. Citizens?" Washington, DC: Pew

Research Center, June 27, 2013. www.pewresearch.org/fact-tank/2013/06/27/if-they-could-how-many-unauthorized-immigrants-would-become-u-s-citizens/.

———. "Latino Voters Support Obama by 3–1 Ratio, but Are Less Certain Than Others about Voting." Pew Hispanic Center, June 15, 2012. www.pbs.org/newshour/bb/politics/jan-june12/dreamact_06-15.html.

Lowell, B. Lindsay, and Zhongren Jing. "Unauthorized Workers and Immigration Reform: What Can We Ascertain from Employers?" *International Migration Review* 28, no. 107 (1994): 427–448.

Mannheim, Karl. *Essays on the Sociology of Knowledge.* London: Routledge and Kegan Paul, 1952.

Marquardt, Marie Friedmann, Timothy J. Steigenga, Philip J. Williams, and Manuel A. Vásquez. *Living "Illegal": The Human Face of Unauthorized Immigration.* New York: The New Press, 2013.

Martin, David A. "Eight Myths about Immigration Enforcement." *Journal of Legislation and Public Policy* 10, no. 3 (2007): 525–533.

Martin, Philip L. *Trade and Migration: NAFTA and Agriculture.* Washington, DC: Institute for International Economics, 1993.

Massey, Douglas S. "America's Immigration Policy Fiasco: Learning from Past Mistakes." 2013. www.mitpressjournals.org/doi/pdf/10.1162/DAED_a_00215.

Massey, Douglas S., Jorge Durand, and Nolan J. Malone. *Beyond Smoke and Mirrors: Mexican Immigration in an Era of Economic Integration.* New York: Russell Sage Foundation, 2002.

Massey, Douglas S., and Fernando Riosmena. "Undocumented Migration from Latin America in an Era of Rising US Enforcement." *The Annals of the American Academy of Political and Social Science* 630, no. 1 (2010): 294–321.

Masuoka, Natalie. "Together They Become One: Examining the Predictors of Panethnic Group Consciousness among Asian Americans and Latinos." *Social Science Quarterly* 87, no. 5 (2006): 993–1011.

Meissner, Doris, Donald M. Kerwin, Muzaffar Chishti, and Claire Bergoni. *Immigration Enforcement in the United States: The Rise of a Formidable Machinery.* Washington, DC: Migration Policy Institute, 2013.

Michelson, Melissa R. "The Corrosive Effect of Acculturation: How Mexican-Americans Lose Political Trust." *Social Science Quarterly* 84, no. 4 (2003): 918–933.

———. "All Roads Lead to Rust: How Acculturation Erodes Latino Immigrant Trust in Government." *Aztlán: A Journal of Chicano Studies* 32, no. 2 (Fall 2007): 21–46.

———. "Political Trust among Chicago Latinos." *Journal of Urban Affairs* 23 (2001): 323–334.

Miranda, Luis. "Get the Facts on the DREAM Act." The White House, December 1, 2010. www.whitehouse.gov/blog/2010/12/01/get-facts-dream-act.

Montejano, David. *Anglos and Mexicans in the Making of Texas, 1836–1986.* Austin: University of Texas Press, 1987.

Montgomery, Dave. "Senate to Vote on Whether to Take Up Limited Immigration Bill." McClatchy, October 23, 2007. www.mcclatchydc.com/2007/10/23/20766/senate-to-vote-on-whether-to-take.html#storylink=cpy.

"My Detainment Story, or: How I Learned to Stop Feeling Safe in My Own Country and Hate Border Agents." *On the Media*, September 30, 2013. www.onthemedia.org/story/my-detainment-story-or-how-i-learned-stop-feeling-safe-my-own-country-and-hate-border-patrol/.

Nakamura, David. "Obama to Refocus Attention on Immigration, Gun Control." *Washington Post*, March 1, 2013. www.washingtonpost.com/politics/obama-to-refocus-attention-on-immigration-gun-control/2013/03/01/64fbe2d0-81ef-11e2-a350-49866afab584_story.html.

———. "With an Immigration Deal Possible, Advocates Mount New Push to End Deportations." *Washington Post*, February 3, 2014. www.washingtonpost.com/politics/with-an-immigration-deal-possible-advocates-mount-new-push-to-end-deportations/2014/02/03/ee6feaa8-8ce7-11e3-98ab-fe5228217bd1_story.html.

Napolitano, Janet. *Exercising Prosecutorial Discretion with Respect to Individuals Who Came to the United States as Children*. Washington, DC: Government Printing Office, 2012.

"New Poll: After SB1070 Decision Obama Widens Lead over Romney among Latinos." Latino Decisions, July 18, 2012. www.latinodecisions.com/blog/2012/07/18/after-sb1070-decision-obama-widens-lead-over-romney/.

Ngai, Mae M., and Jon Gjerde. *Major Problems in American Immigration History*. 2nd ed. Boston: Wadsworth/Cengage Learning, 2011.

Obama, Barack. "Remarks by the President on Immigration." Rose Garden, June 15, 2012. www.whitehouse.gov/the-press-office/2012/06/15/remarks-president-immigration.

———. *The Audacity of Hope: Thoughts on Reclaiming the American Dream*. New York: Knopf, 2008.

"Obama Mocks Border Enforcement: 'They'll Need a Moat with Alligators.'" Real Clear Politics, May 10, 2011. www.realclearpolitics.com/video/2011/05/10/obama_mocks_border_enforcement_theyll_need_a_moat_with_alligators.html.

Ojeda, Raul Hinojosa, and Paule Cruz Takash. *No DREAMers Left Behind: The Economic Potential of DREAM Act Beneficiaries*. Los Angeles: North American Integration and Development Center, University of California, Los Angeles, October 2010.

O'Keefe, Ed. "Jeb Bush: Many Illegal Immigrants Come out of an 'Act of Love.'" *Washington Post*, April 6, 2014. www.washingtonpost.com/blogs/post-politics/wp/2014/04/06/jeb-bush-many-illegal-immigrants-come-out-of-an-act-of-love/.

Olivas, Michael A. *No Undocumented Child Left Behind: Plyler v. Doe and the Education of Undocumented Schoolchildren*. New York: New York University Press, 2012.

Padilla, Felix M. *Latino Ethnic Consciousness: The Case of Mexican Americans and Puerto Ricans in Chicago*. Notre Dame, IN: University of Notre Dame Press, 1985.

Parker, Ashley. "G.O.P. Congressman's Remarks Undermine Party's Immigration Efforts." *New York Times*, July 24, 2013. http://thecaucus.blogs.nytimes.com/2013/07/23/g-o-p-congressman-undermines-partys-immigration-efforts/?_r=0.

Parker, Ashley, and Jonathan Martin. "Senate, 68 to 32, Passes Overhaul for Immigration." *New York Times*, June 27, 2013. www.nytimes.com/2013/06/28/us/politics/immigration-bill-clears-final-hurdle-to-senate-approval.html?pagewanted=all.

Passel, Jeffrey S. "The Size and Characteristics of the Unauthorized Migrant Population in the U.S." Research Report. Washington, DC: Pew Hispanic Center, March 7, 2006. http://pewhispanic.org/files/reports/61.pdf.

Passel, Jeffrey S., and D'Vera Cohn. "Unauthorized Immigrant Population: National and State Trends, 2010." Washington, DC: Pew Hispanic Center, 2011.

Passel, Jeffrey S., and Mark Hugo Lopez. "Up to 1.7 Million Unauthorized Immigrant Youth May Benefit from New Deportation Rules." Washington, DC: Pew Hispanic Center, August 14, 2012. www.pewhispanic.org/2012/08/14/up-to-1-7-million-unauthorized-immigrant-youth-may-benefit-from-new-deportation-rules/.

Pérez, Emma. *The Decolonial Imaginary: Writing Chicanas into History.* Bloomington: Indiana University Press, 1999.

Planas, Roque. "Deportation: More Than 200,000 Parents Removed Who Say They Have a U.S. Citizen Child since 2010." *Huffington Post,* December 17, 2012. www.huffingtonpost.com/2012/12/17/deportation-more-than-200000-parents -removed-citizen-child_n_2316692.html.

Portes, Alejandro, and Rubén G. Rumbaut. *Immigrant America: A Portrait.* Berkeley: University of California Press, 2006.

————. "The Second Generation and the Children of Immigrants Longitudinal Study." *Ethnic and Racial Studies* 28, no. 6 (2005): 983–999.

Preston, Julia. "Program Benefiting Some Immigrants Extends Wait for Others." *New York Times,* February 9, 2014, A20.

Putnam, L. L. "The Interpretive Perspective, an Alternative to Functionalism." In *Communication in Organizations: An Interpretive Approach.* Beverly Hills, CA: Sage, 1983.

Putnam, Robert D., principal investigator. "The Social Capital Community Benchmark Survey." Saguaro Seminar. Cambridge, MA: Cambridge Harvard University, John F. Kennedy School of Government, 2001. www.ropercenter.uconn/edu/data _access/data/datasets/social_capital_community_survey.html#.Ty64hF34QVA.

Ramirez, Hernan, and Pierrette Hondagneu-Sotelo. "Mexican Immigrant Gardeners: Entrepreneurs or Exploited Workers?" *Social Problems* 56, no. 1 (2009): 70–88.

"Reid, McCain Spar over Immigration Add-On in Defense Bill." FoxNews.com, September 16, 2010. www.foxnews.com/politics/2010/09/16/reid-mccain-spar -immigration-add-defense/.

Romo, Ricardo. "Responses to Mexican Immigration, 1910–1930." *Aztlán* 6 (1975): 173–194.

Ruíz, Vicki. *From Out of the Shadows: Mexican Women in Twentieth-Century America.* New York: Oxford University Press, 2008.

Rutenberg, Jim, and Jeff Zeleny. "Perry and Romney Come Out Swinging at Each Other in G.O.P. Debate." *New York Times,* September 22, 2011. www.nytimes.com /2011/09/23/us/politics/perry-and-romney-come-out-swinging-at-each-other-in -gop-debate.html.

Sandel, Michael J. *What Money Can't Buy: The Moral Limits of Markets.* New York: Farrar, Straus and Giroux, 2012.

Santos, Fernanda. "Border Security Rule Costs Bill Support." *New York Times,* June 26, 2013. www.nytimes.com/2013/06/27/us/politics/border-security-rule-costs-bill -support.html?_r=0.

Sawhill, Isabel, and John E. Morton. "Economic Mobility: Is the American Dream Alive and Well?" Economic Mobility Project Report. Washington, DC: Pew Charitable Trusts, 2007.

Schattschneider, E. E. *The Semi-Sovereign People.* New York: Holt, 1960.

Schmidt, Ronald, Sr. *Language Policy and Identity Politics in the United States.* Philadelphia: Temple University Press, 2000.

————. "Racialization and the Unauthorized Immigration Debate." Paper presented at the Western Political Science Association, Portland, March 23, 2012.

————. "Racialization and the Unauthorized Immigration Debate." Paper presented at the annual meeting of the American Political Science Association, Chicago, August 31, 2013.

Schmidt, Ronald, Sr., Yvette M. Alex-Assensoh, Andrew L. Aoki, and Rodney E. Hero. *Newcomers, Outsiders, and Insiders: Immigrants and American Racial Politics in the Early Twenty-First Century.* Ann Arbor: University of Michigan Press, 2010.

Sears, David O., and Sheri Levi. "Childhood and Adult Political Development." In *Oxford Handbook of Political Psychology*, edited by David O. Sears, Leonie Huddy, and Robert Jervis, 60–109. New York: Oxford University Press, 2003.

Shabad, Rebecca. "Obama Says He's Open to Taking Executive Action on Immigration." *The Hill*, January 31, 2014. http://thehill.com/blogs/blog-briefing-room/news/197137-obama-says-hes-open-to-executive-action-on-immigration.

Shear, Michael D., and Julia Preston. "Obama Plan Envisions 8-Year Wait for Illegal Immigrants." *New York Times*, February 17, 2013. www.nytimes.com/2013/02/18/us/politics/white-house-continues-work-on-its-own-immigration-bill.html.

Sierra, Christine Marie, Teresa Carrillo, Louis DeSipio, and Michael Jones-Correa. "Latino Immigration and Citizenship." *PS: Political Science and Politics* 33, no. 3 (2000): 535–540.

Simon, Adam, and Frank Gilliam. "Don't Stay on Message: What 8,000 Respondents Say about Using Strategic Framing to Move the Public Discourse on Immigration." FrameWorks Institute, 2013.

Smith, Lamar. "Immigration Enforcement Key to Success." *USA Today*, March 4, 2013. www.usatoday.com/story/opinion/2013/03/04/lamar-smith-on-immigration-enforcement/1960287/.

Smith, Rogers M. *Civic Ideals: Conflicting Visions of Citizenship in U.S. History.* New Haven, CT: Yale University Press, 1997.

Sotomayor, Sonya. *My Beloved World.* New York: Knopf, 2013.

Strauss, Valerie. "Hispanic High School Graduates Pass Whites in College Enrollment Rate." *Washington Post*, May 11, 2013. www.washingtonpost.com/blogs/answer-sheet/wp/2013/05/11/hispanic-high-school-graduates-pass-whites-in-college-enrollment-rate/.

Takaki, Ronald. *A Different Mirror: A History of Multicultural America.* Boston: Back Bay Books, 1993.

Terriquez, Veronica, and Caitlin Patler. "Aspiring Americans: Undocumented Youth Leaders in California." Policy Brief, California Young Adult Study. Center for the Study of Immigrant Integration, University of Southern California, June 2012.

Thompson, Ginger, and Sarah Cohen. "More Deportations Follow Minor Crimes, Records Show." *New York Times*, April 6, 2014. www.nytimes.com/2014/04/07/us/more-deportations-follow-minor-crimes-data-shows.html?_r=0.

Thoreau, Henry David. *Civil Disobedience* (1849). In *Walden and Civil Disobedience*, edited by Paul Lauter. Boston and New York: Houghton Mifflin, 2000.

Tichenor, Daniel J. *Dividing Lines: The Politics of Immigration Control in America.* Princeton, NJ: Princeton University Press, 2002.

Uhlaner, Carole Jean, and F. Chris Garcia. *Foundations of Latino Party Identification: Learning, Ethnicity, and Demographic Factors among Mexicans, Puerto Ricans, Cubans, and Anglos in the United States.* Irvine, CA: Center for the Study of Democracy Research Monograph Series, 1998.

US Department of Homeland Security. *Yearbook of Immigration Statistics: 2011.* Washington, DC: USDHS, Office of Immigration Statistics, 2012.

Villanueva, Margaret A. "Racialization and the US Latina Experience: Economic Implications." *Feminist Economics* 8, no. 2 (2002): 145–161.

Weisman, Jonathan. "Boehner Doubts Immigration Bill Will Pass in 2014." *New York Times*, February 7, 2014, A1.

Weisman, Jonathan, and Ashley Parker. "Boehner Is Hit from the Right on Overhaul for Immigration." *New York Times*, February 8, 2014, A1. www.nytimes .com/2014/02/08/us/politics/boehner-is-hit-from-the-right-on-immigration.html.

"What Obama's Immigration Move Means for Undocumented Youth, Politics." *PBS NewsHour*, June 15, 2012. www.pbs.org/newshour/bb/politics/jan-june12 /dreamact_06-15.html.

Wolfinger, Raymond E., and Steven J. Rosenstone. *Who Votes?* New Haven, CT: Yale University Press, 1980.

Wong, Janelle S. "The Effects of Age and Political Exposure on the Development of Party Identification among Asian American and Latino Immigrants in the United States." *Political Behavior* 22, no. 4 (2000): 341–371.

Zhou, Min. "Segmented Assimilation: Issues, Controversies, and Recent Research on the New Second Generation." *International Migration Review* 31, no. 4, Special Issue: Immigrant Adaptation and Native-Born Responses in the Making of Americans (Winter 1997): 975–1008.

Zolberg, Aristide R. *A Nation by Design: Immigration Policy in the Fashioning of America*. Cambridge, MA: Harvard University Press, 2006.

Index

Note: Page numbers in italics refer to tables or figures.

About the Authors

Maria Chávez, Associate Professor of Political Science at Pacific Lutheran University, is the award-winning author of *Everyday Injustice: Latino Professionals and Racism.*

Jessica L. Lavariega Monforti is Associate Professor and Associate Dean of the College of Social and Behavioral Sciences at the University of Texas–Pan American. She is co-editor of *Black and Latino/a Politics: Issues in Political Development in the United States.*

Melissa R. Michelson, Professor of Political Science at Menlo College, is co-author of the award-winning *Mobilizing Inclusion: Redefining Citizenship through Get-Out-the-Vote Campaigns.*